CW01082014

Men in Women's Worlds

Laura Coffey-Glover

Men in Women's Worlds

Constructions of Masculinity in Women's Magazines

Laura Coffey-Glover
English, Communications and Philosophy
Nottingham Trent University
Nottingham, UK

ISBN 978-1-137-57554-8   ISBN 978-1-137-57555-5   (eBook)
https://doi.org/10.1057/978-1-137-57555-5

Library of Congress Control Number: 2018959249

This Palgrave Macmillan imprint is published by the registered company Springer Nature Limited
The registered company address is: The Campus, 4 Crinan Street, London, N1 9XW, United Kingdom

For Louis and Rich

Preface and Acknowledgements

As a teenager I was an avid reader of women's magazines. I remember eagerly devouring their advice on how to perfect the latest make-up trends and must-have looks, and, most importantly, how to bag myself a man. It wasn't until I grew up a little, that I was able to reflect that this advice seemed to consistently involve me doing all the hard work, and I suspected that the boys I was interested in weren't slavishly following the same kinds of tips from *FHM* or *Loaded*. I also began to realize that the kinds of men I encountered did not always behave in the same ways that the magazines I read told me they would.

When I embarked on this research project I was no longer an avid reader of women's magazines. Since I began writing this book, I have also become a parent, and as a parent I am concerned with how I can ensure my children will grow up understanding the importance of being able to recognize and call out forms of stereotyping and social discrimination such as those found in the pages of women's magazines.

Although advances in digital technology have certainly changed the landscape of women's magazines (see, for example, Duffy 2013), scholarship in feminist, media and cultural studies indicates women's magazines are still perceived as having salience in women's lives; their potential to influence how women think about themselves and how they 'should' behave is therefore still relevant (see, for example, Ytre-Arne 2011a). In writing this book, I was curious to see if my experiences of how men were talked about in these texts still rang true from my teenage years. I won't spoil the ending, but it's fair to say that there's still a long way to go in tackling some of the assumptions made about both men and women in texts such as these.

This book builds on work done for my doctoral thesis, completed at the university of Huddersfield. I would therefore like to thank my supervisors, Professors Lesley Jeffries and Dan McIntyre, for their help and support during my time there, and to Lesley in particular for encouraging me to write this book. I would also like to thank my friends and colleagues in Linguistics at Nottingham Trent University for their support during the final push. Special thanks must go to friends who listened to me moan and gave me helpful advice (and cake!) along the way: Cleo Hanaway, Jai Mackenzie, Laura Paterson and Kirsty Budds. Finally, thank you to my family for your enduring love and support, and especially to Rich and Louis, the men in my world.

Nottingham, UK   Laura Coffey-Glover

Contents

List of Figures

List of Tables

1

Introduction: Analyzing Gender Construction in Women's Magazines

This book presents a Feminist Critical Stylistic analysis of a large dataset of women's magazines collected in 2008, to examine the ways in which men are 'sold' to women as part and parcel of a successful performance of heterosexual hegemonic femininity. The book is an explicitly feminist endeavor; I am interested in the implications of these constructions for the ways in which women may then perceive themselves, and potentially alter their behavior in line with the standards and expectations set by women's magazines.

Women's magazines have been in circulation since the late 1600s (Braithwaite 1995), and although sales figures for UK print publications are generally in decline, top-ranking women's magazines like *Cosmopolitan* still achieve bi-annual sales figures of around 300,000 (Oakes 2016). Research on reader engagement with online and print versions also shows that, on the whole, readers of women's magazines prefer print versions to their digital counterparts (Edelmen 2010; Ytre-Arne 2011). The fact that women's magazines have such an established history and persistence in the face of digital markets is therefore testament to their popularity among female audiences. It is also for this reason that examining how gender is constructed for their readers is such

© The Author(s) 2019
L. Coffey-Glover, *Men in Women's Worlds*,
https://doi.org/10.1057/978-1-137-57555-5_1

an essential area for feminist study: it is important to examine the kinds of ideologies of gender that women are buying into when they consume these texts, and to interrogate the potentially damaging effects of these.

A critical linguistic analysis of women's magazines is not in and of itself a new idea—there is a healthy body of existing research on women's magazines and other types of media discourse that deals with the various ways in which texts can and do influence their readers (discussed in more depth in Chapter 3), but work on women's magazines is almost exclusively concerned with examining these issues through the lens of how *women* are sold to women (see, for example, Talbot 1995; Jeffries 2007; Ringrow 2016). Feminist linguistic research has shown how women are constrained by what Talbot (1995) refers to as 'consumer femininity', whereby women are encouraged to engage in beautification processes that involve 'fixing' problems in their appearance in order to uphold ideals of femininity and, ultimately, please men. Very little has been said about how men and masculinity are manifested in these texts, despite the fact that much of this research cites men as the motivation for these constructions of women. Choosing to focus solely on women's roles, women's language, or women's writing means that women become marked; studies of gender in discourse analysis demonstrate a phallocentric tendency to analyze 'women's language' as a deviation from the male norm (Mills 2012: 17). It is therefore important to challenge the androcentrism of research which implies the deviancy of women's behavior and implicitly upholds men's status as norm-makers.

Research focusing on the notion of gender-linked speech styles in the past dominated discourse analytical work on gender identity (see Chapter 2 for an in-depth overview). However, studying the ways in which gender stereotypes are created and recirculated through discourse is also a useful contribution to the study of the relationship between language and gender identity. The kinds of ideologies that are valued in a particular culture will most likely have some effect on the members of that culture and therefore have the potential to shape opinions and beliefs. For example, studies in psychology suggest that 'media framing' (Taylor 2008) can affect beliefs and attitudes regarding sex and relationships, as well as sexual behavior (Taylor 2008; Aubrey et al. 2003; Collins et al. 2004).

In recent years there has been increased public interest in how 'lad culture' proliferates in spaces such as university campuses and 'lads mags', where 'lad culture' can be viewed as behavior involving youthful hedonism and participation in 'raunch' or 'sex object' culture, serving as a form of homosocial bonding (Phipps and Young 2015: 3). Feminist interrogation of 'lad culture' is exemplified by, for instance, the 2013 Lose the Lads Mags campaign in the UK, coordinated by feminist organizations UK Feminista and Object. Grassroots feminist campaigns like the Everyday Sexism Project (Bates 2014) and No More Page Three have been successful in making visible the sexualisation and objectifica-tion of women in such spaces, and critical attention has been given to the notion of the 'mainstreaming' of lad culture (see García-Farvaro and Gill 2016), but this book will argue that the ideologies of hegemonic masculinity that circulate in male-targeted media like men's magazines are also prevalent in female-targeted media such as mainstream women's magazines, which makes them an important site for feminist critique.

1.1   Theorizing Gender: The Trouble with Binaries

The distinction between 'sex' as a biological category and 'gender' as a social construction is a fundamental development of Western feminist thought, and can be attributed to feminist writer Simone de Beauvoir's observation that one is not born, but 'becomes' a woman (1949). Asserting a sex/gender binary recognizes that femininity and mascu-linity can be viewed as behaviors or practices that are not shaped by biology: men can exhibit stereotypically feminine qualities (such as a predilection for wearing pink), and women can behave in ways associ-ated with ideological masculinity (such as displays of aggression). On the face of it, this is an attractive proposition for feminist commentators who wish to point out the fallacies of asserting that men or women are biologically destined to be better suited to particular roles or occupa-tions. However, early theorizing in areas like anthropology and sociol-ogy has tended to oversimplify the sex/gender dichotomy to the extent that gender is sometimes viewed as an adornment that can easily be untangled from biological sex—indeed, this is sometimes referred to by feminist theorists as the 'coat-rack' model of gender (Nicholson 1994). The reality is much more nuanced, since gender stereotypes are often based on biological traits. For example, the prevalence of the 'male as breadwinner' script has been largely based on a generalization that men are physically stronger than women, and this has been used as justification for men's dominance in the workplace for centuries.

In her treatment of what she calls 'neurosexism' in scientific research, Cordelia Fine (2011) debunks myths surrounding so-called 'hard-wired' differences between the male and female brain that have been used to justify why men make better scientists than women or why women are naturally suited to caring roles such as nursing or teaching. She argues that the social effects of gender (expectations of gendered behavior) can have an observable impact on the brain, resulting in patterns that we then interpret as sex-based difference. Acknowledging that supposed 'hard-wired' biological differences are often in fact the psychological result of social stereotyping is an important and compelling argument. What this nuanced interpretation of the social constructionist account of gender shows is the highly complex relationship between the biological and the social. As Cameron (2007) argues, what is important is not necessarily whether or not biological differences exist between men and women, but what ideological use is made of (supposed) differences.

1.1.1 Gender as Performative

In her seminal work, *Gender Trouble* (1990, 1999), feminist philosopher Judith Butler interprets gender as 'performative', defining 'gender' as 'the repeated stylization of the body' (1990: 33). Like the coat-rack model, this theorization of gender emphasizes a separation between biological essence and social construction, but this reconfiguration also emphasizes the role of individual and structural agency in the production of gender identity: gender in the performative account treats identity as something which is enacted, something that you *do* rather than something you *have*. This means that gender is not an innate category but something which is *performed* or *achieved* through our interactions with others, and the discourses that we are exposed to in our daily lives.

The notion of performativity is a development of the linguists Austin's (1962) and Searle's (1969, 1979, 1983, 1989) speech act theory. Austin had noted that illocutions like 'I promise' or 'I pronounce you...' are 'performatives', in that they bring a state of affairs into being, rather than describe something that already exists. Such performatives cause changes in the real world. Butler argued, therefore, that language could be used in order to create or *construct* gender identity. In this model, gender is conceived of as a socially constructed process which we are *continuously* engaged in:

> Gender is the repeated stylization of the body, a set of repeated acts within a highly rigid regulatory frame that congeal over time to produce the appearance of substance of a natural sort of being.
> (Butler 1990: 33)

What Butler means by this is that repeated linguistic and non-linguistic acts, such as styles of dress, gesture, posture, ways of talking and so on, over time become naturalized, acquiring cultural intelligibility as 'normal' expressions of gender in a particular society. Crucially, performances of gender are not a 'free for all': permissible gender performances are regulated by institutional norms like the legal system, workplace and media organizations. Women's magazines, in their repetition of culturally intelligible ideologies of gender, are also arguably part of the 'rigid, regulatory frame' (Butler 1990: 33) that polices individual instantiations of gender. If masculinity and femininity are products of what we do, then the meaning of these actions can only be legitimized by their recognition from others: aggression, virility and dominance can only come to index a masculine persona if others acknowledge that these qualities might point to masculinity, and this can only occur if these connections are repeated over time. Women's magazines are an example of texts that reiterate ideas of what are possible and acceptable performances of masculinity, which 'congeal over time to produce the appearance of substance of a natural sort of being.'

(Butler 1990: 33). That these repetitions lead to an illusion of natural-
ness explains how performativity works to hide the performative nature
of gender: repeated performances of, for example, men's sexual pursuit
of women, means that carnality comes to be perceived as an 'essence' of
male identity so that carnality entails masculinity, rather than it being
seen as a potential behavior that may or may not be enacted by a man.
Performativity theory is therefore a useful framework to account for the
ways in which the illusion that 'men are naturally carnal' can be sustained by women's magazines and other mass media texts.

Research adopting this kind of approach has tended to focus on individual performances of gender through interaction (see for instance
Eckert and McConnell-Ginet 1992; Livia and Hall 1997; Zimman
2014). However, one of the main tenets of this book is that media texts'
constructions of gender can also be considered performances of gender
identity, and their potential to influence readers' world-views means
they are an important site for feminist analysis. Because women's magazines (and other written texts) are mediated, the way they construct
gender identities is much less spontaneous than performances of gender
in naturally-occurring speech, and that is the point: they are 'scripted
performances' of gender. This also means that the distinction traditionally made between spoken performance and written representation
needs to be questioned. Particularly, because texts like women's magazines present a 'tissue of voices' (Talbot 1992: 176), the line between
written and spoken discourse becomes blurred.

1.1.2 Indexicality

Related to the notion of performativity is that of 'indexicality', from linguistic anthropology (Ochs 1992). In her research comparing the communicative practices of motherhood in US society with that of Western
Samoa, Ochs employs the notion of indexicality to argue that gender
is either directly or indirectly indexed through language. Direct indexicality refers to language in which the sex of the speaker is explicitly
encoded, such as items like *man/woman* and *husband/wife* or titles such
as *Mr/Mrs*. Indirect indexicality refers to language use that has become

associated with gendered meanings. For example, a competitive interactional style is often associated with masculinity, where more supportive speech styles have come to signal femininity.

While indexicality is usually used in interactional studies of gender (Eckert and McConnell-Ginet 2003; Holmes 2006), it is also a useful concept when analyzing textual constructions of gender, as lexical items have also become imbued with gendered meanings. For example, Caldas-Coulthard and Moon (2010) observe how men's physical appearance is more likely than women to be described in newspaper representations with adjectives such as *handsome, strapping* and *stocky*, where those such as *pretty, sexy* and *glamorous* were used in descriptions of women. While these items do not directly index gender, in that the referents of, for example, *glamorous*, do not necessarily have to be female, they most frequently are, and therefore the word indirectly indexes, or 'points to' femininity. The concept of indexicality is therefore particularly useful for accounting for the relationship between linguistic description and gender stereotyping.

1.2   Discourse and Ideology in Critical Linguistics

This book follows in the tradition of 'critical' linguistic approaches to analyzing text, in that I am interested in interrogating the role of language in the production of gendered discourses. Critical Discourse Analysis (CDA) emerged in the early 1990s as a synthesis of critical approaches to 'analyzing opaque as well as transparent structural relationships of dominance, discrimination, power and control as manifested in language' (Wodak and Meyer 2009: 10). CDA understands texts, and in particular media texts, as simultaneously reflecting and creating ideologies for the reader. As a political approach, it is concerned with 'de-mystifying' ideologies and power via the 'systematic and *retroductable* investigation of semiotic data' (Wodak and Meyer 2009: 3). This means that analyses of data, (whether written, spoken or visual) should be transparent to the reader.

At the core of all CDA approaches is a broadly post-structuralist interpretation of 'discourse' as 'broad constitutive systems of meaning' (Sunderland 2004: 6), which differs from more traditional linguistic definitions as 'language above the sentence'. However, different CDA perspectives do use the term in different ways, something which has attracted a good deal of criticism (see for example Widdowson 1995). In particular, those working explicitly within the dialectical-relational (Fairclough 1996) or social actors (Van Leeuwen 1995, 2008) approach adopt the Foucauldian sense of 'discourse' as referring to 'practices which systematically form the subjects of which they speak' (Foucault 1972: 49). This sense is most similar to the concept of 'ideology' and the two terms are often used interchangeably. I personally have found it helpful to make a distinction between 'discourse' as 'text that is focused on a particular topic' (Mills and Mullany 2011: 76), or 'ways of seeing the world' (Sunderland 2004: 28) and 'ideology' as denoting the *naturalization* of such discourses: the state of being viewed by a particular community or society as *common-sense knowledge*. This interpretation of 'ideology' is in keeping with a performative account of gender that views gender as a set of practices: ideologies of masculinity in women's magazines are thus common-sense ideas about men (those that have the appearance of normality) as a result of their repetition in discourses (repeated linguistic 'acts').

1.3   Feminist Critical Stylistics

Critical Stylistics is a method of analysis which can be viewed as bridging the gap between CDA and stylistics. CDA conventionally aims to show 'non-obvious ways in which language is involved in social relations of power and domination' (Fairclough 2001: 229), and is predominantly used to analyze non-fictional texts. Stylistics, on the other hand, in its attempt to explain the 'relation between language and artistic function' (Leech and Short 2007: 11) has traditionally focused on literary genres.

Critical Stylistics aims to 'assemble the main general functions that a text has in representing reality' (Jeffries 2010: 14), and can be considered as a development of CDA in terms of both theory and methodology (Jeffries 2007, 2010). One of the main criticisms of CDA is that it has not yet developed a full inventory of tools for the analyst to work with, although work in the dialectical-relational tradition often utilizes elements of functional grammar inspired by Halliday (1994). The lack of a standard set of tools is a (perhaps inevitable) consequence of its multidisciplinary theoretical foundations. Indeed, Wodak and Meyer (2009: 2) assert the necessity of eclecticism in their discussion of what distinguishes CDA from other forms of discourse analysis:

> CDA is [...] not interested in investigating a linguistic unit per se but in studying social phenomena which are necessarily complex and thus require a multidisciplinary and multi-methodical approach.

Because of its focus on eclectic theories and methods of analysis, CDA is sometimes less concerned with conducting detailed, linguistic analysis of ideological meaning than with critiquing the socio-political context for the production of texts. This, as Jeffries points out, can result in 'patchy' coverage of linguistic structures, and the lack of a clear, comprehensive toolkit makes it difficult for students of English Language to apply to the analysis of texts (2010: 6). Critical stylistics attempts to counter this by introducing a systematic model of analysis which amalgamates tools from stylistics and critical linguistics, in order to explore the linguistic choices of text producers and their possible ideological implications.

Proponents of CDA assert that it is not in itself a unitary theory or methodology, but rather a 'school' of intellectual inquiry (see Wodak and Meyer 2009: 5), and have therefore been criticized for using the label as more of a political statement or 'act'. Where CDA analysis takes a specifically left-leaning political standpoint, Critical Stylistics is proposed as a method of uncovering the linguistic mechanisms of ideological meaning in any text, regardless of the analyst's political persuasions (Jeffries 2010: 14). The model is based on a series of 'textual–conceptual' functions (outlined in Chapter 4), which address a level of meaning between formal structure, or *langue* and the reader's contextualized meaning, or *parole* (de Saussure 1960). At this level of meaning, the text uses language resources in combination with ideational meaning to present the world in a particular way (Jeffries 2014: 409). The reader has to work out how the text does this, thus the textual–conceptual functions 'are intended to capture the fact that texts can create specific types of meaning in a number of different ways' (Jeffries 2014: 409). Different kinds of linguistic features (such as nouns, pronouns and nominalizations) can 'name' a particular entity in the world, or different types of syntactic structure can be used to create relationships of opposition in texts (see Chapter 6), so the textual–conceptual functions demonstrate that there is no direct relationship between (linguistic) form and (conceptual) function. These textual functions also form part of the 'ideational metafunction' of language (Halliday 1994), in that they are ways of creating worldviews. They help to uncover how ideology is embedded in a text through a consideration of how linguistic form links to higher-level conceptual meaning.

This book also proposes a specifically feminist approach to undertaking Critical Stylistics, in that its ultimate aim is to uncover how particular stylistic practices contribute to structural patterns of gender inequality in society at large. I argue that the stylistic choices made to construct male identities in women's magazines have potentially detrimental effects on women readers, since they recirculate the idea that men are necessarily (biologically) different from women, the heteronormative principle that heterosexual relationships are a defining aspect of female identity (that women *need* men in order to be validated), and that men are naturally driven by 'primal' urges of aggression and sexual carnality that ultimately serve to reaffirm positions of dominance.

1.4   Corpus Linguistics and Gender Performativity

Corpus linguistics is 'the study of language based on examples of real life language use' (McEnery and Wilson 1996: 1). A corpus is defined as a collection of texts that are machine-readable, authentic, and sampled in such a way as to be representative of a particular language or language variety (McEnery et al. 2006: 5). It uses quantitative methods to analyze large bodies of naturally occurring language in order to uncover linguistic patterns, and is widely renowned for its contributions to lexicography and descriptive grammar (Mautner 2007: 54). Corpus linguistic analysis involves feeding digitized texts into corpus interrogation software, which can perform statistical calculations to reveal linguistic phenomena such as keywords and collocations, which are then interpreted manually by the researcher.

Because of its reliance on statistical patterns rather than qualitative analysis and intuition, corpus linguistics aids the rigor and objectivity of analyses. Of course, corpus-based studies also require some qualitative input: it is ultimately the researcher who interprets linguistic patterns (Baker 2006: 18). However, quantitative methods allow the researcher to analyze larger bodies of text, which increases the reliability of findings, and using frequency data can support findings derived from smaller-scale analyses.

Corpus linguistics has a wide range of applications in linguistics, including language teaching and translation studies (Xiao and McEnery 2002); lexicography (Podhakecka and Piotrowski 2003); forensic linguistics (Woolls and Coulthard 1998); discourse analysis (Baker 2006, 2008) and stylistics and literary studies (Semino and Short 2004; Mahlberg 2007; Mahlberg and McIntyre 2011). Corpus-based approaches to text analysis have become increasingly popular over the last few decades, and have previously been applied to the investigation of discourses and ideologies in media texts (Baker et al. 2013; Baker and Levon 2016; Caldas-Coulthard and Moon 2010; Gabrielatos and Baker 2008; Van Dijk 1991).

Of most relevance to the present study is the growing body of corpus-based work that has been carried out in the area of language and gender (for example Baker 2010, 2014; Baker and Levon 2015, 2016; Sigley and Holmes 2002; Koller 2004; Taylor 2017). This may seem to contradict the shift from analyses of large-scale patterns in sociolinguistics to small-scale studies (Swann 2002), and the general trend in feminist thought, which has turned from global notions (for example of sisterhood), to more localized, individual issues (Baker 2006: 9). However, I assert that the recent conceptualization of gender as performative is entirely in alignment with the cumulative focus of corpus linguistics: for instantiations of gender to become recognizable, they have to be reiterated, and corpus linguistics works on the basis of collecting numerous examples of a linguistic feature, allowing the researchers to see its incremental patterning. As Stubbs puts it: '[r]epeated patterns show that evaluative meanings are not merely personal and idiosyncratic, but widely shared in a discourse community' (2001: 215). The effectiveness of corpus linguistic methods in establishing cumulative meanings is therefore a strong rationale for adopting a corpus-based approach, in order to observe the role of media texts as mechanisms of gender performativity.

1.5   Summary and Outline of the Book

This chapter has introduced the aims of this study of masculinity construction in women's magazines and outlined some key concepts for my approach to studying gender identity in the data, including the notion of gender performativity and the importance of viewing language as a tool for constructing gendered discourses in texts. I have also briefly outlined the Feminist Critical Stylistic approach that underpins this research and its relationship to its intellectual cousin CDA.

Chapter 2 provides a brief account of relevant debates in language and gender study, and places this study within the context of a performative approach to gender construction. Chapter 3 contextualizes the study in relation to existing empirical work on women's and men's magazines, identifying key themes in the literature; including the construction of femininity as a consumerist practice, the construction of gender as biologically determined, the relationship between feminism and women's magazines, and the construction of heteronormativity.

Chapter 4 details the methodological processes involved in constructing the magazine corpus and implementing the Critical Stylistics framework: I discuss how I collected and categorized the articles for inclusion in the corpus in terms of different text types and magazine genres, and I explain how I have used corpus linguistic tools to aid my analysis of the different conceptual-textual functions.

Chapters 5 through 8 present the results of the analytical processes described in Chapter 4. Chapter 5 presents the analysis of Naming and Describing, which refers to the ways in which the texts label and describe male identities. I identify lexis which exhibits lexical, social and referential gender, serving as direct and indirect indices of masculinity. Chapter 6 describes how the texts create equivalences and oppositional meanings that construct men as equating to 'cultural ideals' and other metaphorical concepts, including conceptual metaphors. I also discuss how men are presented in terms of various oppositional constructs, including hyponyms of a GOOD/BAD dichotomy. Chapter 7 shows how the texts represent men's actions and states of being, focusing on actions towards women and states of being denoting both physical and personal traits. In the final analysis chapter, I examine how the texts assume and imply ideologies of masculinity through different types of presupposition and implicature.

In Chapter 9 I pull together the findings of the analysis and point to how they reveal five unifying trends: the idea that men are either 'good' or 'bad'; that men are motivated by carnal instincts; that they are naturally aggressive; that men and women are inherently different creatures; and the idea that heterosexuality is normative. I also show how the different textual-conceptual tools work together, by conducting an analysis of an excerpt from the data as a case study. Finally, I evaluate the effectiveness of combining corpus linguistics with the Critical Stylistics model, and offer some suggestions for further research in this area.

References

Aubrey, J. S., Harrison, K., Kramer, L., & Yellin, J. (2003). Variety Versus Timing: Gender Differences in College Students' Sexual Expectations as Predicted by Exposure to Sexually Oriented Television. *Communication Research, 30*(4), 432–460.

Austin, J. L. (1962). *How to Do Things with Words: The William James Lectures Delivered at Harvard University in 1955*. Oxford: Clarendon Press.

Baker, P. (2006). *Using Corpora in Discourse Analysis*. London: Continuum.

Baker, P. (2008). "Eligible" Bachelors and "Frustrated" Spinsters: Corpus Linguistics, Gender and Language. In J. Sunderland, K. Harrington, & H. Saunston (Eds.), *Gender and Language Research Methodologies*. London: Palgrave Macmillan.

Baker, P. (2010). Will Ms Ever Be as Frequent as Mr?: A Corpus-Based Comparison of Gendered Terms Across Four Diachronic Corpora of British English. *Gender and Language, 4*(1), 125–149.

Baker, P. (2014). *Using Corpora to Analyze Gender*. London: Bloomsbury.

Baker, P., Gabrielatos, C., & McEnery, T. (2013). Sketching Muslims: A Corpus Driven Analysis of Representations Around the Word 'Muslim' in the British Press 1998–2009. *Applied Linguistics, 34*(3), 255–278.

Baker, P., & Levon, E. (2015). Picking the Right Cherries?: A Comparison of Corpus-Based and Qualitative Analyses of News Articles About Masculinity. *Discourse & Communication, 9*(2), 221–236.

Baker, P., & Levon, E. (2016). 'That's What I Call a Man': Representations of Racialised and Classed Masculinities in the UK Print Media. *Gender and Language, 10*(1), 106–139.

Bates, L. (2014). *Everyday Sexism*. London: Simon & Schuster.

Braithwaite, B. (1995). *Women's Magazines: The First 300 Years*. London: Peter Owen.

Butler, J. (1990). *Gender Trouble: Feminism and the Subversion of Identity*. London: Routledge.

Butler, J. (1999). *Gender Trouble: Feminism and the Subversion of Identity* (2nd ed.). London: Routledge.

Caldas-Coulthard, C. R., & Moon, R. (2010). "Curvy, Hunky, Kinky": Using Corpora as Tools for Critical Analysis. *Discourse and Society, 21*(2), 99–133.

Cameron, D. (2007). *The Myth of Mars and Venus: Do Men and Women Really Speak Different Languages?* Oxford: Oxford University Press.

Collins, R. L., Elliott, M. N., Berry, S. H., Kanouse, D. E., Kunkel, D., Hunter, S. B., et al. (2004). Watching Sex on Television Predicts Adolescent Initiation of Sexual Behavior. *Pediatrics, 114*(3), 280–289.

de Beauvoir, S. ([1949] 1988). *The Second Sex* (H. M. Parshley, Trans. and Ed.). London: Pan Books.

de Saussure, F. (1960). *Course in General Linguistics* (W. Baskin, Trans.). London: Peter Owen.

Eckert, P., & McConnell-Ginet, S. (1992). Think Practically and Look Locally: Language and Gender as Community-Based Practice. *Annual Review of Anthropology, 21*(1), 461–490.

Eckert, P., & McConnell-Ginet, S. (2003). *Language and Gender*. Cambridge: Cambridge University Press.

Edelman, D. C. (2010). Branding in the Digital Age: You're Spending Your Money in All the Wrong Places. *Harvard Business Review, 88*, 63–69.

Fairclough, N. (1996). A Reply to Henry Widdowson's "Discourse Analysis: A Critical Review". *Language and Literature, 5*(1), 49–56.

Fairclough, N. (2001). *Language and Power* (2nd ed.). London: Longman.

Fine, C. (2011). *Delusions of Gender: The Real Science Behind Sex Differences*. London: Icon.

Foucault, M. (1972). *The Archaeology of Knowledge*. London: Tavistock.

Gabrielatos, C., & Baker, P. (2008). Fleeing, Sneaking, Flooding: A Corpus Analysis of Discursive Constructions of Refugees and Asylum Seekers in the UK Press, 1996–2005. *Journal of English Linguistics, 36*(1), 5–38.

García-Favaro, L., & Gill, R. (2016). "Emasculation Nation Has Arrived": Sexism Rearticulated in Online Responses to Lose the Lads' Mags Campaign. *Feminist Media Studies, 16*(3), 379–397.

Halliday, M. A. K. (1994). *An Introduction to Functional Grammar* (2nd ed.). London: Arnold.

Holmes, J. (2006). *Gendered Talk at Work*. Oxford: Blackwell.

Jeffries, L. (2007). *Textual Construction of the Female Body: A Critical Discourse Approach*. Basingstoke: Palgrave Macmillan.

Jeffries, L. (2010). *Critical Stylistics*. Basingstoke: Palgrave Macmillan.

Jeffries, L. (2014). Critical Stylistics. In M. Burke (Ed.), *The Routledge Handbook of Stylistics* (pp. 408–420). London: Routledge.

Koller, V. (2004). Businesswomen and War Metaphors: "Possessive Jealous and Pugnacious"? *Journal of Sociolinguistics, 8*(1), 3–22.

Leech, G., & Short, M. (2007). *Style in Fiction: A Linguistic Introduction to English Fictional Prose* (2nd ed.). Harlow: Pearson Education.

Livia, A., & Hall, K. (1997). 'It's a Girl!' Bringing Performativity Back to Linguistics. In A. Livia & K. Hall (Eds.), *Queerly Phrased: Language, Gender, and Sexuality* (pp. 3–18). Oxford: Oxford University Press.

Mahlberg, M. (2007). Corpus Stylistics: Bridging the Gap Between Linguistic and Literary Studies. In M. Hoey, M. Mahlberg, M. Stubbs, & W. Teubert (Eds.), *Text, Discourse and Corpora* (pp. 219–246). London: Continuum.

Mahlberg, M., & McIntyre, D. (2011). A Case for Corpus Stylistics: Ian Fleming's Casino Royale. *English Text Construction, 4*(2), 204–227.

Mautner, G. (2007). Mining Large Corpora for Social Information: The Case of Elderly. *Language in Society, 36*(1), 51–72.

McEnery, T., & Wilson, A. (1996). *Corpus Linguistics*. Edinburgh: Edinburgh University Press.

McEnery, T., Xiao, R., & Tono, Y. (2006). *Corpus-Based Language Studies: An Advanced Resource Book*. London: Routledge.

Mills, S. (2012). *Gender Matters: Feminist Linguistic Analysis*. London: Equinox.

Mills, S., & Mullany, L. (2011). *Language, Gender and Feminism: Theory, Methodology and Practice*. London: Routledge.

Nicholson, L. (1994). Interpreting Gender. *Signs, 20*(1), 79–105.

Oakes, O. (2016). Magazine ABCs: Top 100 for First Half of 2016. *Campaign*. Available at http://www.campaignlive.co.uk/article/magazine-abcs-top-100-first-half-2016/1405423. Accessed June 2017.

Ochs, E. (1992). Indexing Gender. In A. Duranti & C. Goodwin (Eds.), *Rethinking Context: Language as an Interactive Phenomenon* (pp. 335–358). Cambridge: Cambridge University Press.

Phipps, A., & Young, I. (2015). "Lad Culture" in Higher Education: Agency in the Sexualisation Debates. *Sexualities, 18*(4), 459–479.

Podhakecka, M., & Piotrowski, T. (2003). Russianisms in English (OED-BNC-LDOCE). In B. Lewandowska-Tomaszczyk (Ed.), *Practical Applications in Language and Computers* (pp. 241–252). Frankfurt am Main: Peter Lang.

Ringrow, H. (2016). *The Language of Cosmetics Advertising*. Basingstoke: Palgrave Macmillan.

Searle, J. R. (1969). *Speech Acts: An Essay in the Philosophy of Language*. Cambridge: Cambridge University Press.

Searle, J. R. (1979). *Expression and Meaning: Studies in the Theory of Speech Acts*. Cambridge: Cambridge University Press.

Searle, J. R. (1983). *Intentionality: An Essay in the Philosophy of Mind*. Cambridge: Cambridge University Press.

Searle, J. R. (1989). Consciousness, Unconsciousness and Intentionality. *Philosophical Topics, xxxvii*(10), 193–209.

Semino, E., & Short, M. (2004). *Corpus Stylistics: Speech, Writing and Thought Presentation in a Corpus of English Writing*. London: Routledge.

Sigley, R., & Holmes, J. (2002). *Looking at Girls in Corpora of English, 30*(2), 138–157.

Stubbs, M. (2001). *Words and Phrases: Corpus Studies of Lexical Semantics*. London: Blackwell.

Sunderland, J. (2004). *Gendered Discourses*. Basingstoke: Palgrave Macmillan.

Swann, J. (2002). Yes, but Is It Gender? In L. Litosseliti & J. Sunderland (Eds.), *Gender Identity and Discourse Analysis* (pp. 43–67). Amsterdam: John Benjamins.

Talbot, M. (1992). The Construction of Gender in a Teenage Magazine. In N. Fairclough (Ed.), *Critical Language Awareness* (pp. 174–199). London: Longman.

Talbot, M. (1995). A Synthetic Sisterhood: False Friends in a Teenage Magazine. In K. Hall & M. Bucholtz (Eds.), *Gender Articulated: Language and the Socially Constructed Self* (pp. 143–165). London: Routledge.

Taylor, C. (2017). Women Are Bitchy, but Men Are Sarcastic? Investigating Gender and Sarcasm. *Gender and Language, 11*(3), 415–445.

Taylor, L. D. (2008). Cads, Dads, and Magazines: Women's Sexual Preferences and Articles About Sex and Relationships. *Communication Monographs, 75*(3), 270–289.

Van Dijk, T. (1991). *Racism and the Press*. London: Routledge.

Van Leeuwen, T. (1995). Representing Social Action. *Discourse & Society, 6*(1), 81–106.

Widdowson, H. G. (1995). Discourse Analysis: A Critical Review. *Language and Literature, 4*(3), 157–172.

Wodak, R., & Meyer, M. (2009). Critical Discourse Analysis: History, Agenda, Theory and Methodology. In R. Wodak & M. Meyer (Eds.), *Methods of Critical Discourse Analysis* (2nd ed., pp. 1–33). London: Sage.

Woolls, D., & Coulthard, R. M. (1998). Tools for the Trade. *Forensic Linguistics, 5*(1), 33–57.

Xiao, Z., & McEnery, A. (2002, August 8–11). *A Corpus-Based Approach to Tense and Aspect in English-Chinese Translation*. Paper Presented at International Symposium on Contrastive and Translation Studies Between Chinese and English, Shanghai.

Ytre-Arne, B. (2011). 'I Want to Hold It in My Hands': Readers' Experiences of the Phenomenological Differences Between Women's Magazines Online and in Print. *Media, Culture and Society, 33*(3), 467–477.

Zimman, L. (2014). The Discursive Construction of Sex: Remaking and Reclaiming the Gendered Body in Talk About Genitals Among Trans Men. In L. Zimman, J. Raclaw, & J. Davis (Eds.), *Queer Excursions: Retheorizing Binaries in Language, Gender, and Sexuality* (pp. 13–34). Oxford: Oxford University Press.

2

Approaches to Studying Language and Gender

This chapter frames the current study within the context of existing discourse analytic research on the relationship between language and gender. Early empirical work in language and gender is often categorized according to the '3 D's' model, referring to Deficit, Dominance and Difference. These research paradigms have tended to address the issue of men and women's use of language in talk, rather than how gender is conceptualized *through* language, which is the primary concern of this study. More recent work is characterized by a concern with the discursive construction of gender, often underpinned by the notion of performativity (outlined in Chapter 1), which conceptualizes 'gender' as something a person 'does', as opposed to something one 'has'. Here I first outline the 'three D's' approaches to language and gender, then consider work adopting more discursive approaches to gender construction in text and talk.

© The Author(s) 2019
L. Coffey-Glover, *Men in Women's Worlds*,
https://doi.org/10.1057/978-1-137-57555-5_2

2.1   Gender as Difference: The '3Ds' Model

Danish linguist Otto Jespersen is often cited as the first scholar to give credence to observing women's language use, and his work is characteristic of the 'deficit' approach to language and gender which views women's speech as deficient to men's. Jespersen's chapter on 'women's language' from his 1922 book *Language: Its Nature, Development and Origin*, polarized male and female language use. Jespersen asserted that while women function to maintain the 'purity' of language, men are responsible for its innovation and creativity. His interpretation of 'purity' was related to the notion that women avoid 'coarse and vulgar expressions', preferring 'refined (and in certain spheres) veiled and indirect expressions' (1922: 246). This androcentric view posited 'women's language' as a lesser deviation from men's speech, and relied purely on Jespersen's own intuitions about language use, anecdotal evidence and literary texts, rather than empirical investigation.

The relationship between gender identity and language use would later be addressed more empirically by variationist sociolinguists, using gender, or more accurately, biological sex, as an independent social variable (Labov 1990; Milroy 1980; Trudgill 1972, 1974). However, like the feminist-inspired 'dominance' and 'difference' approaches, variationist sociolinguists tended to assume a deterministic model of 'gender', and looked for differences, rather than possible similarities, between men and women's use of language. Sociolinguistic studies have received significant critique from feminist linguists for what they perceive as sexism in sociolinguistic research, where male speech is theorized as a positive norm, and women's speech is treated as a negative deviation (see Cameron 1992). For example, in Trudgill's study of dialect use in Norwich, women are interpreted as exhibiting more 'conservative' speech habits because they are said to aspire to a higher social class, where men's use of vernacular speech acquires the more positively valued 'covert prestige' (Mills 2012: 17–18).

The 'dominance' model of language and gender, which developed out of second wave feminism in the 1960s and 1970s, is exemplified by the notion that differences between men's and women's speech are a product of, and affirmation of, male dominance in society. The most influential and controversial research straddling both 'deficit' and 'dominance' approaches is Robin Lakoff's pioneering work *Language and Woman's Place* (1975). Lakoff argued that there are two styles of speech: 'neutral language' and 'women's language.' She asserted that women's speech style was marked by the use of particular linguistic features, including hedges such as 'you know', 'sort of' and 'well' and so on, that reduce the force of an utterance; intensifiers like *very, really, so*; tag questions; rising intonation on declaratives and 'trivial' lexis and 'empty' adjectives, including evaluative adjectives like *lovely, divine*, and *charming*, which Jespersen had also claimed were features of women's speech (Lakoff 1975, 2004: 78–80). Lakoff claimed that these features are linked in terms of their communicative function, which is to weaken the force of an utterance. For example, rising intonation is interpreted as showing tentativeness; tag questions are associated with a desire for confirmation and approval; and qualifiers and intensifiers are said to function as hedges in conversation (Lakoff 1975, 2004: 79). Lakoff concluded that this 'unassertive' speech style is a symptom of patriarchal society, in which women are brought up to think of assertion and authority as masculine qualities, and taught instead to display 'feminine' qualities of weakness, passivity and deference to men. She argues that young girls acquire Women's Language in the course of childhood socialization as a way of preparing them for their subordinate place in adult society.

Many sociolinguists have acknowledged the methodological flaws in Lakoff's work; like Jespersen's work in the 1920s, the 'features' of women's language she observes were based mainly on her own intuitions, and the few participants she did include were all educated, white, middle class subjects. Despite these criticisms, it is important to recognize the importance of Lakoff's work in aligning feminism with the study of language and gender, and in considering power as the direct index that explains women's use of language. While her work was empirically dubious, Lakoff is often credited as the first person to give serious intellectual space to the relationship between language and women's subordinate position in society. Because of this, her work is considered by many feminist language and gender scholars as signifying the birth of feminist linguistics. The publication of *Language and Woman's Place* sparked a number of empirically based discourse analytic studies seeking evidence for features of Women's Language (for example Fishman 1983; Holmes 1984; O'Barr and Atkins 1980; Zimmerman and West 1975).

At the heart of the 'dominance' approach lies the issue of power: women's use of language is perceived as 'powerless' language, because of the subordinate position of women in society. Pamela Fishman, in her classic study of talk between three heterosexual couples (1980, 1983) found that:

> as with work in its usual sense, there appears to be a division of labor in conversation. The people who do the routine maintenance work, the women, are not the same people who either control or benefit from the process.
>
> (Fishman 1983: 99)

Fishman interpreted women's low status interactional work, or 'interactional shit-work', as a symptom of the low-status jobs they are pushed into. This kind of explanation was an attractive one to some feminist researchers, but as several commentators have pointed out, there are problems with the notion that conversational dominance is analogous to patriarchal dominance: to assert that a linguistic feature is 'powerful' or 'powerless' necessitates being able to establish meanings unequivocally, but since linguistic forms are 'multifunctional'—they can mean different things in different contexts and be interpreted in different ways depending on context—it is not possible to state than one particular form always functions in a particular way; for example that tag questions communicate unassertiveness, or that interruptions always function as assertions of power.

Asserting that differences in language use can be attributed to the unequal power relations of patriarchal society also assumes that all men have power over all women. Whilst power relations are clearly an important part of interaction, they are context dependent. As Talbot points out, if we want to talk about male dominance, we need to be more specific, and consider how patterns of male dominance might vary in different cultures, or across different contexts within a particular culture (2010: 111).

The current of research often termed the 'difference' approach to language and gender asserts that men and women speak differently, not because of power differentials, but because they belong to different social subcultures, and therefore use language to fulfil different social roles (see, for example, Coates 1989; Maltz and Borker 1982; Tannen 1990). This suggested that gendered talk needed to be understood via the study of single-sex as well as mixed-sex groups, which prompted the investigation, and positive re-evaluation of women's talk (Holmes 1984), and later, investigation of men's talk (Coates 2003; Johnson and Meinhoff 1997).

The main proponent of this approach is Deborah Tannen, who wrote *You Just Don't Understand*, a popular book about the conversational rules men and women adhere to (Tannen 1990). Her theory was based on Gumperz's (1982) work on ethnically distinct subcultures, and Maltz and Borker's work on children's playground interactions. Maltz and Borker found that boys and girls tended to have different norms of interaction in segregated play: boys usually play in hierarchical groups and use a more competitive speech style, where girls play in small groups of 'best friends', where they use a more supportive speech style. Maltz and Borker argued that these speech styles developed in youth result in a form of 'cross-cultural miscommunication' between males and females, analogous to that which Gumperz found in his research on miscommunication between different ethnic groups. Gumperz showed that subtle differences in the way two ethnic groups used language could lead to what he called 'crosstalk': systematic misunderstandings of which neither group was conscious.

Tannen appropriated this idea of crosstalk and applied it to male-female communication. She argued that men grow up in a world where conversation is a contest, but for women talk is a way to exchange confirmation and support, and used the term 'genderlect' to describe these different gendered 'dialects'. Tannen argues that differing activities and social norms of boys' and girls' peer groups teach them different rules for talking, and that childhood segregation makes the two sexes as different in their ways of communicating as people of different ethnicities: 'conversation between men and women is cross-cultural communication' (Tannen 1990: 47). Tannen asserts that it is not the genderlects themselves that are a problem, but that expectations that one must conform to their genderlect are likely to restrict men and women in different situations, and not being aware of one another's genderlect will result in communicative stalemates. Critics of Tannen's work have argued that her position is apolitical, and thus ignores how differing power relations between men and women might affect their communicative behavior (see, for example, Uchida 1992). In the context of women's magazines, the idea that men and women do not understand one another because they are inherently different is echoed, for instance, in the inclusion of articles like 'Man Talk' (see Chapter 9, Sect. 9.3.1), where the text implicitly implies that men's utterances are in need of explanation, because women cannot understand them.

There are numerous problems with the cross-cultural miscommunication argument, and the 'difference' approach in general. As Cameron (2007: 44) observes, a major problem with the difference model is that in its focus on *differences* between men and women's linguistic behavior, it ignores the *similarities* between men and women. For example, studies surveying work on male and female differences have actually found little evidence for sex differences in language use (Canary and Hause 1993; Hyde 2005). Janet Hyde examined the results of 46 studies on sex variation, covering 20 years of data, and found that on most psychological characteristics, men and women were more alike than different. Her findings for studies on gender differences in verbal behavior also show that men and women are more similar than they are different (Hyde 2005: 186).

To argue that men and women belong to distinct subcultures implies that men and women are inherently different creatures, which can have serious consequences. For example, Henley and Kramarae explain how the two-cultures argument could allow for acquaintance rape and domestic abuse to be interpreted as extreme cases of miscommunication (Henley and Kramarae 1991). Sociolinguist Susan Ehrlich (2001) recorded the proceedings of a sexual harassment case which demonstrates how the folklinguistic idea that men don't understand women's indirectness can result in women being blamed for instances of sexual assault. She recorded the proceedings of a Canadian university tribunal concerning two women students who had made allegations of sexual assault against the same male student. Both incidents had begun consensually, but the women claimed that he had forced them into further sexual activity. This contradicted the male's account, since he insisted that the women had consented. Ehrlich analyzed the proceedings, and noted how members of the tribunal interpret the incident as a case of miscommunication, and the woman complainants were held responsible for the breakdown in communication—in other words that the women should have indicated that they didn't want to have sex more directly.

This idea also features prominently in sex education and rape prevention programs, which instruct women that if they do not want to have sex, they should 'just say no' (Cameron 2007: 93). It is stressed that a woman's refusal should take the form of a firm, unequivocal 'no'— the idea being that only by keeping the message short and simple can you be sure it will not be misunderstood. However, conversation analysts Celia Kitzinger and Hannah Frith (1999) conducted focus-group interviews with 58 women and asked them how, in practice, they communicated to men that they did not wish to have sex. Despite being familiar with the 'just say no' maxim, most of the women said they felt this strategy would be more likely to aggravate men—the strategies they actually reported were designed to mitigate the force of the refusal, such as giving excuses like 'I've got a headache', 'I'm tired', 'I'm on my period'. Cameron points out that all the strategies the women reported are ones used by *both* sexes in any situation where it is necessary to refuse something, and that studies of interaction show that in everyday contexts, refusing is never done by 'just saying no': 'Most refusals don't even contain the word 'no'. Yet in non-sexual situations, no one seems to have trouble understanding them' (Cameron 2007: 94). As Kitzinger and Frith assert, this undercuts the notion that men misunderstand 'indirect' refusals on the basis that they have been socialized to only respond to direct forms of language. In the case recorded by Ehrlich (2001), the women were held responsible for the actions of the male assailant because they failed to communicate directly in a way that the two cultures approach asserts men would have been better equipped to understand.

Like the 'deficit' and 'dominance' models, the difference approach is also necessarily essentialist, because it relies on the concepts of 'male/female' and 'masculinity/femininity' as fixed, relational binaries. All three models are ultimately based on the notion of difference, assuming essential or generalizable differences in language use that could be mapped onto gender and sexuality and focusing on one side of a supposed binary distinction (gay people or women) at the expense of the 'normal' other (heterosexuals, men) (Baker 2008: 58).

2.2   Beyond 'Difference': Discourse and Diversity

The '3 D's' typology presupposes that gender identity is reflected through language use. However, developments in social constructionism and post-structuralism induced a change in the way research into gender construction conceptualizes 'gender', influenced particularly by Butler's notion of 'performativity'. The shift in perceiving gender as something we embody to something we 'do' (consciously or unconsciously), consequently signaled a shift in emphasis from 'gendered speakers' to 'what is communicated by, to and about women, men, boys and girls' (Sunderland and Litosseliti 2008: 4), in other words, gendered discourses (Sunderland 2004).

The discursive approach to gender identity views language as a tool for constructing, challenging and signaling orientation towards particular gendered subjectivities (Eckert and McConnell-Ginet 2003). This approach crucially recognizes the diversity of gender performance: rather than treating 'men' and 'women' as discrete, homogeneous social categories, work that goes beyond a focus on 'difference' emphasizes the role that context plays in gender performance, such as social setting or membership of particular communities of practice (Eckert and McConnell-Ginet 1992), as well as the ways that different facets of social identity (such as class, age, ethnicity) intersect with gender in the production of different masculinities, femininities and non-binary gender identities (Levon and Mendes 2016).

Analyzing gendered discourses involves considering the ways of talking about men and women that are made available to speaker-readers in a particular text or context, and research in this tradition has demonstrated the important role that media genres play in producing and reproducing ideological gender scripts (Baker 2008; Ringrow 2016; Sunderland 2004; Talbot 2014). Work focusing on the construction and representation of gendered discourses in the media employs a wide range of methodological approaches including corpus linguistics (Baker 2014) and Feminist Critical Discourse Analysis (CDA) (Lazar 2005; Ringrow 2016). A post-structuralist understanding of 'gender' necessitates approaches that privilege 'function' over 'form', that is, approaches that acknowledge the *variability* of language practices. This means that rather than focusing on large-scale quantitative studies of the differences between men's and women's speech, research influenced by discourse analysis is more likely to focus on smaller-scale studies of how language practices come to index particular understandings of gender identity. Indeed, even corpus linguistic work on language and gender is more concerned with identifying statistically salient patterns that might be associated with particular gendered identities in specific contexts, rather than trying to find evidence for global gender patterns (for example Baker and Levon 2015). The 'shift to discourse' also entails an increased interest in the gendered meanings of different semiotic modes, including visual images (Brookes et al. 2016). Feminist linguistic analysis of any methodological persuasion is concerned with challenging the gender inequalities that are often at the heart of these constructed ideological gender norms (Mills and Mullany 2011).

2.3   Hegemonic Masculinity

Alongside the theoretical shift in perspective from a conception of gender as who we *are* to 'effects we produce by what we *do*' (Cameron 1997: 48) in discourse analytic work, was a consideration of the relationship between language and masculinity(ies). Until the 1990s, the focus of language and gender study was mainly on women's speech and mixed-sex talk. For some this reflects a wider androcentrism in scholarship, betraying an assumption that men's language represents the 'neutral' benchmark by which women's language should be measured (see, for example, Mills 1995: 44). Studies of all-male interaction can be seen in part as an attempt to challenge the sexism and androcentrism of earlier research and bring male language into focus, since unless we challenge how gender norms are produced and sustained, there can be no 'subversive confusion' of them (Butler 1990: 34).

Language and Masculinity (Johnson and Meinhoff 1997) was the first book-length consideration of the relationship between masculinity and language use. Since then research into language and masculinities has focused predominantly on men's interactional behavior, examining how both formal features and topic content might index different forms of masculine performance in different contexts or communities of practice (for example Balirano and Baker 2018; Holmes 2009; Kiesling 2002; Milani 2015), although research in (critical) discourse analysis and related disciplines also turned to how written texts construct ideologies of masculinity for their readers (Attenborough 2011; Baker and Levon 2016; Benwell 2003; Gill 2014).

The literature on language and masculinity reveals a concern with how language can be seen to construct what is conventionally termed 'hegemonic masculinity'. This term was popularized by sociologist Raewyn Connell (1995, 2005) to refer to forms of masculinity that rely on 'a correspondence between cultural ideal and institutional power' (Connell 1995: 77). The term 'hegemony' is appropriated from Gramsci (1971, 1985), who used it to refer to compliance towards a dominant person or group. The notion of dominance, both cultural and physical, is therefore a key aspect of hegemonic masculinity. Frosh et al. (2002) describe hegemonic masculinity as an amalgamation of various concepts and practices, such as: 'heterosexuality, toughness, power and authority, competitiveness and the subordination of gay men' (2002: 75–76). Hegemony is what naturalizes culturally valued forms of masculinity and subordinates masculinities that conflict with these dominant forms.

Coates (2003) uses the concept of hegemonic masculinity to explain the patterns of talk she found in her analysis of 32 informal interactions in all-male friendship groups, focusing in particular on story-telling. Her interest in men's linguistic behavior was in part a reaction to the tendency to focus on 'women's language' and assumptions made about men's language based on mixed-sex interaction. Coates concludes that the men in her study align themselves with hegemonic masculinity, exhibiting qualities of toughness, competitiveness, power, a lack of self-disclosure and heterosexuality (2003: 197). In terms of topics of conversation, she found that 'beer-talk', heterosexual encounters, modern technology, sport and cars were prominent themes. These may be recognizable to the reader as things which stereotypically index masculinity, and are also present in my data: the magazines also presuppose men's heterosexuality, virility and interest in things like drinking, sport and cars (see Chapter 8). As mentioned above, the concept of heterosexual display is a prominent theme in the literature on language and masculinity, and this is largely supported by my analysis of constructions of masculinity in women's magazines: oppositional meanings construct sexuality as a binary construct (see Chapter 6); homosexuality is associated with femininity, and heterosexuality is an assumed norm (see Chapter 8).

Research into men's language also asserts that men are less prone to self-disclosure and to discuss emotions (Coates 2001, 2003). Men are largely seen as unemotional in my data, although the desirability of self-disclosure, or at least an acknowledgement of the possibility of emotionality, is also evident: for example, the true-life story 'My girlfriend jilted me at the altar' is a first-person narrative which is part of a regular series of stories prefaced by the tagline 'Men Cry too…'. This story could be said to function in part as an example of male disclosure, but there is of course an implicit assumption here that for men to cry is unusual.

As the 'norm', hegemonic masculinity is also the 'ideal' form of masculinity, which is endemic in phenomena like celebrity culture, and therefore a natural presence in commercial women's magazines. Part of the importance of studying hegemonic masculinity in women's magazines is the idea that women also contribute to its construction (both as writers and readers), because '[m]en do not take up positions of dominance by their own efforts alone' (Talbot 1998: 198). Women's magazines instruct women on how men should behave and be treated, as well as how women should present themselves to the world.

2.4 Summary

This chapter has provided the necessary intellectual context for discussing women's magazines as conduits of gender performance. I have shown how language and gender scholars usually uphold a distinction between spoken interaction and written representation, and that scholarship has concentrated mainly on the *use* of language as linked to gendered speech styles, rather than how masculinity or femininity is constructed *through* language, which is the focus of this study. In the following chapter I consider some of the existing research on gender representation in women's and men's magazines, as an appropriate empirical backdrop for the present study.

References

Attenborough, F. T. (2011). Complicating the Sexualisation Thesis: The Media, Gender and 'Sci-Candy'. *Discourse & Society, 22*(6), 659–676.

Baker, P. (2008). *Sexed Texts: Language, Gender and Sexuality*. London: Equinox.

Baker, P. (2014). *Using Corpora to Analyze Gender*. London: Bloomsbury.

Baker, P., & Levon, E. (2015). Picking the Right Cherries?: A Comparison of Corpus-Based and Qualitative Analyses of News Articles About Masculinity. *Discourse & Communication, 9*(2), 221–236.

Baker, P., & Levon, E. (2016). 'That's What I Call a Man': Representations of Racialised and Classed Masculinities in the UK Print Media. *Gender and Language, 10*(1), 106–139.

Balirano, G., & Baker, P. (2018). *Queering Masculinities in Language and Culture*. Basingstoke: Palgrave Macmillan.

Benwell, B. (Ed.). (2003). *Masculinity in Men's Lifestyle Magazines*. Oxford: Blackwell.

Brookes, G., Harvey, K., & Mullany, L. (2016). "Off to the Best Start"? A Multimodal Critique of Breast and Formula Feeding Health Promotional Discourse. *Gender and Language, 10*(3), 340–363.

Butler, J. (1990). *Gender Trouble: Feminism and the Subversion of Identity*. London: Routledge.

Cameron, D. (1992). *Feminism and Linguistic Theory* (2nd ed.). Basingstoke: Macmillan.

Cameron, D. (1997). Performing Gender Identity: Young Men's Talk and the Construction of Heterosexual Masculinity. In S. Johnson & U. H. Meinhoff (Eds.), *Language and Masculinity* (pp. 47–64). Oxford: Blackwell.

Cameron, D. (2007). *The Myth of Mars and Venus: Do Men and Women Really Speak Different Languages?* Oxford: Oxford University Press.

Canary, D. J., & Hause, K. S. (1993). Is There Any Reason to Research Sex Differences in Communication? *Communication Quarterly, 41*(2), 129–144.

Coates, J. (1989). Gossip Revisited: Language in All-Female Groups. In J. Coates & D. Cameron (Eds.), *Women in Their Speech Communities* (pp. 94–121). London: Longman.

Coates, J. (2001). Pushing at the Boundaries: The Expression of Alternative Masculinities. In J. Cotterill & A. Ife (Eds.), *Language Across Boundaries* (pp. 1–24). London: BAAL/Continuum.

Coates, J. (2003). *Men Talk*. Oxford: Blackwell.

Connell, R. W. (1995). *Masculinities*. Berkeley: University of California Press.

Connell, R. W. (2005). Hegemonic Masculinity: Rethinking the Concept. *Gender & Society, 19*(6), 829–859.

Eckert, P., & McConnell-Ginet, S. (1992). Think Practically and Look Locally: Language and Gender as Community-Based Practice. *Annual Review of Anthropology, 21*(1), 461–490.

Eckert, P., & McConnell-Ginet, S. (2003). *Language and Gender*. Cambridge: Cambridge University Press.

Ehrlich, S. (2001). *Representing Rape: Language and Sexual Consent*. London: Routledge.

Fishman, P. M. (1980). Conversational Insecurity. In H. Giles, W. P. Robinson, & P. M. Smith (Eds.), *Language Social Psychological Perspectives* (pp. 127–132). New York: Pergamon Press.

Fishman, P. M. (1983). Interaction: The Work Women Do. In B. Thorne, C. Kramarae, & N. Henley (Eds.), *Language, Gender and Society*. Rowley, MA: Newbury House.

Frosh, S., Phoenix, A., & Pattman, R. (2002). *Young Masculinities: Understanding Boys in Contemporary Society*. Basingstoke: Palgrave Macmillan.

Gill, R. (2014). Powerful Women, Vulnerable Men and Postfeminist Masculinity in Men's Popular Fiction. *Gender and Language, 8*(2), 185–204.

Gramsci, A. (1971). *Selections from Prison Notebooks* (Q. Hoare & G. Nowell-Smith, Trans.). London: Lawrence and Wishart.

Gramsci, A. (1985). *Selections from the Cultural Writings 1921–1926* (D. Forgacs & G. Nowell-Smith, Eds. and W. Boelhower, Trans.). London: Lawrence and Wishart.

Gumperz, J. (Ed.). (1982). *Language and Identity*. Cambridge: Cambridge University Press.

Henley, N., & Kramarae, C. (1991). Gender, Power and Miscommunication. In N. Coupland, H. Giles, & J. Wiemann (Eds.), *"Miscommunication" and Problem Talk* (pp. 18–43). Newbury Park, CA: Sage.

Holmes, J. (1984). Hedging Your Bets and Sitting on the Fence: Some Evidence for Hedges as Support Structures. *Te Reo, 27,* 47–62.

Holmes, J. (2009). Men, Masculinities and Leadership: Different Discourse Styles at Work. In P. Pichler & E. M. Eppler (Eds.), *Gender and Spoken Interaction* (pp. 186–210). Basingstoke: Palgrave Macmillan.

Hyde, J. (2005). The Gender Similarities Hypothesis. *American Psychologist, 60*(6), 581–592.

Jespersen, O. (1922). *Language, Its Origin and Development*. London: Allen & Unwin.

Johnson, S., & Meinhoff, U. (Eds.). (1997). *Language and Masculinity*. Oxford: Blackwell.

Kiesling, S. (2002). Playing the Straight Man: Displaying and Maintaining Male Heterosexuality in Discourse. In K. Campbell-Kibler, R. J. Podesva, S. J. Roberts, & A. Wong (Eds.), *Language and Sexuality: Contesting Meaning in Theory and Practice* (pp. 249–266). Stanford, CA: CSLI Publications.

Kitzinger, C., & Frith, H. (1999). Just Say No? The Use of Conversation Analysis on Developing a Feminist Perspective on Sexual Refusal. *Discourse & Society, 10*(3), 293–316.

Labov, W. (1990). The Intersection of Sex and Social Class in the Course of Linguistic Change. *Language, Variation and Change, 2*(2), 205–254.

Lakoff, R. T. (1975). *Language and Woman's Place*. New York: Harper & Row.

Lakoff, R. T. (2004). *Language and Woman's Place: Text and Commentaries* (M. Bucholtz, Ed., Rev. Exp. ed.). New York: Oxford University Press.

Lazar, M. (2005). *Feminist Critical Discourse Analysis*. Basingstoke: Palgrave Macmillan.

Levon, E., & Mendes, R. B. (2016). *Language, Sexuality and Power: Studies in Intersectional Sociolinguistics*. Oxford: Oxford University Press.

Maltz, D., & Borker, R. (1982). A Cultural Approach to Male-Female Miscommunication. In J. Gumperz (Ed.), *Language and Social Identity* (pp. 196–216). Cambridge: Cambridge University Press.

Milani, T. (Ed.). (2015). *Language and Masculinities: Performances, Intersections, Dislocations*. London: Routledge.

Mills, S. (1995). *Feminist Stylistics*. London: Routledge.

Mills, S. (2012). *Gender Matters: Feminist Linguistic Analysis.* London: Equinox.

Mills, S., & Mullany, L. (2011). *Language, Gender and Feminism: Theory, Methodology and Practice.* London: Routledge.

Milroy, L. (1980). *Language and Social Networks.* Oxford: Basil Blackwell.

O'Barr, W., & Atkins, B. (1980). "Women's Language" or "Powerless Language"? In S. McConnell-Ginet, R. Borker, & N. Furman (Eds.), *Women and Language in Literature and Society* (pp. 93–110). New York: Praeger.

Ringrow, H. (2016). *The Language of Cosmetics Advertising.* Basingstoke: Palgrave Macmillan.

Sunderland, J. (2004). *Gendered Discourses.* Basingstoke: Palgrave Macmillan.

Sunderland, J., & Litosseliti, L. (2008). Current Research Methodologies in Gender and Language Study: Key Issues. In K. Harrington, L. Litosseliti, H. Sauntson, & J. Sunderland (Eds.), *Gender and Language Research Methodologies* (pp. 1–18). Basingstoke: Palgrave Macmillan.

Talbot, M. (1998). *Language and Gender: An Introduction.* Cambridge: Polity Press.

Talbot, M. (2010). *Language and Gender* (2nd ed.). Cambridge: Polity Press.

Talbot, M. (2014). Language, Gender and Popular Culture. In S. Ehrlich, M. Meyerhoff, & J. Holmes (Eds.), *The Handbook of Language, Gender and Sexuality* (pp. 604–624). Malden, MA and Oxford: Wiley-Blackwell.

Tannen, D. (1990). *You Just Don't Understand.* London: Virago.

Trudgill, P. (1972). Sex, Covert Prestige and Linguistic Change in the Urban British English of Norwich. *Language in Society, 1*(2), 179–195.

Trudgill, P. (1974). *The Social Differentiation of English in Norwich.* Cambridge: Cambridge University Press.

Uchida, A. (1992). When "Difference" Is "Dominance": A Critique of the 'Anti-Power-Based' Cultural Approach to Sex Differences. *Language in Society, 21*(4), 547–568.

Zimmerman, D., & West, C. (1975). Sex Roles, Interruptions and Silences in Conversation. In B. Thorne & N. Henley (Eds.), *Language and Sex: Difference and Dominance* (pp. 105–129). Rowley, MA: Newbury House.

3

Women's and Men's Magazines

Women's magazines have been studied from a wide range of perspectives and geographical contexts. Earlier work focused exclusively on content analysis and the role of ideology in shaping reader responses, where more recent work encompasses analysis of audience response, as well as sites of production (see, for example, Ytre-Arne 2011; Favaro 2017). Analyses of content have focused explicitly on ideologies of femininity, although studies of magazines for girls and young women have acknowledged that the ability to attract boys is seen as an important step in girls' ascendency to womanhood (Firminger 2006; McLoughlin 2000). The study of magazines for adolescent girls has concentrated on the pedagogical role of magazines, the potential influence of these on girls' self-perception and their socialization into traditional gender roles (Duke and Kreshel 1998; McRobbie 1982; McLoughlin 2008). Magazines for women are described as gatekeepers of advice for women on fashion and beauty, sexual relationships with men and careers (McRobbie 1996; Talbot 1995; Gill 2009), and idealized images of the female body (Jeffries 2007; Gill and Elias 2014; Ringrow 2016).

Existing scholarship acknowledges the heteronormative nature of mainstream women's magazines, and that these publications are

© The Author(s) 2019
L. Coffey-Glover, *Men in Women's Worlds*,
https://doi.org/10.1057/978-1-137-57555-5_3

heavily engaged in instructing women on how to please men (Firminger 2006; Litosseliti 2006; McLoughlin 2000; Jeffries 2007; Ménard and Kleinplatz 2008). For example, McRobbie acknowledges the ubiquity of men in the pages of *Jackie* magazine: 'even the enjoyment of fashion and pop music seemed to be defined in terms of the presence or absence of a "boyfriend"' (1996: 182). Commentators also recognize that women are constructed as actively pursuing heterosexual relationships, and as primarily responsible for their relationships with men (Eggins and Iedema 1997; Litosseliti 2006: 100). However, limited research has been carried out explicitly on the role of men in women's magazines, and how masculinity is negotiated in these texts. In addition, the majority of textual analyses of women's magazines, while adopting concepts like 'discourse' and 'ideology', are often nevertheless focused on content analysis, which privileges thematic convenience over the rigor of linguistic form. I argue that analyzing linguistic structure is imperative for an understanding of how texts communicate to their readers, whether or not readers actually take up the positions offered to them by the text. That is because if we do not interrogate the *mechanisms* of sexist, misogynistic or homophobic discourse, we cannot begin to challenge harmful ideologies.

3.1   Gendered Discourses in Women's Magazines

There is a substantial body of work on the women's magazine genre that cuts across disciplines including linguistics, sociology, media and communication studies, cultural studies and psychology (Ballaster et al. 1991; McRobbie 1982, 1991, 1996; Talbot 1992, 1995; Machin and Thornborrow 2003; Ticknell et al. 2003; Gill 2007, 2009; Jeffries 2007; Hasinoff 2009; Ringrow 2016). This body of research addresses a number of discernible themes: the idea that femininity is a consumerist practice, gender as biologically determined, the relationship between feminism and women's magazines, and constructions of heteronormativity and female sexuality.

Although language is often the analytical focus in textual analyses from these disciplines, little attention is paid to grammatical structure or lexical choice, in other words, of how language actually works to *produce* these representations. If we can understand the mechanics of *how* a text constructs linguistic images of masculinity, then we can understand more about how readers might reach these possible interpretations of the texts, and therefore the kinds of effects they may have on the reader. There is *some* linguistics-based research on women's magazines that has proved invaluable in the design and implementation of this study (Jeffries 2007; Eggins and Iedma 1997; del-Teso-Craviotto 2005; Motschenbacher 2009); the present study represents a small contribution to this growing body of work.

3.1.1 Consumer Femininity

Among the literature on women's magazines are a number of studies that focus on the idea of femininity as a consumerist practice; the notion that femininity is a product that can be bought, because 'women's bodies are always imperfect. They always need fixing' (Smith 1988: 47). According to this research, women's magazines promote the idea that women's bodies can be 'fixed' through the use of cosmetics and other 'curing' processes.

McRobbie's (1982, 1991) analyses of *Jackie*, a magazine aimed at young women, denigrated women's magazines as conforming to patriarchal societal structures, producing a 'culture of femininity' centering around the concept of romance and the repetition of beautification processes in order to attract a male suitor. Talbot (1992: 172) also describes women's magazines as a tool of 'consumer femininity', where achieving feminine identity is represented as reliant on undertaking 'feminizing practices', which involves the consumption of various material and visual resources for 'creating' femininity (1992: 173). Ringrow's (2016) book-length treatment of cosmetics advertising discourse in French and English women's magazines also shows how cosmetics are offered as 'tools' for creating the ideal body (in identifiable Problem-Solution patterns), but, crucially, the products are often described in a way that emphasizes they are a 'natural' beauty aid with positive sensory effects, which serves to disguise their synthetic properties. As a discursive strategy this is rather canny, since it encourages women to consume products without feeling that they are 'tampering' with their natural bodies. Scientific language is also used to describe cosmetics and other beauty products, which emphasize the authenticity of the products and their feminizing effects (Jeffries 2007; Ringrow 2016).

As well as the youthful, ideal body, some scholars also acknowledge the ways in which female sexuality is offered to the reader for consumption. Talbot, for example, shows how the headlines of a series of sex-related instructional features on the cover of magazines serve as 'sell lines' for the magazines themselves (1992: 174). McCracken also notes that 'women's magazines repeatedly succeed in linking desire to consumerism' (1993: 301), and Gill's (2009) analysis of sexual relationships in *Glamour* magazine notes how discourses of consumerism can be traced through the use of metaphorical expressions like 'investing in' or 'snapping up' men, as though they were products for consumption (2009: 352). Machin and Thornborrow (2003) similarly discuss discourses of consumerism in *Cosmopolitan*, observing how the magazine represents women's sexual and work practices, and found that women are constructed as able to access agency and independence through a manipulation of male sexuality; power is achieved through the exploitation of men and their bodies. The authors argue that female empowerment is represented as a product for consumption, and that it is a discourse of consumerism which allows women to forge feminine identities. These accounts therefore acknowledge that the desire to please men is represented as a primary motivation for indulging in feminizing practices. I would therefore argue that particular discourses of masculinity are being sold to women as part and parcel of consumer femininity.

3.1.2 Sociobiology

Hasinoff (2009) discusses discourses of 'sociobiology' in *Cosmopolitan*, a model of gender essentialism in which 'men are driven by psychological and physiological urges' and women are associated with 'domestic labor, nurturing behaviors, and [adhere] to ideals of white middle-class Western femininity' (2009: 267–268). She argues that the magazine presents this essentialism as indisputable scientific 'fact', which in turn justifies the maintenance of 'normative' gender practices. Firminger's (2006) study of American teenage girls' magazines also discusses essentialist definitions of gender in the texts. She found that where teenage boys are represented as unemotional, sexually driven and superficial, girls are encouraged to pursue boys, but are less sexualized. They are also responsible for the maintenance of relationships and construct their identities based on what is attractive to boys.

Through textual analysis, Hasinoff argues that 'scientific common sense consistently offers anti-feminist justifications for the practices and techniques of normative femininity' (2009: 269). Hasinoff's (2009) survey shows how references to expert research on sociobiology are used to assert that norms of female bodily appearance reflect men's genetically-determined subconscious desire for fertility, effectively 'biologizing' heterosexuality (2009: 273). Hasinoff's examples demonstrate how *Cosmopolitan* uses sociobiological statements to encourage the reader to work out what men find attractive and create a simulated natural version for male consumption.

In a recent study of online women's magazines, García-Favaro (2015) shows how peer-to-peer and editorial advice on men's use of pornography relies on evolutionary accounts of gender. Advice from both user discussions and editorial content emphasizes that men and women are 'equal-but-different', and (all) men's assumed use of porn is attributed to the 'fact' that 'men need porn' because they are 'programmed' differently. Like in Hasinoff's study, the ultimate advice to women in García-Favaro's data is to change their own behavior in response to men's sexual 'needs', which points to the 'biological inevitability of male sexuality' (2015: 371). The pseudo-scientific discourse evident in these kinds of arguments are also found in my data. While the texts in my corpus do not make explicit reference to genetically-determined behavior in men in a way that is linked to the idea of 'hard-wired' differences, there are many examples in my data that do make generalizations about male behavior that can be read as deterministic, underpinned by a discourse of gender differences, and this is particularly pertinent when it comes to constructions of men's assumed biological need for sex (see Chapter 8).

3.1.3 Feminism and Women's Magazines

Feminist movements are commonly conceptualized in terms of 'waves', with First Wave feminism beginning in the late nineteenth century, characterized by the suffragette movement. Second Wave feminism developed in the late 1960s in response to inequalities in areas such as the workplace, childcare, contraception and abortion (Mills 2003). The question of whether women's magazines launched following the development of Second Wave feminism are informed by feminist ideas has been a prominent theme in studies of women's magazines (Gill 2007: 198). Third Wave feminism developed during the 1990s in response to the notion of global 'sisterhood' and favored individualism and local activism, or what Lazar refers to as a shift from 'we-feminism' to 'I-feminism' (2009: 397). This focus on individualism has arguably allowed women's magazines to appropriate feminist ideas in a way that upholds ideological femininity while at the same time paying lip-service to notions of individual agency and empowerment. Caldas-Coulthard notes that 'glossy' magazines demonstrate 'an acceptance and incorporation of some basic feminist and liberal principles', but that '[t]he conservative discourse of separate spheres between men and women and of female passivity [...] continue to coexist with a liberal discourse of the independent woman' (1996: 253). This flux between female passivity and independence, between empowerment and subordination, problematizes the notion of women's magazines as articulating feminist discourses.

Earlier studies, influenced by the Second Wave, provided textual analyses highlighting the ways in which women's magazines are in contradiction with feminist principles (see, for example, Friedan 1963; Tuchman et al. 1978). These studies were therefore motivated by a desire to uncover 'unreal' images of women and promote more positive images that were more in line with the feminist movement (Gough-Yates 2002: 8). Media scholars in the 1980s began to adopt more ideologically-driven analyses of women's magazines, asserting that they were 'instruments of domination' (Gough-Yates 2002: 9) influenced by Althusser's work on ideology (for example Glazer 1980; Leman 1980).

However, McRobbie (1996) argues that the 'conventional' feminist critique of women's magazines as exemplifying oppression—one that her earlier work on *Jackie* magazine in the 1970s and 1980s subscribed to—is unhelpful, as it 'generates an enormous polarization between 'the feminists' and the magazines and their readers' (1996: 180). In a similar vein, Winship argues that: 'we shouldn't just contemplate the many and inevitable ways [women's magazines] are not feminist, but also consider what they might say to feminism' (Winship 1987: 139). In other words, she asks what women's magazines can tell us that might enhance a feminist politics and praxis. Winship's work (1983, 1985, 1987) charted the changing content of women's magazines form the 1950s to the 1980s, and she is one of a number of scholars who acknowledges the 'pleasure' of women's magazines, but asserts that the pleasure derived from them 'depends on being familiar with the cultural codes of what is meant to be pleasurable, and on occupying the appropriate spaces' (Winship 1987: 52).

In light of this, a more coherent, and reflexive dialogue between feminism and women's magazines could contribute significantly to the development of feminist movements. For example, women's magazines could helpfully contribute to feminist activism if their producers could provide coherent, consistent content addressing feminist issues, such as the gender pay gap, equal parental rights, and violence against women. While there is evidence that some of the glossy magazines are influenced by feminist thought, by the inclusion of articles on domestic violence and career advice, there are paradoxes here: for instance, women are represented as assertive, yet increasingly sexually available to men (Ticknell et al. 2003).

3.1.4 (Hetero)Sexuality and Women's Magazines

Aside from a focus on essentialist gender roles, there is a thread of research focusing on sexuality in women's magazines which has identified the presence of a presupposed universal heterosexuality, or what Warner (1993) refers to as 'heteronormativity': 'the assumption that everyone is heterosexual and the recognition that all social institutions [...] are built around a heterosexual model of male/female relations' (Nagel 2003: 49–50). Heteronormativity is therefore aligned with essentialist definitions of gender and the notion that all human beings can be categorized along a male/female binary, and promotes the notion that 'sexual relations are only normal when they occur between two people of the opposite sex' (Baker 2008: 109). Existing scholarship on women's magazines acknowledges their role as arbiters of heterosexual romance; for instance, Gill's (2009) analysis of mediated intimacy in *Glamour* magazine shows how the majority of articles in the magazine are devoted to sex, with an assumed heterosexual 'true romance" endemic in the texts (2009: 352).

Since heteronormative discourses privilege heterosexuality as the accepted status quo, heteronormativity is also engaged in the marginalizing of non-heterosexual practices, which has also been identified in women's magazines. For example, in an analysis of a problem page from *Bliss* magazine, McLoughlin (2008) demonstrates how the agony aunt's reply frames homosexuality as a stage that the letter writer will grow out of, thereby confirming the perceived normality of heterosexuality. Gill (2007: 200) also notes that where they are mentioned, homosexual men are presented as 'style accessories' for young women. This renders them desexualized, further reiterating a heterosexist ideology.

Studies of sex advice in men's and women's magazines shows how this advice promotes the achievement of 'great sex', with discussions of sex contributing to constructions of gender-role stereotypes that promote heteronormative discourses (see, for example, Ménard and Kleinplatz 2008; McLoughlin 2008). My own analysis also shows how mainstream women's magazines promote heteronormative discourses via a number of linguistic and visual strategies, including the use of male pronouns to refer to objects of sexual desire and 'eroticized' images of men, through the use of adjectival descriptions focusing on sexual attractiveness (see Chapter 5); these in turn discount sexualized images of women or the possibility for female bodies to be positioned as objects of desire for the (ideal) female reader.

Sexuality and female empowerment
Existing work on women's magazines acknowledges an increasing focus on female (hetero)sexuality (Gill 2007, 2009; Ticknell et al. 2003). This is no doubt symptomatic of a general increased awareness of female sexuality triggered by, inter alia, third wave feminist movements. Gill (2007) argues that since the 1990s, there have been a number of discernible shifts in the content of women's magazines, including a greater emphasis on heterosexual sex (2007: 184). She identifies three prevailing discourses of sexuality in 'glossy' women's magazines:

* Emphasis on pleasing your man
* Sexual frontierism – women are encouraged to try new things to avoid getting 'stuck in a rut'.
* Feminist (postfeminist) discourse about taking charge sexually
                                        (Adapted from Gill 2007: 192)

Discussions of female sexuality in women's magazines acknowledge that although women are often represented as sexually confident, this is couched in a necessity to please men (Firminger 2006; Jeffries 2007; Litosseliti 2006; McLoughlin 2008). This is reflective of what Holloway (1984) refers to as a 'male sexual drive' discourse, where men 'cannot help' having a high sex drive. This ideology of masculinity is also mirrored in my data, where men's natural virility is assumed via the processes of presupposition and implicature (see Chapter 8). The construction of an essentialist binary between male and female sexuality has also been considered in much research on gender representation in women's magazines. For example, McLoughlin (2008) found that in teenage girls' magazines, girls are constructed as passive recipients of male sexual activity. Additionally, Farvid and Braun's (2006) thematic study of male and female sexuality in six issues of *Cleo* and *Cosmopolitan* found that men are represented as more sexually adventurous than women. This also reflects the distinction between representations of male activity and female passivity that linguists using transitivity analysis have observed in women's magazines (Eggins and Iedema 1997;

Jeffries 2007), and other genres such as romance fiction (Mills 1995; Wareing 1990, 1994).

The degree to which magazines focus on sexuality and relationships depends on the magazine genre in question. For example, del-Teso-Craviotto (2005) uses corpus linguistic techniques in her analysis of the vocabulary of a corpus of four women's magazines. She argues that while lexical items like 'man' and 'woman' are shared across all four magazines, an examination of their contexts of use reveals that they are used differently depending on the genre. For example, in the 'progressive' magazines such as *Cosmopolitan*, forms of MAN (*man/men/men's*) co-occurred with words indicating a romantic interest in men, including 'romantic', 'perfect' and 'sexy', 'whereas in more 'traditional' magazines like *Ms*, MAN appeared close to words relating to social categorization, such as 'young', 'gay', 'black', and 'managers' (2005: 2015). In my own corpus, in the glossy magazines, naming strategies were focused more on the reader's romantic relationships with men than kinship relations (see Chapter 5). This reflects the different target readerships of the two genres; as magazines like *Cosmopolitan* are targeted at younger readers than the more traditional, domestic weeklies, it is expected that these readers will be single and in search of a (male) suitor.

Ultimately though, the literature on women's magazines suggests that 'finding and keeping a man' is presented as a primary concern for women readers. McLoughlin's textual analysis of 'sex specials' shows how the magazines assume that men are afraid of committing to women (2008: 181), but that for women, long-term relationships are privileged over short-term sexual encounters (2008: 179). This correlates with Farvid and Braun's findings, where women are presented as in pursuit of 'The One', which is in turn presented as women's ultimate goal (2006: 299). McLoughlin (2008) asserts that men are represented as ignorant when it comes to issues like contraception and menstruation (2008: 180). Stibbe's study on *Men's Health* magazine also supports this, where 'instructions on the best way to have sex and [...] descriptions of great sex, condoms are never mentioned, creating a positive image of unsafe sex' (2004: 47). The practicalities of sexual health in both men's and girls' magazines is also therefore constructed as women's responsibility.

3.2   The 'Voice of a Friend'

Aside from gender ideologies, there have also been a handful of studies examining the stylistic form of women's magazines, which also involves considering the constructed relationship between the implied reader and the magazine writers. Talbot (1992) examines the 'text population' of real and imaginary characters, investigating the text as a 'tissue of voices' for indices of people addressing one another (1992: 176). She shows how, in order to simulate friendly face-to-face interaction with the reader, text producers use what Fairclough terms 'synthetic personalization', which is the 'tendency to give the impression of treating each of the people "handled" en masse as an individual' (1989: 62). This involves techniques such as using informal vocabulary to set up a friendly, 'chatty' relationship with the reader, and the inclusive *we* to refer to both the writer and reader. These strategies minimize the social distance between themselves and the reader in order to address the reader as a friend (1992: 189). Other linguistic (and non-linguistic) studies of women's magazines have made similar points about how the texts simulate friendly relationships between the reader and text producers (Jeffries 2007; McLoughlin 2000).

McLoughlin's (2000) account of magazines considers some of the linguistic features which make up the discourse of men's and women's lifestyle magazines. She explores similar features to Talbot in her analysis of how magazines address their mass audience in a way which gives the impression of knowing the reader personally. Her account also includes an analysis of femininity construction in women's magazines, and representations of masculinity in men's magazines: she compares two advertorials, one from *FHM* promoting skincare products, and one from *Cosmopolitan* advertising a make-up brand. She notes how in *FHM* the text producers encourage the male 'ideal reader' to commence a beauty regime, but behind closed doors, whereas in the *Cosmopolitan* article it is assumed that the female reader will already have a beauty regime. Her findings are evidence for a wider gender ideology that the consumption of beauty products is a necessary part of femininity construction, but is treated as in opposition to traditional masculinity construction. There is similar evidence for this in my data (see Chapters 5 and 8).

3.3   Reading Women's Magazines: Audience Response

As well as text-based analyses, a number of studies have investigated the relationship between magazines and their readers, using ethnographic data to analyze reader's responses to the texts (Frazer 1987; Ballaster et al. 1991; Hermes 1995; McLoughlin 2008; Ytre-Arne 2011). The empirical studies discussed in this chapter so far address magazines' potential effects on the 'ideal reader': one who accepts the 'messages' in the texts wholesale (see, for example, Fillmore 1982). Audience response studies aim to measure the impact of ideologies of femininity suggested by scholars of textual analyses on 'real' readers. The results of these studies are inconclusive, some proposing that readers are able to adopt 'critical' or 'conscious' approaches to content (such as Frazer 1987; McLoughlin 2008), others asserting that the texts ultimately have 'no meaning' for their readers (Hermes 1995).

Ballaster et al. (1991) concluded from their interviews with women that readers were acutely aware of the magazines as 'bearers of particular discourses of femininity' (1991: 127), and reported that some readers were able to adopt a critical approach to reading the texts (1991: 37). Frazer also reports on the 'self-conscious and reflexive approach to texts' of the young readers of *Jackie* magazine she spoke to, and there is evidence of the readers being aware of the ideologies of femininity constructed by the texts, and their own resistance to them (1987: 419). The idea of the 'conscious reader' is also reflected in McLoughlin's (2008) study of 'sex specials' in British teenage girls' magazines *Bliss* and *Sugar*. Using a combination of CDA and ethnographic interviews, she found that while most of the comments from the younger group of readers (14 years old) aligned with the magazines' 'ideal' readers, in that they felt the publications were reliable sources of information, they occasionally showed 'awareness' of 'the text producer's schemes' (2008: 190). Additionally, most of the comments from the older group (15 years old) were coded as 'critical' (2008: 190).

Hermes conducted 80 interviews with Dutch and British readers of women's magazines, and found that, interestingly, the readers imbued the texts with meanings that were independent of the content of the magazines themselves. Her interviewees talked about how reading the magazines fitted into the context of their everyday lives, but did not expound much on the content of the texts themselves. Hermes therefore concluded that the 'messages' of women's magazines are not significant (1995: 504).

In a more recent study, Ytre-Arne (2011) analyzed reading practices of consumers of the Norwegian weekly magazine *KK* through a combination of a questionnaire survey and individual research interview data. The analysis focuses on participants' interactions with the medium of print magazine, whereby readers associate magazine reading either with processes of relaxation and reward, or with 'skimming' in between other day-to-day activities, what Ytre-Arne describes as a more 'fragmented' reading practice (2011: 219). Although reading practices had the potential to be fleeting, or what Hermes (1995) refers to as the 'easily put down' nature of women's magazines, in terms of content, participants reported valuing content that was 'relevant' to their lives and rather than being 'trivial and superficial' were in fact more often seen as a reflection of 'the way things are' (Ytre-Arne 2011: 222). The research on audience engagement with women's magazines suggests therefore that while for some, magazines are 'just for entertainment', they are consumed by large numbers of readers, and have the potential to influence how women perceive themselves, as well as the role of men in their lives.

3.4   Masculinity and Men's Magazines

While women's magazines have a long history in Western cultures, men's lifestyle magazines are, in comparison, a relatively recent development. The first attempt at a British men's lifestyle magazine was *Men Only* launched in 1935 (Greenfield et al. 1999: 458). Other magazines that followed, such as *Playboy* and *Esquire*, focused primarily on sexual content, and *Playboy* in particular brought pornographic material into mainstream culture (Osgerby 2001: 76). These magazines are associated in cultural and media studies with the figure of the 'Old Man' as typifying pre-feminist sexism (Edwards 2003).

Titles such as *Arena* and *GQ* emerging in the 1980s shifted the focus of content to encompass an increased emphasis on fashion and health. These magazines are often cited as marking the rise of the 'New Man', perceived as a challenge to traditional forms of masculinity: 'an avid consumer and unashamed narcissist' who had 'also internalized and endorsed the principles of feminism', such as a rejection of traditional gender roles and a renewed commitment to the responsibilities of fatherhood (Benwell 2003a: 13). The 'New Lad' is linked to the launch of 'lads' mags' like *FHM* and the (now defunct) *Loaded* in the mid-1990s, which replaced this focus on fashion and style with a celebration of more 'laddish' forms of masculinity, associated with 'drinking, sport and sex' (Jackson et al. 2001: 1).

The fact that there is also an abundance of research on masculinity in men's magazines formed part of the rationale for this study: I was interested in finding out whether the kinds of images of masculinity 'sold' to consumers of men's magazines would also be present in women's magazines.

3.4.1   New Laddism in Men's Magazines

Feminist writers on masculinity and men's magazines have documented the rise of the New Lad in 'lads' mags' in terms of a 'backlash' against the New Man and his 'pro-feminist' principles (Benwell 2003b; Edwards 2003; Whelehan 2000). In this narrative, the kind of masculinity promoted in these magazines is perceived as a return to 'traditional', or 'hegemonic' forms, veiled under a 'mischievous knowingness (commonly termed *irony*) which enables it to survive in a post-feminist era' (Benwell 2001: 19). This attempt at ironic distance can be interpreted as promoting sexist values, 'disguised' as harmless humor (Mills 2008: 11). Feminist response to lads mags and 'New Lad' masculinity was also profoundly felt outside of the academy: in 2013 UK feminist organizations UK Feminista and Object launched the 'Lose the Lads' Mags' campaign, which sought to remove magazines like *Loaded, Nuts* and *Zoo* from the shelves of the major retailers. This was done in direct response to the sexualization of women in 'lads mags' which forms part of a broader 'sexualization of culture' (García-Favaro and Gill 2016: 381).

As with studies of women's magazines, the majority of the available literature on men's magazines has been conducted in fields like cultural and media studies (Breazeale 1994; Nixon 1996; Jackson et al. 2001; Crewe 2003; Edwards 2003), although there is a small body of work adopting more linguistic approaches (such as Benwell 2001, 2003b, 2004; Conradie 2011; Stibbe 2004; Taylor and Sunderland 2003). Despite differences in foci, unifying trends identified in these accounts acknowledge the presence of different facets of hegemonic masculinity corresponding to lad culture in men's magazines, including discourses of heterosexual prowess, heroism, anti-heroism and indirect sexism.

Male heterosexuality

Commentators on the men's magazine market have noted how the increasing visibility of the male body in men's style magazines of the 1980s revealed tensions between sexualized images of masculinity in fashion and advertising, and the need to assert unambiguously heterosexual representations (Simpson 1994). Adopting Laura Mulvey's concept of the 'male gaze' from psychoanalysis, Nixon (1996, 1997) and Edwards (1997) analyze practices of spectatorship in menswear retailing, advertising, marketing and magazine culture. They argue that as the implied gaze of images in magazines like *GQ* and *Arena* is potentially homoerotic, this gives rise to tensions between these and textual content of the magazines. In the 'lads' mags' of the 1990s, however, the glaring focus on 'drinking to excess, adopting a predatory attitude towards women and obsessive forms of independence' (Jackson et al. 2001: 78) pointed to an unambiguously heterosexual implied reader. In my own study, the most prevalent discourses of masculinity seem to align with those documented in men's magazine studies; the difference is in how they are valued by the magazine writers. For example, while it is assumed that men adopt a 'predatory attitude' towards women (see Chapter 8), it is not presented as an ideal aspect of masculinity, but one which must be tolerated as a fundamental 'truth' of masculine identity. This finding demonstrates one of the ways in which the magazines reformulate the New Lad for a specifically female audience in women's magazines.

Jackson et al. (2001) show how the concept of marriage and long-term relationships are viewed as 'a form of social constraint' in men's magazines, preventing men from 'living a life of consumptive and sexual freedom' (2001: 81). Being single is therefore celebrated, as autonomy and independence are highly valued. The reverse is true in women's magazines, which promote the idea of long-term relationships, and in particular marriage, as the ideal goal for any woman. Taylor and Sunderland (2003) analyze an article from *Maxim* about a male sex worker, Peter, showing how positive representations construct him as a sex expert and in control (2003: 176). They also suggest that the absence of references to a long-term partner means that Peter is represented as a free agent, aligning with the prevailing discourses of *Maxim*, where men are represented as seasonally single (2003: 177). This differs considerably from the article on female sex workers analyzed by Caldas-Coulthard (1996), in which long-term heterosexual relationships were implicitly constructed as the desired goal. Being an escort is treated here as unproblematic for men, where for women it is seen as 'degrading' (Taylor and Sunderland 2003: 178).

The idea that men are afraid of commitment is certainly mirrored in my corpus. However, interestingly, while there is much evidence to suggest that a similarly 'laddish' attitude to relationships is presented in women's magazines, images of more caring, sensitive masculinities are also visible. For example, an analysis of naming strategies demonstrates that men are seen to occupy roles of father and husband, and modified positively with lexis connoting nurturing or emotional behavior (see Chapter 5).

Heroism and anti-heroism

The interdisciplinary edited collection *Masculinity and Men's Lifestyle Magazines* (Benwell 2003a) is one of the most comprehensive treatments of men's magazines, and contains studies dedicated to the linguistic construction of masculinities (Baker 2003; Benwell 2003b; Taylor and Sunderland 2003). Adopting a broadly Faircloughian CDA approach, Benwell's (2003b) study describes the 'perpetual oscillation' between traditional, idealized forms of masculinity and 'ironic, fallible and anti-heroic masculinity' (2003b: 157). She defines 'heroic' or 'traditional' masculinity as that associated with 'muscularity, physical labor, outdoor settings, heroic activities, sport and violence', and anti-heroism as forms associated with 'ordinariness, weakness, and self-reflexiveness' (2003b: 157). She analyzes an extract from a tribute to Clint Eastwood from *GQ* magazine, demonstrating how the writer presents him as the agent of material action intention processes, physical actions which have a direct affect on objects in the world. Benwell asserts that while heroic masculinity is what the magazine writer aspires to, anti-heroism is 'what he inevitably falls back on' (2003b: 157). I found a similar distinction between heroic and anti-heroic representations of men in women's magazines, but for women, heroic behavior also involves the promise of 'happily ever after': metaphorical nouns evoking fairy-tale romance label men as 'princes' and 'heroes' (see Chapter 5, Sect. 5.2.3).

Indirect sexism and 'banter'

In an earlier study, Benwell (2001) analyzed a letters page from *Loaded* magazine to show how ritual insults function as a cohesive device that promotes the 'hegemonic subculture' of laddish modes of masculinity, which exclude women and gay men, and promote drinking, heterosexual sex and sexism. Her analysis also makes a connection between 'male gossip' in spoken discourse (Johnson and Finlay 1997) and the 'banter' present in men's magazines. She reports on the high frequency of taboo language in men's magazines, which is also supported by more quantitative studies such as del-Teso-Craviotto's (2005) comparative corpus study. In another study, Benwell (2002) analyses how humor and irony in conjunction with visual images allows for hegemonic forms of masculinity to dominate, while appearing to offer alternatives. This aligns with Mills' (2008) concept of 'indirect sexism', which she defines as sexist language use that operates at the discourse level of a text, realized by humor and irony. This kind of sexism is more difficult to challenge, because it is less explicit than, for example, insult terms directed at women, and also less specific: it is easier to 'point to' lexical items that serve as direct insults than instances where it is implied that women are the butt of the joke (see, for example, Sunderland 2007).

3.5   Comparing Worlds: Comparative Magazine Studies

As well as studies focusing solely on men's or women's magazines, there is also a collection of studies comparing gender representation/construction in both men's and women's magazines (for example del-Teso-Craviotto 2005; Moschenbacher 2009). These serve to highlight how the lifestyle magazine market promotes a 'Mars-Venus' model of gender, where men and women are viewed as existing in entirely different worlds. For example, Malkin et al.'s (1999) comparative content analysis of 21 women's and men's magazine covers demonstrated that while women's magazine covers use 'sell lines' that focus on improving physical appearance, men's magazine covers emphasize entertainment, expanding knowledge and pastimes.

In their study of social agency and moral discourse in teenage and men's magazines, Ticknell et al. (2003) observe that where men are central to constructions of normative femininity in teenage girls' magazines, women serve a peripheral role in men's magazines, functioning solely as objects of desire. In girls' magazines, men are both sexual objects and owners of social agency, which results in 'a constant and profoundly anxious solicitation of male opinion and approval that fits uneasily with the assertion of 'girl power" (Ticknell et al. 2003: 59).

Psychological research into male body image in men's and women's magazines shows that degree of muscularity is a determining factor in how the ideal male body is marketed and consumed. For example, in their study of representations of male body image, Frederick et al. (2005) compared images of men from the front covers and centrefolds of *Cosmopolitan, Men's Health, Men's Fitness* and *Muscle and Fitness* to see if the contrast between men's perceptions of women's preferences and women's actual preferences were reflected in differences in the visual representations of men. Female-audience magazines presented less muscular images of men than male-audience magazines, which implies that male physical appearance in general is constructed as less important to women than men's behavioral or mental attributes in women's magazines. In my own analysis, behavior, in particular sexual behavior, is similarly lexicalized more frequently than physical appearance (see Chapters 5–8).

Motschenbacher (2009) investigates the performative construction of masculinity and femininity via body-part vocabulary in a corpus of advertising texts taken from *Cosmopolitan* and *Men's Health*. He found that lexis such as *muscles* and *six pack* occurred more frequently in *Men's Health* than *Cosmopolitan*, and concluded that while these terms are not lexically gendered (Hellinger and Bussmann 2001–2003), in other words, there is nothing in their denotative meanings that directly index gender, they are associated with masculine performance, or what Ochs (1992) would term 'indirect' indices of gender. While most comparative studies of men's and women's magazines take the notion of gender difference as a starting point, Motschenbacher places his study of body-part vocabulary more firmly within a poststructuralist framework by stating that he takes *similarity* between men's and women's bodies as a basic assumption (2009: 5). His theoretical approach to the texts is therefore very similar to my own in wanting to investigate kinds of lexis that have come to 'mean' masculinity in women's magazines.

3.6   Summary

This chapter has reviewed some of the key literature on women's and men's magazines, from various disciplines and methodological approaches. I have identified some key themes arising from text analyses of women's magazines, some of which my own analysis attends to, such as the construction of heterosexuality, and an ideology of gender as a biological construct. The discussion of the New Lad introduced here in relation to men's magazines will also inform subsequent discussion of masculinity in the data corpus in Chapters 5–8, which shows how some of the behaviors and practices associated with men in the glossy genre of women's magazines in this study can be interpreted as constructions of New Lad masculinity for a female audience. In the next chapter, I discuss my methods of data collection, and describe the analytical processes used to explore gender construction in the women's magazine corpus.

References

Baker, P. (2003). No Effeminates Please: A Corpus-Based Analysis of Masculinity via Personal Adverts in Gay News/Times 1973–2000. In B. Benwell (Ed.), *Masculinity and Men's Lifestyle Magazines* (pp. 243–260). Oxford: Blackwell.

Baker, P. (2008). *Sexed Texts: Language, Gender and Sexuality*. London: Equinox.

Ballaster, R., Beetham, M., Frazer, E., & Hebron, S. (1991). *Women's Worlds: Ideology, Femininity and Women's Magazines*. Basingstoke: Palgrave Macmillan.

Benwell, B. (2001). Male Gossip and Language Play in the Letters Pages of Men's Lifestyle Magazines. *Journal of Popular Culture, 35*(1), 19–33.

Benwell, B. (2002). "Is There Anything 'New' About These Lads?" The Textual and Visual Construction of Masculinity in Men's Magazines. In L. Litosseliti & J. Sunderland (Eds.), *Gender Identity and Discourse Analysis* (pp. 149–174). Amsterdam: Benjamins.

Benwell, B. (Ed.). (2003a). *Masculinity in Men's Lifestyle Magazines*. Oxford: Blackwell.

Benwell, B. (2003b). Ambiguous Masculinities: Heroism and Anti-heroism in the Men's Lifestyle Magazine. In B. Benwell (Ed.), *Masculinity and Men's Lifestyle Magazines* (pp. 151–168). Oxford: Blackwell.

Benwell, B. (2004). Ironic Discourse: Evasive Masculinity in British Men's Lifestyle Magazines. *Men and Masculinities, 7*(1), 3–21.

Breazeale, K. (1994). In Spite of Women: *Esquire* Magazine and the Construction of the Male Consumer. *Signs, 20*(1), 1–22.

Caldas-Coulthard, C. R. (1996). "Women Who Pay for Sex. And Enjoy It": Transgression Versus Morality in Women's Magazines. In C. R. Caldash-Coulthard & M. Coulthard (Eds.), *Texts and Practices: Readings in Critical Discourse Analysis* (pp. 250–270). London: Routledge.

Conradie, M. (2011). Masculine Sexuality: A Critical Discourse Analysis of *FHM. South African Linguistics and Applied Language Studies, 29*(2), 167–185.

Crewe, B. (2003). *Representing Men: Cultural Production and Producers in the Men's Magazine Market*. London: Bloomsbury.

del-Teso-Craviotto, M. (2005). Words That Matter: Lexical Choice and Gender Ideologies in Women's Magazines. *Journal of Pragmatics, 38*(11), 2003–2021.

Duke, L., & Kreshel, P. (1998). Negotiating Femininity: Girls in Early Adolescence Read Teen Magazines. *Journal of Communication Inquiry, 22*(1), 48–71.

Edwards, T. (1997). *Men in the Mirror: Men's Fashion, Masculinity and Consumer Society*. London: Cassell.

Edwards, T. (2003). Sex, Booze and Fags: Masculinity, Style and Men's Magazines. In B. Benwell (Ed.), *Masculinity and Men's Lifestyle Magazines* (pp. 132–146). Oxford: Blackwell.

Eggins, S., & Iedema, R. (1997). Difference Without Diversity: Semantic Orientation and Ideology in Competing Women's Magazines. In R. Wodak (Ed.), *Gender and Discourse* (pp. 165–196). London: Sage.

Fairclough, N. (1989). *Language and Power*. London: Longman.

Fairclough, N. (1992). *Critical Language Awareness*. London: Longman.

Farvid, P., & Braun, V. (2006). "Most of Us Guys Are Raring to Go Anytime, Anyplace, Anywhere": Male and Female Sexuality in *Cleo* and *Cosmo*. *Sex Roles, 55,* 295–310.

Favaro, L. (2017). Mediating Intimacy Online: Authenticity, Magazines and Chasing the Clicks. *Journal of Gender Studies*. Available at http://dx.doi.org/10.1080/09589236.2017.1280385. Accessed June 2017.

Fillmore, C. (1982). Ideal Reader and Real Readers. In D. Tannen (Ed.), *Analyzing Discourse: Text and Talk* (pp. 248–270). Washington, DC: Georgetown University Press.

Firminger, K. B. (2006). Is He Boyfriend Material? Representations of Males in Teenage Girls' Magazines. *Men and Masculinities, 8*(3), 298–308.

Frazer, E. (1987). Teenage Girls Reading *Jackie*. *Media, Culture and Society, 9*(4), 407–425.

Frederick, D., Fessler, D., & Haselton, M. (2005). Do Representations of Male Muscularity Differ in Men's and Women's Magazines? *Body Image, 2*(1), 81–86.

Friedan, B. (1963). *The Feminine Mystique*. New York: Dell.

García-Favaro, L. (2015). 'Porn Trouble': On the Sexual Regime and Travels of Postfeminist Biologism. *Australian Feminist Studies, 30*(86), 366–376.

García-Favaro, L., & Gill, R. (2016). "Emasculation Nation Has Arrived": Sexism Rearticulated in Online Responses to Lose the Lads' Mags Campaign. *Feminist Media Studies, 16*(3), 379–397.

Gill, R. (2007). *Gender and the Media*. Cambridge: Polity Press.

Gill, R. (2009). Mediated Intimacy and Postfeminism: A Discourse Analytic Examination of Sex and Relationships Advice in a Woman's Magazine. *Discourse and Communication, 3*(1), 345–369.

Gill, R., & Elias, A. S. (2014). "Awaken Your Incredible": Love Your Body Discourses and Postfeminist Contradictions. *International Journal of Media and Cultural Politics, 10*(2), 179–188.

Glazer, N. (1980). Overworking the Working Woman: The Double Day in a Mass Magazine. *Woman's Studies International Quarterly, 3*(1), 79–93.

Gough-Yates, A. (2002). *Understanding Women's Magazines.* London: Routledge.

Greenfield, J., O'Connell, S., & Reid, C. (1999). Fashioning Masculinity: *Men Only*, Consumption and the Development of Marketing in the 1930s. *Twentieth Century British History, 10*(4), 457–476.

Hasinoff, A. (2009). It's Sociobiology, Hon! Genetic Gender Determinism in *Cosmopolitan* Magazine. *Feminist Media Studies, 9*(3), 267–283.

Hellinger, M., & Bussmann, H. (2001–2003). *Gender Across Languages: The Linguistic Representation of Women and Men* (3 Vols.). Amsterdam: John Benjamins.

Hermes, J. (1995). *Reading Women's Magazines: An Analysis of Everyday Media Use.* Cambridge: Polity Press.

Holloway, W. (1984). Gender Difference and the Production of Subjectivity. In J. Henriques, W. Holloway, C. Urwin, C. Venn, & V. Walkerdine (Eds.), *Changing the Subject: Psychology, Social Regulation and Subjectivity* (pp. 227–339). London: Methuen.

Jackson, P., Stevenson, N., & Brooks, K. (2001). *Making Sense of Men's Magazines.* Cambridge: Polity Press.

Jeffries, L. (2007). *Textual Construction of the Female Body: A Critical Discourse Approach.* Basingstoke: Palgrave Macmillan.

Johnson, F., & Finlay, F. (1997). Do Men Gossip? An Analysis of Football Talk on Television. In S. Johnson & U. Meinhoff (Eds.), *Language and Masculinity* (pp. 130–143). Oxford: Blackwell.

Lazar, M. (2009). Entitled to Consume: Postfeminist Femininity and a Culture of Post-Critique. *Discourse & Communication, 3*(4), 371–400.

Leman, J. (1980). "The Advice of a Real Friend": Codes of Intimacy and Oppression in Women's Magazines 1937–1955. *Woman's Studies International Quarterly, 3*(1), 63–78.

Litosseliti, L. (2006). *Gender and Language: Theory and Practice.* London: Hodder Arnold.

Machin, D., & Thornborrow, J. (2003). Branding and Discourse: The Case of Cosmopolitan. *Discourse and Society, 14*(4), 453–471.

Malkin, A., Wornian, K., & Chrisler, J. (1999). Women and Weight: Gendered Messages on Magazine Covers. *Sex Roles: A Journal of Research, 40*(7–8), 647–655.

McCracken, E. (1993). *Decoding Women's Magazines: From 'Mademoiselle' to 'Ms'.* London: Macmillan.

McLoughlin, L. (2000). *The Language of Magazines.* London: Routledge.

McLoughlin, L. (2008). The Construction of Female Sexuality in the "Sex Special": Transgression or Containment in Magazines' Information on Sexuality for Girls? *Gender and Language, 2*(2), 171–195.

McRobbie, A. (1982). *Jackie*: An Ideology of Adolescent Femininity. In B. Waites, T. Bennett, & G. Martin (Eds.), *Popular Culture: Past and Present* (pp. 263–283). London: Croom Helm.

McRobbie, A. (1991). *Feminism and Youth Culture: From 'Jackie' to 'Just Seventeen'.* Basingstoke: Macmillan Education.

McRobbie, A. (1996). *More!*: New Sexualities in Girls' and Women's Magazines. In J. Curran, D. Morley, & V. Walkerdine (Eds.), *Cultural Studies and Communications* (pp. 172–194). London: Arnold.

Ménard, A., & Kleinplatz, P. (2008). "Twenty-One Moves Guaranteed to Make His Thighs Go Up in Flames": Depictions of 'Great Sex' in Popular Magazines. *Sexuality and Culture, 12*(1), 1–20.

Mills, S. (1995). *Feminist Stylistics*. London: Routledge.

Mills, S. (2003). Third Wave Feminism and the Analysis of Sexism. *Discourse Analysis On-line*. Available at https://extra.shu.ac.uk/daol/articles/open/2003/001/mills2003001.html. Accessed January 2018.

Mills, S. (2008). *Language and Sexism*. Cambridge: Cambridge University Press.

Motschenbacher, H. (2009). Speaking the Gendered Body: The Performative Construction of Commercial Femininities and Masculinities via Body-Part Vocabulary. *Language in Society, 38*(1), 1–22.

Nagel, J. (2003). *Race, Ethnicity and Sexuality: Intimate Intersections, Forbidden Frontiers*. Oxford: Oxford University Press.

Nixon, S. (1996). *Hard Looks: Masculinities, Spectatorships, and Contemporary Consumption*. London: UCL Press.

Nixon, S. (1997). Exhibiting Masculinity. In S. Hall (Ed.), *Representation: Cultural Representations and Signifying Practices* (pp. 291–330). London: Sage.

Ochs, E. (1992). Indexing Gender. In A. Duranti & C. Goodwin (Eds.), *Rethinking Context: Language as an Interactive Phenomenon* (pp. 335–358). Cambridge: Cambridge University Press.

Osgerby, B. (2001). *Playboys in Paradise: Masculinity, Youth and Leisure-Style in Modern America*. Oxford: Berg.

Ringrow, H. (2016). *The Language of Cosmetics Advertising*. Basingstoke: Palgrave Macmillan.

Simpson, M. (1994). *Male Impersonators: Men Performing Masculinity*. London: Cassell.

Smith, D. (1988). Femininity as Discourse. In L. G. Roman & L. K. Christian-Smith (Eds.), *Becoming Feminine: The Politics of Popular Culture* (pp. 37–59). New York: Falmer Press.

Stibbe, A. (2004). Health and the Social Construction of Masculinity in *Men's Health* Magazine. *Men and Masculinities, 7*(1), 31–51.

Sunderland, J. (2007). Contradictions in Gendered Discourses: Feminist Readings of Sexist Jokes? *Gender and Language, 1*(2), 207–228.

Talbot, M. (1992). The Construction of Gender in a Teenage Magazine. In N. Fairclough (Ed.), *Critical Language Awareness* (pp. 174–199). London: Longman.

Talbot, M. (1995). A Synthetic Sisterhood: False Friends in a Teenage Magazine. In K. Hall & M. Bucholtz (Eds.), *Gender Articulated: Language and the Socially Constructed Self* (pp. 143–165). London: Routledge.

Taylor, Y., & Sunderland, J. (2003). "I've Always Loved Women": The Representation of the Male Sex Worker in *Maxim*. In B. Benwell (Ed.), *Masculintiy and Men's Lifestyle Magazines* (pp. 169–187). Oxford: Blackwell.

Ticknell, E., Chambers, D., van Loon, J., & Hudson, N. (2003). Begging for It: "New Femininities", Social Agency and Moral Discourse in Contemporary Teenage and Men's Magazines. *Feminist Media Studies, 3*(1), 47–63.

Tuchman, G., Daniels, A. K., & Benet, J. (1978). *Hearth and Home: Images of Women in Mass Media*. Oxford: Oxford University Press.

Wareing, S. (1990). Women in Fiction: Stylistics Modes of Reclamation. *Parlance, 2*(2), 72–85.

Wareing, S. (1994). And Then He Kissed Her…. In K. Wales (Ed.), *Feminist Linguistics in Literary Criticism* (pp. 117–136). Cambridge: D.S. Brewer.

Warner, M. (Ed.). (1993). *Fear of a Queer Planet*. Minneapolis: University of Minnesota Press.

Whelehan, I. (2000). *Overloaded: Popular Culture and the Future of Feminism*. London: Women's Press.

Winship, J. (1983). Femininity and Women's Magazines. Unit 6, *U221 The Changing Experience of Women*. Milton Keynes: Open University.

Winship, J. (1985). "A Girl Needs to Get Street-Wise": Magazines for the 1980s. *Feminist Review, 21*, 25–46.

Winship, J. (1987). *Inside Women's Magazines*. London: Pandora.

Ytre-Arne, B. (2011). Women's Magazines and Their Readers: The Relationship Between Textual Features and Practices of Reading. *European Journal of Cultural Studies, 14*(2), 213–228.

4

Data and Method

In this chapter I outline the methods used to interrogate discourses of masculinity in my corpus of women's magazines. First, I discuss the data selection process, outlining how I built the corpus of magazine data. I provide a breakdown of the corpus contents, including a consideration of the different magazine genres and text types that make up the dataset. I talk about the different target demographics of the magazines in relation to the distinction made between the 'glossy' and 'domestic weekly' (Hermes 1995) genres. I then discuss the analytical process, detailing how I have combined Jeffries' (2010b) model of Critical Stylistics with some basic tools from corpus linguistics.

4.1   The Data: A Corpus of Women's Magazines

The data for this study consists of a corpus of women's magazines sold in the UK in 2008. I went to a popular high-street retailer in Huddersfield, West Yorkshire, and bought all the women's magazines relevant to my research questions that were available on that particular day. Given this 'opportunistic' method of data collection, the magazine

© The Author(s) 2019
L. Coffey-Glover, *Men in Women's Worlds*,
https://doi.org/10.1057/978-1-137-57555-5_4

sample cannot be said to be representative of *all* UK women's magazines, but serves as a useful snapshot of the lifestyle publications available from a specific mainstream retailer, at a specific point in time. Only general lifestyle magazines were chosen, and only those which would be likely to reveal something about men and gender relations; beauty magazines were excluded, as were parenting magazines, on the basis that fatherhood is an aspect of masculinity outside the scope of this study.

I collected 21 magazines in total, and 148 articles were selected from these based on whether the topic in some way related to men or relationships, including interviews with or profiles of celebrities. Therefore, the data includes articles concerning both collective and individual male identities. The magazines cover a wide range of target readerships, with differences in age, ethnicity, social class and sexuality. Following Hermes, the magazines can also be grouped into two different subgenres: 'glossy' magazines and 'domestic weeklies' (1995: 6). The more traditional 'domestic weeklies' place an emphasis on celebrity and true life stories, and tend to be produced on a weekly basis, such as *Best*, *That's Life* and *Woman's Own*. The glossy magazines have a larger and wider range of content, use high quality 'glossy' print, and are usually published on a monthly basis, such as *Cosmopolitan*, *Glamour* and *Woman & Home*. These two categories also comply with different target demographics according to socio-economic class: the glossy magazines are on the whole marketed at middle-class readerships, whereas the weekly magazines are generally read and targeted at working-class women (Hermes 1995: 6). The 'domestic' magazine category also aligns with what Caldas-Coulthard terms 'traditional' magazines, where women are situated in a domestic sphere and the concept of femininity is 'bound to family ideals of affection, loyalty and obligation and domestic production or housekeeping' (1996: 253).

To assist in classifying the magazines according to this distinction, I obtained information about the target demographics for each magazine from publishing company press packs, available from the magazine publishers' websites. *More* magazine, which went out of circulation in 2013, proved to be an interesting anomaly in this categorization, as it contained elements of both the glossy and weekly genres: for example, it was targeted at younger readerships and contained instructional feature articles like the other glossies, but was produced on a fortnightly basis, and included a focus on celebrity culture. It has been categorized here as a 'domestic weekly' for ease of reference, but this highlights the fact that these are by no means clear-cut labels. The resulting corpus contains articles from 10 glossy magazines and 11 domestic weeklies (see Table 4.1).

The print magazines were digitized using Optical Character Recognition software, and then manually edited for errors made at the scanning stage and stored as separate text files. I then used the wordlist function in WordSmith Tools (Scott 2008), to gather statistical information about the distribution of words across the corpus, as shown in Tables 4.1 and 4.2.

Table 4.1 Total frequencies of articles and words in each of the magazine sub-corpora

Magazine	Articles		Words	
	Number	% of corpus	Number	% of corpus
Asiana	16	10.8	17,333	10.7
Best	7	4.7	6600	4.1
Company	8	5.4	9115	5.6
Cosmopolitan	14	9.5	10,998	6.8
Diva	9	6.1	11,283	7
Easy Living	4	2.7	5094	3.1
Ebony	9	6.1	9224	5.7
Glamour	7	4.7	6536	4
Love It	8	5.4	10,798	6.7
More	10	6.8	7641	4.7
My Weekly	5	3.4	6619	4.1
Pick Me Up	6	4	8140	5
Pride	4	2.7	3330	2.1
Real People	5	3.4	6995	4.3
Scarlet	9	6.1	9187	5.7
Take a Break	3	2	4446	2.7
That's Life	6	4	6327	3.9
Woman	5	3.4	3770	2.3
Woman & Home	4	2.7	7185	4.4
Woman's Own	4	2.7	3347	2.1
Woman's Weekly	5	3.4	8186	5
Total	148	100	162,154	100

Table 4.2 Frequency of words in the magazine genre sub-corpora

Magazine genre	Word frequency	% of corpus
Domestic weeklies	72,870	45
Glossies	89,288	55

Table 4.1 provides word frequencies for each magazine and Table 4.2 shows the number of words in each of the two genres. I anticipated that because magazines in the domestic weekly category are targeted at an older readership than the glossy magazines, these texts would be more likely to represent men in terms of their roles as fathers or husbands, rather than boyfriends. This was largely borne out in the data (see Chapter 5).

4.1.1 Text Types

As well as magazine genre, I also anticipated that there may be differences in the kinds of masculinity evident depending on text type. To identify the different text types I used a combination of 'internal' and 'external' criteria: 'internal' criteria refers to the linguistic components of a text, for example grammatical structure or lexical features; 'external' criteria relate to the perceived communicative functions of the texts. For example, in terms of internal criteria, the 'problem page' is based on a series of 'adjacency pairs': pairs of utterances in sequence produced by different 'speakers' (Schegloff and Sacks 1973). These adjacency pairs constitute questions from the reader with corresponding answers from the resident 'agony aunt' or 'uncle'; the purpose of problem pages is therefore to provide a forum for readers to disclose their personal problems and seek and get advice from experts. The external criteria can be used to differentiate different text types that contain the same internal criteria. For example, one thing that differentiates problem pages from interviews is that the adjacency pairs in interviews are representations of a conversation between the interviewer and a celebrity interviewee, with the dual purpose of providing the reader with information on that celebrity and promoting the commercial outputs that they are currently involved in, such as their latest film, television program, or album.

I predicted that the different stylistic functions of the text types would give rise to some general differences in the textual representation of men worthy of further analysis, which did turn out to be the case. For example, I found that the true-life stories were more likely to present violent images of men, and the fictional texts were more likely to present men meronymically in terms of their body parts (see Chapters 5 and 7 below).

The text-types which make up the largest proportions of the corpus are the features, interviews and true-life stories, each constituting around a quarter of the corpus (see Table 4.3). The amount of space given to these text types is indicative of their status as staples of the wider magazine genre.

The fact that so much space is dedicated to interviews, features and true-life stories also suggests that these are the kinds of texts which are most concerned with representing men, given that the articles were chosen on the basis of whether or not they feature male identities or refer to men in some way.

Table 4.3 Number of articles and word frequencies in the women's magazine corpus per text type

Text type	Number of articles	% of corpus	Total word frequency	% of corpus
Interviews	33	22	35,046	22
Features	26	18	35,459	22
True-life stories	26	18	34,226	21
Problem pages	15	10	14,447	9
Opinion columns	13	9	9204	6
Fiction	8	5	14,860	9
Reports	6	4	8298	5
Survey reports	6	4	4160	3
Letters	4	3	2315	1
Profiles	4	3	1379	1
Advertorials	3	2	1536	1
Listicles	3	2	967	1
Reviews	1	1	261	0
Total	148	100	162,158	100

Advertorials

Advertorials are advertisements that are presented as editorial content, written to encourage readers to buy the products featured (McLoughlin 2000: 101). There are only three in the women's magazine corpus: 'A man for all seasons' (*Easy Living*), 'The men who make you look good' (*Easy Living*) and 'My Place' (*Woman*). This is likely a reflection in itself of the fact that the kinds of products usually advertised in women's magazines are related to fashion and beauty, topics that are incompatible with hegemonic masculinity, as the analysis in Chapters 5–8 indicates.

Opinion Columns

Opinion columns are narrated from the point of view of one individual, in the first person, and have a persuasive rhetorical strategy. Of the 13 opinion pieces, seven are written by women, and six by men. Most of the columns are related to sex and relationships in some way. *Asiana* is interesting in that it contains two columns, one where the 'implied author' is a man and the other in which the implied author is a woman. The two pages are visually very similar, which suggests that they are intended to be read as male and female counterparts. This implies that men and women have naturally different opinions, emphasizing a discourse of gender difference. The column narrated from the perspective of a female writer is about how the fashion world is prejudiced against plus-size women; the one written from the point of view of a male writer argues that women are only interested in money when it comes to selecting a suitable partner. These are stereotypically gendered topics, in that fashion is associated with femininity, and finances and careers are stereotypically perceived as male domains, indexing masculinity.

Features

Delin (2000) identifies three key values of feature writing in women's magazines: evidentiality, discursivity and point of view. 'Evidentiality' refers to writers' use of varied authoritative sources of information, such as direct quotations from experts; 'discursivity' refers to the explanatory and elaborative function of feature writing, as opposed to the representation of 'facts'; and 'point of view' relates to their evaluative style—they represent opinions of the writer via 'affective' vocabulary, such as lexis indicating positive or negative evaluation (2000: 112). Features are similar to columns in their use of evaluative lexis, but differ from them in the amount of space given to expert voices, which also causes them to serve a more pedagogical function.

Out of the 26 features in the corpus, 17 are on the topic of sex and relationships. Most of these adopt an instructional tone, and include advice from 'experts' giving advice to readers on how to obtain and keep a male partner, with the exception of the features in *Diva*, which are about gay marriages and lesbian dating; they are included in the corpus because they also discuss men and heterosexual relationships.

Fiction

Fictional texts in women's magazines are creative narratives purportedly sent in by readers of the magazines, although some are also published authors who use the fiction pages of the magazines as a platform for promoting their material. While only two could really be described as 'romance' fiction, in that the central character is a young woman with a male love interest whom she finds 'mysterious and domineering' (Wareing 1994: 118), most are also centered on romantic relationships. I predicted that fiction would be the text type most likely to include features such as body part agency, and metonymic representation of men via body part terms; this is discussed in Chapter 5.

Interviews

The interviews are representations of conversations between a magazine writer and a celebrity; they consist of adjacency pairs, following a question-answer format. I have included interviews with male celebrities, but also interviews with female celebrities which make reference to men, most often to do with romantic relationships.

Letters
The letters pages are a forum for the readers to 'have their say'; the ones included in the corpus are letters pages specifically on the topic of men, and feature exclusively in the domestic weekly genre: 'You've got Male' from *Love It* magazine exploits the homophonic properties of *male* and *mail* to indicate that the letters included in it are all about men; *That's Life*'s 'Aren't Men Daft' is a regular feature dedicated to displaying readers' pictures and anecdotes of their male partners' 'daft' exploits, and while 'Him Indoors' from *Pick Me Up* magazine forms just one section of a page, it is also a dedicated space where women can write in about the 'silly' behavior of their partners. The fact that this type of letters page exists at all is exemplary of the idea that men are seen as an integral part of women's worlds, and that they are not just viewed as objects of desire, but also objects of amusement and ridicule.

Listicles
The term 'listicle' is a blend of 'list' and 'article'; listicles consist of a numbered list of items, either instructional or informative (Favaro 2017: 8), such as '14 things you should never ask a man to do' (*More*) or 'Six secrets of a man's wallet' (*Cosmopolitan*). Listicles concerning information about men are more likely to appear in the glossy genre, an indication of the fact that this genre is the more concerned with explaining the 'mystery of man' and how to behave around him. (The assumption in the domestic magazines is that the reader has already successfully found a partner, and therefore has no further interest in 'understanding' men.)

Problem Pages
The problem pages are based on a 'question and answer' format, and feature the personal problems of readers who write in for advice from their resident 'agony aunts' (or less commonly, 'agony uncles'). The problem page is viewed as a staple feature of women's magazines

(McLoughlin 2000), and indeed all the magazines in the women's magazine corpus include one. They differ only in terms of the kinds of experts giving advice: for example, rather than the traditional agony aunt figure, *Scarlet*'s problem page has 'pleasure aunts', who are 'sex and relationship experts,' which fits in with this magazine's explicit focus on sex. *Glamour* also makes use of a panel of 'experts', while *Take a Break* describes their agony aunts as 'buddies': 'real' women who can offer advice as a 'friend'. Domestic weekly magazines *Best* and *Pick Me Up* both have celebrity agony aunts: Lorraine Kelly and Jeremy Kyle, respectively. (Jeremy Kyle is a UK television chat show host who presents *The Jeremy Kyle Show*, in which members of the public divulge their personal problems and dilemmas, often related to family feuds, in front of a live studio audience.) The choice of 'agony uncle' in this case is therefore reflective of the magazines' focus on drama and gossip.

Profiles

The profiles are similar to celebrity interviews, in that they are intended to put a particular celebrity individual in the 'spotlight', with the overarching aim of promoting products or media associated with that celebrity. They differ from interviews in that the voice of the interviewer is often not present; presumably these are based originally on some form of interview, in which the interviewer's questions have been excluded, to give the impression of proximity between the celebrity concerned and the reader. Occasionally the questions are reformulated into declarative statements, for example in *Scarlet*'s 'Top 5 X-Factor Loin Throbs,' pictures of five previous contestants from television talent show *X-Factor* are accompanied by 'vital statistics'-style facts about the celebrity in question, detailing information such as their age, where they live, and whether or not they are single.

Survey Reports

The survey reports are based around questions addressed to samples of readers, or 'real' men accosted on the street, in order to discover 'what goes through men's minds'. For example, a survey from *Glamour* centers around the single question 'What's your favourite erogenous zone?', while another survey from *More* asks 'Should a girl ever make the first move?' As with the listicles, the surveys are more likely to appear in the glossy magazines, as these are the texts most concerned with telling single women what men think, in order that they may successfully obtain a man for themselves.

These articles also often include statistics, indicating what percentages of the sample voted in a particular way. For example, *Glamour*'s survey 'Would you rather…', reports the results of a series of scenarios presented to a sample of readers, and shows what percentage voted for each scenario, which is then followed by a comment on the results:

> Would you rather…
> He's too pale 62%
> He's too tanned 38%
> Really now? A lily-white indie boy over a Ready Brek glow? But what about er, um, Peter Andre and, uh, Andy Scott-Lee and… OK, we see your point.

The comment is supposed to represent the collective 'voice' of the magazine, indicated by the use of inclusive pronoun *we*. In this case however the 'we' is exclusive, as it does not include the reader in its reference. The survey reports are one of the few text types in which distance is created between the writer and the reader; the rest of the time, techniques such as direct address using second-person pronouns *you* and *your* serve to reduce the social distance between the reader and text producers (see Talbot 1992; McLoughlin 2000).

True-Life Stories
True-life stories are narratives which are often written from the first-person perspective of a female narrator, and are intended to narrate 'real life' events. They are a staple feature of women's magazines (McLoughlin 2000: 60). True-life stories make up 18% of the texts in the women's magazine corpus. 25 of these (96%) are found

in the gossip sub-corpus, and the true-life story makes up the largest proportion of text-types in the gossip genre (39%). This not only suggests that true-life stories are distinctive to the gossips, but also that the representations of men found in the true-life stories may be distinctive to that particular text-type, and perhaps to the gossip genre itself.

Direct speech is also used to reduce the visibility of authorial point of view in the true-life stories, where first-person pronouns such as *I* and *my* indicates a character's point of view in the title of the story, as in 'I love the Man Who Knifed You' (*That's Life*); 'My arm was wrenched clean off' (*Pick Me Up*). The first-person pronouns indicate that the stories are being narrated from the point of view of the (female) characters, therefore 'hiding' the editors' point of view. In this way, they are similar to fictional narratives. True-life stories and fictional narratives differ from features in that their narrators can be described as 'omniscient'; much less space is given to the representation of characters' thoughts in features.

Reports

Report articles were identified by the use of factual information, often including statistical information. For example, *More's* 'Man Facts' was defined as a report because it lists a series of 'facts' about men, using statistical information gathered from various sources. They can also be treatments of a more serious topic, for example, *Company* runs articles that are headed as 'reports' as a regular feature, and the one in my corpus is about women who turned to working in the sex industry to finance their travels around the world. However, most of my reports are on arguably more trivial topics: *More* reports on 'What it's like Living with a Man' and *Scarlet's* 'Sex, Lies and Videotape' provides statistics about men's and women's porn viewing habits.

Reviews

Reviews provide an evaluation of media products, such as books, television programs or films. The only magazine containing this text type was *Diva*, and there was only one relevant review for inclusion in the corpus.

All the magazines are addressed at heterosexual women apart from *Diva*, which is aimed at women in lesbian readerships. The fact that *Diva* was the only magazine to include a review is indicative of its differing focus: this magazine also features articles relating to politics, art and culture, topics not present in the magazines aimed at heterosexual women. Heterosexual women are thus constructed as inherently different to lesbian women by the producers of these magazines.

4.2   Combining Corpus Linguistics and Critical Stylistics

This study combines the CDA-inspired Critical Stylistics framework with quantitative techniques from corpus linguistics. Much of the work that has been done on women's magazines in linguistics comes from a CDA-inflected or otherwise critical linguistic perspective (Talbot 1995; Eggins and Iedema 1997; del-Teso-Craviotto 2005; Jeffries 2007; Motschenbacher 2009). However, most of this research constitutes small-scale, qualitative analyses of the texts, with the exception of del-Teso-Craviotto (2005) and Motschenbacher (2009), who also incorporate corpus techniques. Jeffries' (2007) study can also be regarded as a 'corpus' study, as she examined a large dataset of 86 texts, although she did not explicitly employ quantitative techniques to explore linguistic patterns. Jeffries' analysis of women's magazines aimed to investigate the 'problem' of the texts' representations of women's bodies, as a reflection of wider ideologies concerning idealized femininity. Jeffries' work presented a coherent, systematic model for analyzing texts, and the textual-conceptual functions that the model is based on are useful for thinking about what any text is 'doing', in other words, the ideological effects it produces.

Although a number of critical linguistic studies in CDA utilize corpus techniques (such as Caldas-Coulthard and Moon 2010; Baker et al. 2013; Mautner 2016), this study is one of the few which adopt a Critical Stylistics model (López Maestre 2013; Tabbert 2016).

The corpus tools were used as a way of organizing the data in order to facilitate the application of this Critical Stylistics framework to the texts. Before describing the methods of analysis, I will first outline the tools of Critical Stylistics, and how I have used them in combination with corpus linguistic tools such as frequency wordlists, concordances and collocations.

4.2.1 The Tools of Critical Stylistics

The tools of Critical Stylistics as outlined by Jeffries (2007, 2010b), are given in Table 4.4.

The model expands on linguistic features frequently adopted in other critical approaches, particularly critical linguistics (Fowler 1991) and CDA (Fairclough 1989, 1992, 1995). The tools are displayed here according to textual function and some of their possible formal

Table 4.4 The tools of Critical Stylistics (Jeffries 2007, 2010b)

Conceptual-textual function	Formal realizations
Naming and describing	Choice of nominals to denote a referent; nominalizations; the construction of noun phrases with modifiers (in pre- and post-positions) to further identify the referent
Equating	Noun phrase apposition; parallel structures indicating synonymous relationships; relational transitivity choices
Contrasting	Lexical or structurally constructed opposition (antonymous sense relations or syntactic triggers); negation
Enumerating and exemplifying	Two, three or four-part lists indicating hyponymous and meronymous sense relations
Assuming and implying	Presupposition and implicature
Prioritizing	Transformation of grammatical constructions (such as active to passive voice); clefting
Constructing time and space	Choices of tense; adverbials of time; deixis; metaphor.
Representing actions/events/ states	Transitivity choices
Presenting opinions	Modality choices; speech and thought presentation

realizations. It is not intended to be an exhaustive list, but to provide a coherent model that directly addresses the functional aspect of text analysis. By thinking about the conceptual functions of a particular linguistic form, the reader is more likely to be able to make links between linguistic form and ideological meaning, and it is partly for this reason that I have found Jeffries' model a particularly illuminating toolkit. Another advantage that Critical Stylistics has over other CDA methodologies is the logical cohesion and interconnectivity of the tools themselves: for example, a consideration of how oppositional and equivalent meanings are constructed may also rely upon the processes of presupposition or implicature. For reasons of clarity, I have separated the functions where possible, providing cross-references to the other tools where relevant; I demonstrate this interrelation of the tools in the construction of meaning via an analysis of a longer data extract in the final chapter.

Naming and Describing

'Naming and describing' involves examining how entities and events are labelled and modified, and is realized through the noun phrase. Acknowledging the significance of how a person or event is defined and evaluated via naming practices is not in itself a new concept, and is similar to the concept of 'referential strategies' in CDA (see, for example, Van Leeuwen 1996; Reisigl and Wodak 2001). Nominalization, one realization of naming, is also frequently considered in CDA studies (see Fowler 1991). What makes Jeffries' approach unique is the use of the noun phrase as the basic unit of analysis. For reasons of space, I have focused my analysis here on the text producers' choice of nouns to refer to men, and modifying adjectives, either attributive adjectives premodifying the head noun or functioning as the Complements of intensive verbs in predicative form. In Jeffries' analysis of women's magazines, she also examines the use of determiners and pronouns in categorizing the reader, but narrows the focus of adjectival descriptions to those premodifying the head noun. I have expanded her analysis of adjectives to those in propositional form, as these also function to categorize male identities, particularly in categorical, generalizing forms, such as 'men are…', which also proved fruitful for uncovering discourses of the 'ideal man'.

Previous studies of gender construction using corpus techniques have used male nouns such as MAN, MEN and pronouns as search terms for finding statistical patterns (such as Koller 2004; Pearce 2008). Although this would have facilitated quantitative analysis of nominal reference, it would not however have revealed ideological differences in the choice of noun. Therefore, in order to conduct an analysis of naming strategies, I used Wmatrix (Rayson 2008), a web-based corpus interrogation program which automatically encodes corpora for Part-of-Speech (POS) metadata. This meant that I could search for nominal tags to find male pronouns, and search through concordance lines of common nouns in order to find nouns with male referents.

I searched for adjectival descriptions of men in a similar manner, by using the POS tag of different categories of adjectives to find those modifying a male referent. This allowed me to record instances of attributive adjectives, premodifying male referents in noun phrases, as well as predicative adjectives, functioning as the grammatical Complement in clauses with male Subjects. I also decided to conduct a more quantitative study of how men are described in the corpus, by calculating statistical collocates of male identities (see Sect. 4.2.2).

Equating and Contrasting
'Equating and contrasting' refers to how texts construct oppositional and equivalent meanings. It develops work in lexical semantics on (decontextualized) sense relations between words (see Lyons 1977; Cruse 1986, 2004; Murphy 2003). After Jeffries' (2010a) and Davies' (2013) work in this area, the Critical Stylistic approach to opposition construction acknowledges how processing new opposites often relies on an understanding of higher-level, conventional opposites, such as GOOD/BAD; MALE/FEMALE. The concept of superordinate opposites, and the specific categories of opposition used in this study, are described in more detail in Chapter 6.

Oppositional and equivalent meanings are often signalled via syntactic triggers, including co-ordinating and subordinating conjunctions (such as *and, but, or, yet* and so on). In order to search for instances of equivalence and opposition, I searched through concordance lines of the POS conjunction tags in Wmatrix, recording those which created equivalent or oppositional relationships relevant to the representation of men. However, not all equivalence or opposition is signalled by syntactic means, as they sometimes rely on semantic relationships or parallel clause structures. Appositional equivalence, for example, involves the juxtaposition of two noun phrases, as in 'Kirsty, the brilliant psychologist.' There are no searchable lexical triggers here, and Wmatrix is only able to tag individual words, not parse whole phrases or clauses. Manual analysis of equivalence would have been unfeasible given the size of the corpus, therefore appositional equivalences created via the juxtaposition of noun phrases were not recorded.

As with Naming and Describing, the corpus tools were mainly used as an organizational aid to help me to find relevant data for analysis. As well as recording instances of different types of opposition, I also made a note of any underlying higher-level opposites, following Davies' (2013) approach to the analysis of opposition construction.

Representing Actions/Events/States

'Representing Actions/Events/States' involves the analysis of transitivity choices, which is based on Simpson's (1993) presentation of Halliday's (1994) model of transitivity, due to its accessibility and ease of application to both literary and non-literary texts. Transitivity forms part of Halliday's functional grammar, which is based on the idea that language is shaped by the social functions it has come to serve. Halliday proposes three 'metafunctions': the interpersonal metafunction, concerned with interactions between the writer/speaker and reader/hearer; the ideational metafunction, which is concerned with the expression of our experiences of the world, both internally and externally to the conscious self, and the textual metafunction, which concerns grammatical systems related to the organization of text (Halliday and Matthiessen 2004).

Transitivity is a realization of the ideational metafunction: the system of transitivity construes experiences into a set of process types and relates them to the participants and circumstances involved in the production of the clause. By analyzing syntax in this way we can observe how texts employ linguistic devices to direct, question and inform the reader, which is extremely useful for exposing ideology in texts. There is a long tradition of analyzing transitivity patterns in stylistics and critical linguistics for uncovering the linguistic construction of world-views (for example, Burton 1982; Fowler 1991; Simpson 1993; Van Leeuwen 1995). Transitivity analysis is useful for observing 'who is doing what to who' in a text, and therefore facilitates an analysis of power relations and the types of actions men perform in women's magazines.

In order to find instances of transitivity, I searched concordance lines of lexical verb POS tags in Wmatrix. As I was only interested in how male social actors were represented, I only recorded instances of male participants acting as the agents of verbs; I concluded that an analysis of the kinds of actions men are seen to perform in the texts would be of most use, and would also make the task more manageable. I coded these for process type, and any other kinds of participants involved in the clause. This involved looking at whether 'recipients' of the verb phrase were male or female, or represented as inanimate objects, cognitions, events, or places. I also analyzed the semantic properties of the verbs themselves, in order to ascertain what *kinds* of material actions or intensive processes, and so on, that men are seen to perform in the texts.

Assuming and Implying

The metafunction 'assuming and implying' refers to how knowledge is either treated as background information or implied. This textual-conceptual function is realized by the processes of presupposition (Levinson 1983) and implicature (Grice 1975). Presuppositions assume the existence of an entity or event, or assume the occurrence of an action. For example, in the noun phrase 'his beer drinking', the possessive pronoun 'his' presupposes both the existence of the nominalized action of drinking, and the existence of a male referent. In 'he stopped snoring', the verb 'stopped' presupposes that the man previously snored. Conversational implicatures are meanings implied by the text which the reader infers via a process of 'reading between the lines.' These are based on occasions where a speaker flouts one or more of Grice's 'maxims of conversation' (1975), giving rise to implicatures: implied meanings that must be uncovered by the reader (the processes of presupposition and implicature are discussed in more detail in Chapter 8).

The analysis of semantic presupposition is to an extent more amenable to automatic analysis than conversational implicature, as presupposition is signaled in the text by specific linguistic triggers. Implicature is a more pragmatic concept; uncovering implicatures relies much more heavily on contextual information and the reader's own schematic knowledge. Schemata are elements of background knowledge which the reader draws on in order to construct meaning from texts (Semino 1997). Because of this reliance on context and background knowledge in the retrieval of implicatures, this aspect of textual meaning proved the most difficult to examine using corpus techniques. I thus relied on manual analysis of the sentences captured for my analysis of transitivity processes.

4.2.2 Corpus Linguistic Processes

This study uses corpus linguistic tools as an organizational aid to find evidence of how the texts represent men in terms of the four metafunctions of Critical Stylistics (outlined in Sect. 4.2.1). The discussion below focuses on concepts and tools most relevant to this study: frequency, concordances and collocation.

Frequency

Basic frequency analyses are central to corpus linguistics. Studies of discourse analysis using corpus linguistic methods often begin with the frequency word list. In WordSmith Tools, the Wordlist function allows the user to create a single list of all the words in a corpus or sub-corpus, which the analyst can then use to derive statistical information about individual words or lemmas (all possible forms of a word) in a corpus. Wordlists are a useful starting point for any corpus analysis; if you have an idea of which particular lexical items you want to investigate, a wordlist will tell you both their raw frequency and proportional representation (relative frequency) in the corpus. For example, in their analysis of the representation of refugees in the press, Gabrielatos and Baker (2008) used REFUGEE, ASYLUM, IMMIGRANT, ILLEGAL ALIEN, and DEPORT as search terms as a starting point for their analysis of racialized discourses. I used the Wordlist function in WordSmith initially to calculate frequencies of the different genres and text types: I made a wordlist for each of the glossy and domestic weekly genres, which allowed me to find out how big each of the two sub-corpora were. I also made Wordlists of the different text types, which allowed me to see the prevalence of different text types across the corpus.

However, when it came to undertaking the first part of the analysis, identifying processes of naming and describing, I decided not to use a wordlist to find instances of male reference. This is because I wanted to use the noun phrase as a starting point. Since noun phrases can consist of different combinations, such as proper noun (*David*), determiner + adjective + noun (*the sexy footballer*) or pronoun + noun (*my bloke*) and contain both pre- and post-modifying elements (such as *the man with the pink moustache*), this was best facilitated by considering relevant word classes that appear in noun phrases, and so I based my search on grammatical rather than lexical categories. I did use wordlists in the analysis of body part agency (Chapter 7, Sect. 7.5), where I searched wordlists of the different text types to find body part terms, and then computed concordances in order to see how the body parts behaved in context.

Concordances

A concordance is a list of all the instances of a particular search word in a corpus, presented within its co-text, which is usually a few words either side of the 'node' item (Baker 2006: 71). In my study, concordances of body part terms were used to examine the kinds of actions 'performed' by them in the analysis of body part agency (Chapter 7,

Sect. 7.5), but elsewhere I used POS searches in Wmatrix to find the relevant lexis under examination. In WordSmith it is possible to sort concordance lines within a specified span to the left and right of the search term, which can make analyses of long lists of concordance lines much easier to search through. Wmatrix also allows the user to compute concordances to examine the contexts of use, but it is not possible to sort concordance lines in Wmatrix. However, WordSmith does not have the capability to tag words for POS information, so most of the analysis had to be done in Wmatrix. WordSmith Tools has the facility to calculate collocational information about pairs of lexis from concordances, so the Concordance function was used in WordSmith to calculate collocates of adjectives describing men (see Chapter 5, Sect. 5.4).

Another way in which I have taken advantage of the Concordance tool is when looking at the contexts of specific lexical items in a reference corpus, in order to test my intuitions about common contexts of use. Baker also discusses the usefulness of consulting reference corpora as a means of triangulation in the analysis of discourses (2006: 16). The British National Corpus (BNC) is a 100 million-word general corpus of English, compiled in the early 1990s and designed to be representative of British English in general. The BNC can therefore be usefully utilized as reference corpus to corroborate interpretations of particular words or phrases. The BYU-BNC is an online interface that allows the user to interrogate the BNC, generating a random sample of up to 50 concordance lines of a chosen word or phrase. I used this facility for checking the validity of hypotheses about the meanings of words. For example, in my analysis of naming and describing, I suspected that the phrase 'bad boy' is often used to describe male promiscuity and violent behavior; by searching for 'bad boy' in the BNC, I was able to look at the co-text of the randomly generated concordance lines and confirm that it indeed seems to indicate discourses of male violence and womanizing. Because the BNC is a general corpus, and therefore contains representative samples of texts from a wide range of genres and text types, this meant that the meanings of 'bad boy' that I had identified in the women's magazine corpus could be interpreted as reflective of wider use in the language, and not specific to women's magazines.

Collocation

'Collocation' refers to 'the occurrence of two or more words within a short space of each other in a text' (Sinclair 1991: 170). Statistical collocation specifically refers to 'the above-chance frequent co-occurrence of two words within a pre-determined span' (Baker et al. 2008: 278). The collocates of a word contribute to its meaning, providing information about the most frequent concepts associated with a word. Collocation may be calculated in WordSmith Tools using a number of different statistical measures: Specific Mutual Information (MI); MI3; Z-score; log-likelihood or T-score. The different measures favour different types of words: the MI score tends to give high scores to low frequency words—lexical, rather than functional items—whereas algorithms like MI3 and log-likelihood tend to privilege high-frequency function words (Baker 2006: 102). The MI test calculates the expected probability of two words occurring near to each other, based on their relative frequencies and overall size of the corpus. It compares this figure with the actual frequency and converts the difference into a number indicating the strength of collocation. In this calculation, a score of three or more is considered to indicate a strong collocation (Baker 2006: 101).

My analysis of how the texts describe men in Chapter 5 includes a consideration of both statistical and manually derived collocates. Computing collocates using corpus linguistic tools only allows the user to calculate the relationship between specific words, rather than a set of semantically related words. I wanted to be able to find out what kinds of descriptions were consistently used with reference to men, pointing to ideologies of masculinity, which I knew would not necessarily entail the use of the *same* adjectives, but low frequency instances of different but semantically-related lexis. For example, *hot, fit* and *eye candy* are synonyms relating to physical attractiveness that individually occur infrequently in the corpus, but taken together build up a picture of how physical attractiveness, and certain kinds of attractiveness, are privileged as desirable aspects of masculinity for the reader. However, it is not possible to do this using corpus methods, because the software cannot identify this semantic relationship and treat these as one category of collocate.

Additionally, because the calculation of collocation involves examining how concepts are related to a single lexeme, it was not possible to calculate statistical collocates for all the different nominal references to men together. So, in order to compute statistical collocates, I decided to calculate collocates of the lemmas MAN and MEN. To do this, I created a wordlist of the corpus articles in WordSmith Tools, and lemmatized the forms of *man* and *men* using a lemma match list. This meant that MAN and MEN would be treated as one entry. I then filtered the results of these to find adjectival collocates that functioned to categorize male referents, discarding those that did not serve some kind of modifying function.

4.3   Summary: Using Corpus Linguistics to Analyze Discourses of Gender

Although quantitative methods are on the whole extremely fruitful for the analysis of gendered discourses, limitations make a combination of both quantitative and qualitative approaches desirable. The first of these relates to objectivity. Both methods are still heavily reliant on the intuitions of the individual researcher and manual analysis. For example, whilst knowing that the central concept I wanted to focus on was men, I could not simply use 'man' or 'men' as key search terms to acquire frequency information, as this would have eliminated other nominal references to men and masculinity, such as 'fella', 'guy' or 'bloke'.

Secondly, just because a word occurs frequently in a text, this does not necessarily mean it is semantically central to the text's meaning; while high frequency patterns are clearly salient to the cumulative effect of ideology (in that the more something is repeated the more potential there is for it to become normalized in discourse), it could be argued that some constructions which occur less frequently can have more ideological impact than those with a higher statistical significance. For example, while the ideology that team sports are a predominantly male pastime does not occur frequently enough to warrant being labelled as statistically significant in the corpus, this idea will be instantly recognized by many readers of this book, because of its ubiquity in other domains (such as sports journalism, Physical Education curricula in schools, and so on). It is of course for this reason that corpus analyses should always be combined with a consideration of the social, political and historical contexts in which they occur. Corpus linguistics has received criticism for 'abstracting text from its context' (Baldry 2000: 36); it is therefore important to complement quantitative results with qualitative interpretation. Detailed analysis can provide the context for quantitative patterns and allows us to answer questions related to text production—who authored the text and for what purpose.

Chapters 5–8 below present the results of the analysis, beginning with an analysis of how the text producers name and describe men in the magazine data.

References

Baker, P. (2006). *Using Corpora in Discourse Analysis*. London: Continuum.

Baker, P., Gabrielatos, C., & McEnery, T. (2013). Sketching Muslims: A Corpus Driven Analysis of Representations Around the Word 'Muslim' in the British Press 1998–2009. *Applied Linguistics, 34*(3), 255–278.

Baker, P., Gabrielatos, C., Khosravinik, M., Krzyzanowski, M., McEnery, T., & Wodak, R. (2008). A Useful Methodological Synergy? Combining Critical Discourse Analysis and Corpus Linguistics to Examine Discourses of Refugees and Asylum Seekers in the UK Press. *Discourse and Society, 19*(3), 273–306.

Baldry, A. (2000). *Multimodality and Multimediality in the Distance Learning Age*. Campobasso: Palladino.

Burton, D. (1982). Through Glass Darkly: Through Dark Glasses: On Stylistics and Political Commitment. In R. Carter (Ed.), *Language and Literature* (pp. 195–214). London: Allen & Unwin.

Caldas-Coulthard, C. R. (1996). "Women Who Pay for Sex. And Enjoy It": Transgression Versus Morality in Women's Magazines. In C. R. Caldash-Coulthard & M. Coulthard (Eds.), *Texts and Practices: Readings in Critical Discourse Analysis* (pp. 250–270). London: Routledge.

Caldas-Coulthard, C. R., & Moon, R. (2010). 'Curvy, Hunky, Kinky': Using Corpora as Tools for Critical Analysis. *Discourse and Society, 21*(2), 99–133.

Cruse, A. (1986). *Lexical Semantics*. Cambridge: Cambridge University Press.

Cruse, A. (2004). *Meaning in Language: An Introduction to Semantics and Pragmatics*. Oxford: Oxford University Press.

Davies, M. (2013). *Oppositions and Ideology in News Discourse*. London: Bloomsbury.

Delin, J. (2000). *The Language of Everyday Life: An Introduction*. London: Sage.

del-Teso-Craviotto, M. (2005). Words That Matter: Lexical Choice and Gender Ideologies in Women's Magazines. *Journal of Pragmatics, 38*(11), 2003–2021.

Eggins, S., & Iedema, R. (1997). Difference Without Diversity: Semantic Orientation and Ideology in Competing Women's Magazines. In R. Wodak (Ed.), *Gender and Discourse* (pp. 165–196). London: Sage.

Fairclough, N. (1989). *Language and Power*. London: Longman.

Fairclough, N. (1992). *Critical Language Awareness*. London: Longman.

Fairclough, N. (1995). *Critical Discourse Analysis*. London: Longman.

Favaro, L. (2017). Mediating Intimacy Online: Authenticity, Magazines and Chasing the Clicks. *Journal of Gender Studies*. Available at http://dx.doi.org/10.1080/09589236.2017.1280385. Accessed June 2017.

Fowler, R. (1991). *Language in the News: Discourse and Ideology in the Press*. London: Routledge.

Gabrielatos, C., & Baker, P. (2008). Fleeing, Sneaking, Flooding: A Corpus Analysis of Discursive Constructions of Refugees and Asylum Seekers in the UK Press, 1996–2005. *Journal of English Linguistics, 36*(1), 5–38.

Grice, P. (1975). Logic and Conversation. In P. Cole & J. L. Morgan (Eds.), *Syntax and Semantics 3: Speech Acts* (pp. 41–58). New York: Academic.

Halliday, M. A. K. (1994). *An Introduction to Functional Grammar* (2nd ed.). London: Arnold.

Halliday, M. A. K., & Matthiessen, C. (2004). *An Introduction to Functional Grammar* (3rd ed.). London: Arnold.

Hermes, J. (1995). *Reading Women's Magazines: An Analysis of Everyday Media Use*. Cambridge: Polity Press.

Jeffries, L. (2007). *Textual Construction of the Female Body: A Critical Discourse Approach*. Basingstoke: Palgrave Macmillan.

Jeffries, L. (2010a). *Opposition in Discourse*. London: Continuum.

Jeffries, L. (2010b). *Critical Stylistics*. Basingstoke: Palgrave Macmillan.

Koller, V. (2004). Businesswomen and War Metaphors: "Possessive Jealous and Pugnacious"? *Journal of Sociolinguistics, 8*(1), 3–22.

Levinson, S. C. (1983). *Pragmatics*. Cambridge: Cambridge University Press.

López Maestre, M. D. (2013). Narrative and Ideologies of Violence Against Women: The Legend of the Black Lagoon. *Language and Literature, 22*(4), 299–313.

Lyons, J. (1977). *Semantics* (Vol. 1). Cambridge: Cambridge University Press.

Mautner, G. (2016). Checks and Balances: How Corpus Linguistics Can Contribute to CDA. In R. Wodak & M. Meyer (Eds.), *Methods of Critical Discourse Studies* (3rd ed., pp. 154–179). London: Sage.

McLoughlin, L. (2000). *The Language of Magazines*. London: Routledge.

Motschenbacher, H. (2009). Speaking the Gendered Body: The Performative Construction of Commercial Femininities and Masculinities via Body-Part Vocabulary. *Language in Society, 38*(1), 1–22.

Murphy, L. (2003). *Semantic Relations and the Lexicon*. Cambridge: Cambridge University Press.

Pearce, M. (2008). Investigating the Collocational Behaviour of MAN and WOMAN in the BNC Using Sketch Engine. *Corpora, 3*(1), 1–29.

Rayson, P. (2008). From Key Words to Key Semantic Domains. *International Journal of Corpus Linguistics, 13*(4), 519–549.

Reisigl, M., & Wodak, R. (2001). *Discourse and Discrimination: Rhetorics of Racism and Anti-Semitism*. London: Routledge.

Schegloff, E. A., & Sacks, H. (1973). Opening Up Closings. *Semiotica, 7*(1), 289–327.

Scott, M. (2008). *WordSmith Tools Version 5*. Liverpool: Lexical Analysis Software.

Semino, E. (1997). *Language and World Creation in Poems and Other Texts*. London: Longman.

Simpson, P. (1993). *Language, Ideology and Point of View*. London: Routledge.

Sinclair, J. (1991). *Corpus, Concordance, Collocation*. Oxford: Oxford University Press.

Tabbert, U. (2016). *Language and Crime: Constructing Offenders and Victims in Newspaper Reports*. London: Palgrave Macmillan.

Talbot, M. (1992). The Construction of Gender in a Teenage Magazine. In N. Fairclough (Ed.), *Critical Language Awareness* (pp. 174–199). London: Longman.

Talbot, M. (1995). A Synthetic Sisterhood: False Friends in a Teenage Magazine. In K. Hall & M. Bucholtz (Eds.), *Gender Articulated: Language and the Socially Constructed Self* (pp. 143–165). London: Routledge.

Van Leeuwen, T. (1995). Representing Social Action. *Discourse & Society, 6*(1), 81–106.

Van Leeuwen, T. (1996). The Representation of Social Actors. In C. R. Caldas-Coulthard & M. Coulthard (Ed.), *Texts and Practices: Readings in Critical Discourse Analysis* (pp. 32–70). London: Routledge.

Wareing, S. (1994). And Then He Kissed Her.... In K. Wales (Ed.), *Feminist Linguistics in Literary Criticism* (pp. 117–136). Cambridge: D. S. Brewer.

5

Lads, Blokes and Monsters: Strategies of Naming and Description

This chapter examines the ideological impact of how men are labelled and categorized by the magazine producers. Writers make decisions about how to refer to men in women's magazines, and the choice of label indicates which aspects of male identity the writer wishes to foreground. For example, a noun like *hottie* focuses on physical appearance, *boyfriend* on relationship roles, and *soldier* on occupational roles. These choices can reveal attitudes towards particular ways of being that are potentially ideologically harmful, from a feminist perspective. For example, in some contexts, the decision to use the word *lad* or *bloke* in place of a more evaluatively 'neutral' noun like *man* may serve to indicate a discourse of 'bad behavior', since terms like *lad* are often associated with activities such as heavy drinking and womanizing (Phipps and Young 2015). This kind of choice is potentially significant, because it feeds into a broader ideology that (young) men are irresponsible. As I will argue, this is potentially dangerous when the notion of irresponsibility is framed as something that men 'cannot help', particularly when the 'bad behavior' relates to non-consensual sexual activity.

Given the ideological potential of naming choices, naming analysis is often the starting point for Critical Discourse Analysis (CDA) analyses

© The Author(s) 2019
L. Coffey-Glover, *Men in Women's Worlds*,
https://doi.org/10.1057/978-1-137-57555-5_5

of identity construction. The discussion of naming I present here takes the noun phrase as the basic unit for analysis, following Jeffries' (2007) work on magazines and female identity construction, and focuses on the following types of nominal and adjectival choices:

- common nouns
- body part nouns
- adjectives.

The most ideologically salient nominal categories for naming men in the data were the common nouns and body part nouns, and so these are the main focus of my analysis of naming. I consider the positive and negative connotations associated with these choices and ideologies of masculinity that they can be seen to promote.

Pronouns either function as anaphoric references, or as a collective term, as in: 'Where to spend Christmas Day – your place or his?' (*Company*). The writers' decision to use a noun that usually denotes a specific referent to refer to a collective identity, what Fairclough terms 'synthetic personalization' (1989: 62), is one of the strategies women's magazines adopt in order to make them appear as though they are addressing the individual reader and her life personally, and is a well-documented characteristic of women's magazines (Talbot 1992: 175). The significance of using male pronouns to construct a collective male identity is that they presuppose that these qualities and attributes are applicable to *all* men. This is particularly the case with the possessive pronoun *his*, which produces existential presuppositions in noun phrases (see Chapter 8). Pronouns therefore serve to construct the reader as heterosexual, and to create an image of men as a homogeneous group.

5.1   Gender and Labels: Lexical, Social and Referential Gender

In analyzing the types of nouns used to label men in the corpus, I draw on Hellinger and Bussman's (2001) categories of linguistic gender construction: lexical gender, social gender and referential gender.

Proper nouns and pronouns are 'lexically' gendered in that they include the semantic feature [+male] or [+female] in their denotative meanings. Personal nouns referencing men and women in general (such as *man, bachelor*), and address terms (*Mr, sir*) are also lexically gendered, in that they directly index the sex of the speaker, and include the component [+male] in their denotation. Common nouns such as *soldier, mechanic* or *truck driver* are 'socially' gendered, because although they are technically gender-neutral, in reality they have connotations of male reference. The analysis of socially gendered labels is particularly illuminating for feminist analyses, because it reveals the constructedness of gender: words come to 'mean' masculinity or femininity through repeated use over time. Referential gender refers to the actual referent of a particular lexeme. This is a useful category for describing nouns that usually index femininity, but in context have a male referent, such as the use of 'diva' to label a male speaker (*Woman & Home*).

In this chapter I treat the processes of naming and describing separately for reasons of clarity, but in fact we can view pre-modifying adjectives (such as 'hot bloke') as part of the naming process, so they actually work together to produce certain effects.

5.2   Naming: Common Nouns

The first step in uncovering the ideological potential of common nouns used to label men was to group these into semantic categories. As Table 5.1 demonstrates, the majority of common nouns served as some kind of social classification, such as sex, age, class, sexuality, ethnicity or religion.

These are more permanent aspects of identity, because they are more difficult to change than more temporary aspects, such as occupation, or other behavioral roles, such as 'interviewer', or 'contender', and are therefore arguably reified. The largest sub-category of social classification are nouns whose primary semantic purpose is to express the quality [+male], and includes words like 'boy', 'bloke', 'man' and 'lad'. I anticipated that some instances of terms like 'lad' and 'bloke' would

Table 5.1 Semantic categories of male common nouns

Semantic category	Frequency (tokens)	% of male common noun tokens
Social classification	805	39.9
Relational roles	755	33.8
Occupation	230	13.2
Metaphor	103	5.1
Behaviour/personality	104	5.1
Human	29	1.4
Appraisement	17	0.8
Quantification	1	0.05

have additional connotative meanings that index the kinds of hegemonic masculinity associated with the New Laddism of men's magazines (Benwell 2003, 2004; Jackson et al. 2001) and 'lad culture' more broadly. Closer examination of the contexts of the lemmas LAD and BLOKE revealed that in the majority of cases, LAD and BLOKE could be interpreted simply as informal or colloquial synonyms for *man*. However, approximately a third of these are used in contexts where men are behaving in ways that are culturally associated with New Lad masculinity (21 instances, 32%).

5.2.1 Personifying 'Lad Culture' in Women's Magazines

As discussed in Sect. 3.4 above, the practices and behaviors associated with the New Lad in men's magazines include excessive drinking, sexism, and a rejection of beautification processes like using skincare products or cosmetics ('male grooming' in advertising discourse). The following examples from *Company* magazine demonstrate the anti-beautification connotations of 'lad':

And it's not just the super-fashion-forward metrosexual types who love their lipsticks - men all over the UK are getting involved (remember this summer, when even the laddy **lads** on *Shipwrecked* wore eyeliner for the beach party every week?).

Aside from the nominal label, the pre-modifying adjective 'laddy' is also instrumental in indexing the anti-beautification sentiment, partly because it suggests that there are degrees of laddish behavior, and those at the far end (most 'lad-like'?) of the scale would not be expected to engage in beautification processes. This is compounded by the conventional implicature of the adverb *even*, a feature of pragmatic meaning (the mechanics of pragmatic meaning are discussed in Chapter 8).

Grooming is also negatively evaluated by the 'real-life' interviewee in the following example, who rejects cosmetic products for a legitimate performance of masculinity.

> I've grown up thinking it's better for us **lads** to be seen not to care much about grooming. Surely that's better than caring too much! (Jason, 27, Newcastle)

Here it is assumed that it is possible to care 'too much' about one's appearance, equated with grooming practices, and this acquires negative status via the conventional meaning of *too*, as implying negative evaluation of the propositions involved.

The term 'bloke' is also associated with a hegemonic masculinity that involves rejecting make-up:

> Blokes should look like **blokes**, and in my opinion, we look better natural. (James, 26, Manchester)

This example contains a tautological proposition. The reader can infer from this that *bloke* does not just denote [+male] but has additional, connotative meanings, which in this case are that 'real' men do not wear make-up, because wearing make-up is not viewed as constituting authentic masculinity due to its associations with femininity.

As well as a rejection of beautification processes, the New Lad is also said to be a womanizer, afraid of long-term commitment in relationships (Jackson et al. 2001: 81; Taylor and Sunderland 2003: 177). The 'laddish' connotations of 'bloke' often contributes to the ideology that men are commitment-phobes, and also adopt a predatory approach to women, as in the following extracts from *Cosmopolitan* magazine:

> So girls have got to go out with a guy for 11 years before they can get them down the aisle? Dec: "Well, you don't want to rush into anything, do you?" [...]
>
> Ant: "**Blokes** are renowned for taking their time... "
>
> (*Cosmopolitan*)

The mouthpiece for 'blokes' in the first example here is celebrity TV presenter Ant McPartlin, who is being questioned about men's assumed propensity to postpone marriage, because of their fear of 'rushing into' long-term relationships.

In the following example from the same magazine, short-term sexual encounters are glossed as hyponyms of 'running wild':

> From snogs in the stationery cupboard to naked bums on the photocopier – do **blokes** really run wild at the office bash?
>
> (*Cosmopolitan*)

The idiomatic phrase 'run wild' connotes unfettered, animal behavior, drawing on the conceptual metaphor MEN ARE ANIMALS. Conceptual metaphors are those that operate on a cognitive level, in which one concept is understood in terms of another (Gibbs 1994: 6). The use of conceptual metaphor was an interesting although infrequent technique, and is discussed further in Sect. 5.2.3.

The final example is from a survey of male respondents to the question of whether women should initiate sexual encounters/relationships:

> Should a girl ever make the first move? [...]
>
> "Yes. I can't imagine any **bloke** having a problem with it." (Paul, 23, Oxford)
>
> (*More*)

The response implies that no (modern) man would take issue with this, because all men are interested in being in heterosexual relationships. The pre-modifying quantifier 'any' denotes inclusive reference, which has the ideological effect of assuming all men are the same, in this respect.

All of the examples in this section come from articles in magazines aimed at single women. The instances of 'bloke' in the domestic weeklies do not occur in the context of 'laddish' masculinity, and seem to function more simply as colloquial synonyms for *man*. This suggests that the glossy magazines may be more influenced by the forms of masculinity found in men's magazines than the domestic weeklies are, that is, they are more deeply imbricated in 'lad culture'. Given that the domestic weeklies have older target markets than the glossies, we can surmise that New Laddism is specifically a youthful construct.

5.2.2 Occupational Nouns: What the Ideal Man Does

The third largest category of nouns denoting male referents are those that refer to occupations. The majority of occupational nouns belong to the field of culture and creative arts (53 tokens, 23%), probably reflecting the presence of celebrity identities, who are mainly actors and musicians. The second largest category is that of the emergency services and armed forces, most of which (21, 78%) denote occupations in the police force. This seems to reflect a wider cultural gender divide in the workplace: jobs in the armed forces and emergency services are traditionally associated with men, and the occupations with the lowest frequencies are those in areas like fashion, beauty and education, which are conventionally associated with women. From this perspective, the magazines are constructing a stereotypical male population, where men perform roles that are in alignment with traditional hegemonic masculinity.

Given the strong presence of occupations associated with men and traditional forms of masculinity in the corpus, it is useful to consider occupational nouns in terms of lexical and social gender. There were a small number of lexically gendered nouns, marked with the suffix –*man* or –*men* (Table 5.2).

It is notable that while the manual labor terms here ('repairman', 'gas man') are those that have not been subject to anti-sexist language reform, the others all have gender-neutral alternatives codified in

Table 5.2 Frequencies of lexically gendered occupational
nouns

Lexically gendered occupatiobal nouns	Raw frequency
Businessman	6
Fireman	1
Gas man	1
POLICEMAN	4
Postman	1
Repairman	1

dictionaries as a result of feminist campaigning, for example: *fire fighter,
police officer, businessperson.*

As well as occupations that are lexically marked for male reference,
a number of the occupational terms indicate social gender: 'a matter of
entrenched social stereotypes that tie certain role scripts to women and
men' (2009: 3). For example, whereas a term like *nurse* is more likely
to be interpreted as having female reference, *soldier* is more likely to be
perceived as male. Table 5.3 provides examples of lexis that can be interpreted as exhibiting social gender:

In Table 5.3, 120 instances of occupational nouns arguably exhibit
social gender, comprising 52% of the total number of occupational
nouns with male referents. The occupational nouns in the emergency

Table 5.3 Socially gendered occupational nouns used to label men

Job sector	Socially gendered lexis	Frequency
Culture and creative arts	ACTOR; composer; DJ; movie producer	21
Emergency services and armed forces	Cop; SOLDIER; spy; agent; OFFICER	21
Science and medicine	Doctor; GP; engineer; surgeon; consultant; physician	21
Government and politics	Mayor; president; governor	18
Business and management	BOSS; CEO; entrepreneur	9
Sport	Athlete; baseball player; basketball analyst; boxer; F1 champion; footballer; motocross driver; racing driver	9
Law	Judge; lawyer; QC; solicitor	7
Security	Bouncer; guards; security guard; security official	7
Transport and logistics	Lorry driver; truck driver; trucker	4
Manual labor	Joiner; mechanic	3
		119

services and armed forces, sport, manual labor and security categories are all terms that are traditionally associated with male occupations. This is a reflection of the ideology that men are physically stronger than women, and therefore roles like fire fighter and police officer, which are physically demanding, have become associated with men. It could be argued that some of these terms, such as 'basketball analyst' or 'DJ' are less obviously linked to social stereotypes; others, such as 'footballer', 'soldier', and 'lorry driver', are very well established as gendered roles, and therefore serve as indirect indices of masculinity. The fact that the majority of male identities that populate women's magazines occupy stereotypically gendered roles demonstrates the magazines' part in reifying these socio-cultural scripts.

The distribution of occupational nouns across the different text types shows that the majority of words in the 'emergency services and armed forces' category come from the true-life stories (20 tokens, 74%). The majority of the occupational nouns in the 'culture and creative arts' category come from the interviews text type, which would be expected, given that the interviewees in these texts are celebrities. While occupations associated with traditional hegemonic masculinity are clearly present and relatively high frequency in women's magazines, it is interesting that the kinds of men who are idealized in women's magazines are actually more often actors and musicians, which counters research on the male populations of men's magazines which has shown that the kinds of men who are idolised in those texts are often associated with 'dangerous spheres', such as war photographers or members of the armed forces, who serve as heroes for the aspiring male (Benwell 2003: 157).

5.2.3 Monsters and Heroes: Metaphorical Nouns

Nouns with metaphorical meanings fit into two broad categories: cultural stereotypes based on particular behaviors or appearance, such as 'boy-about-town', or 'hero', and more specific culturally defined figures, such as 'bogeyman' or 'devil'. There are also a small number of fictional metaphors, based on characters from mythical and fairy-tale genres or romance fiction, for example:

1. Remember, you will date a few **frogs** before you find your prince.

   (*Pride*)

2. You've heard the saying: You have to kiss a lot of Eric Banas before you find your **prince**.

   (*Glamour*)

3. Michelle Obama knows how to keep the twinkle in her husband's eye while pushing him to the top. I used to be **Prince Charming** too, but baby, why did you have to change the happy ending?

   (*Pride*)

All these focus on the notion of physical attractiveness and chivalry. The first two contain intertextual references to the Brothers Grimm fairy tale *The Frog Prince*, in which a young princess grudgingly agrees to befriend a frog, who consequently transforms into a prince. The 'ideal reader' here is one who is familiar with the story, and the related proverbial phrase 'you have to kiss a few frogs before you find your prince', and who will therefore interpret 'frogs' and 'Eric Banas' as a metaphor denoting an unattractive or undesirable man, and 'prince' as referring to an attractive, highly desirable man. The reader will likely infer that 'Eric Banas' is intended to denote an undesirable man, due to the negative connotations usually associated with 'frogs', and the conversely positive associations of 'prince'. The final example includes reference to 'Prince Charming', the stock protagonist of most fairy-tales. This comes from an opinion column written by a male writer who is complaining that, since marrying his wife, their relationship has changed. Here he is comparing their relationship with that of fairy-tales, drawing on the conceptual metaphor LOVE IS A FAIRY-TALE, also indicated by the intertextual reference to the 'happy ending'. The writer also draws parallels between their relationship and that of Barack and Michelle Obama's, comparing himself with the then Presidential candidate Barack Obama, stating that they are both Prince Charmings, signaled by the conventional implicature of *too*. The reader must rely on her schematic knowledge of fairy-tales to interpret the label 'Prince Charming' as referring to an idealized form of masculinity associated with desirability and wealth.

Other metaphorical labels specify romantic behavior towards women, but sometimes have conflicting connotations:

> He has this **Romeo** look about him and you can immediately tell he's a **ladies man**. He made me feel immediately at ease.
>
> (*Asiana*)

Being a 'ladies' man' appears to be perceived by the female narrator as a positive description here, as it is equated with being made to feel comfortable. The proper noun 'Romeo' is used as a pre-modifier to head noun 'look', suggesting that *Romeo* does not just denote the fictional character from Shakespeare's *Romeo and Juliet*, but also refers to a set of behaviors and can therefore serve as a descriptive category. The dictionary definition of 'ladies' man' is 'a man who enjoys female company, *esp.* one who is sexually successful with women' (*OED Online*). Shakespeare's Romeo is successful in courting Juliet, thus 'Romeo' and 'ladies' man' can be interpreted as roughly synonymous.

However, in the following example, the writer uses the compound 'ladies' man' negatively:

> 'It's hard posing naked with fit men: I admitted to Joe one night. He nodded. 'Being a **ladies' man** comes with my job', he confessed.
>
> (*Love It*)

The reader can infer this negative meaning from the conventional negative associations of the reporting verb 'confessed'.

The noun *Lothario* comes from the name of a male character who seduces women in Nicholas Rowe's *The Fair Penitent* (1703), but is used as a common noun in these examples:

> If he's a **Lothario** who's working his way through as many women as possible, make sure he's having safe sex. If he likes putting on women's pants, although you both might be embarrassed, it's not the end of the world.
>
> (*Best*)

> *Company* reports on the rise of the mascara man. It all started with cheeky Noel Fielding and wicked **lothario** Russell Brand. Now, it seems, boys everywhere are delving into their very own make-up bags.
>
> (*Company*)

By extension, *Lothario* is often used as a term for 'a man whose chief interest is seducing women' (*Merriam-Webster Online* 2013). This term is evaluated negatively in these examples, as indicated for instance by pre-modifying adjective 'wicked'. However, whether these terms are really intended to invoke whole-hearted negative associations is debatable.

A small number of metaphorical nouns with explicitly negative connotations, such as 'beast', 'monster', and 'bogeyman', refer to men who have committed immoral acts, specifically in the true-life story text type:

> Better to end up in hospital than be raped by that **beast** again…
> (*Real People*)

> I put that ad in the paper looking for love. But all I found was a **monster**.
> (*Real People*)

> The **BOGEYMAN**'S here … Jodie was dragged naked from her bed. What did her kidnapper want and where was he taking her?
> (*That's Life*)

The first example is from a story in which the female narrator was sexually abused by her father. The choice of noun 'beast' has animalistic connotations, drawing on the conceptual metaphor MEN ARE ANIMALS. The second excerpt is from a narrative in which the female narrator embarks on a relationship with a male respondent to a personal ad, only to discover that he murdered his wife. 'Love' is used metonymically here and is constructed as in opposition to 'monster', the male antagonist of the narrative. The final example comes from a story in which the female narrator's ex-partner becomes jealous of her relationship with a new lover, breaks into the house, attacks her new boyfriend, then abducts her. According to one dictionary, the *bogeyman* is 'a monstrous imaginary figure used in threatening children' (*Merriam-Webster*). It is interesting that this should be the chosen noun, given that the victim of the male perpetrator is not a child, but an adult woman.

In these stories, the men have all committed acts of violence; the use of metaphorical nouns with animalistic connotations is a way of dehumanizing them. The magazine writers' decision to include such nominal references is characteristic of tabloid news discourse, particularly in cases of male sexual violence. For example, in her study of news reporting in *The Sun*, Clark (1992) found that where men are the agents of acts of violence against women, they are referred to as 'maniacs' or 'monsters', making them appear extreme and abnormal (Clark 1992: 210). Naylor's (2001) study of reports of sexual violence in the British press found that male offenders in sex murder cases are often labelled 'fiend' or 'monster' (2001: 190). Soothill and Walby (1991) also discuss tabloid newspapers' appropriation of nicknames like 'beast' and 'monster' to denote such offenders.

5.2.4 Divas and Fashionistas: Indexing Femininity

As stated at the beginning of this chapter, the term 'referential gender' serves as a direct index for whoever a particular noun refers to in a given context, and can be a particularly useful category for observing the subversion of gender stereotypes (Motschenbacher 2009: 4). For example, the words *fashionista* and *diva* are typically gendered as feminine in English, but are used with male referents in the magazine corpus in order to attribute 'feminine' behaviors to the referents in question. In the case of 'diva', this attribution is intended as an insult:

> Whenever someone offered commiserations or made a comment about the tackiness of Todd's post-divorce rush to the altar, I'd bat it away with a comment like: "You are looking at a happily divorced woman." Or I'd resort to irony: "In private Todd was always a diva… so I'm not surprised he simply had to marry one."
>
> (*Woman & Home*)

This extract is taken from a fictional story narrated from the point of view of a female character called Anne, who is Todd's ex-wife. Todd is a lawyer who divorced Anne to marry an opera singer. The narrator describes Todd as a 'diva' in an effort to counter-act previous descriptions of Todd as 'hard-nosed'. Here the narrator exploits the connotative meanings of 'diva' to imply that Todd is controlling and demanding. A negative appraisal of being a 'diva' is implied by the proposition that Todd keeps his diva-ish behavior a secret; the reader is to infer that such behavior is shameful. The word *diva* has the component [+female] in its denotative meaning, and therefore usually directly indexes femininity. It is often used to describe demanding women, particularly those who work in theatre; these negative connotative meanings are transferred to the male referent here. Part of the illocutionary force of the insult therefore is that Todd is behaving *like a woman*. The idea that behaving 'like a woman' is insulting, sexist and essentialist, as it assumes, firstly, that it is possible to behave 'like a (typical) woman', and secondly that it is undesirable to do so. On the other hand, it would also be possible to interpret the use of 'diva' in Butler's terms as a 'subversive act' (1990), if we view signifying a male body with a female signifier as beginning to break down the sex-gender equation.

In the following example, the author of the opinion column 'Supersize Fashion' uses the term 'fashionista' to refer to a man, implied by the pre-modifying compound adjective 'woman-hating':

> I refuse to believe that I'm a size 32 or whatever just because some twisted woman-hating fashionista has decreed anyone with a big butt and big boobs must necessarily be.
>
> (*Asiana*)

The *Oxford English Dictionary* defines 'fashionista' as 'A person employed in the creation or promotion of high fashion, as a designer, photographer, model, fashion writer, etc. Also: a devotee of the fashion industry; a wearer of high-fashion clothing' (*OED Online*). Examining a list of concordance lines for 'fashionista' in WebCorp, a concordancer that allows the user to interrogate internet search engines, revealed that the term is usually used to refer to women who follow high fashion, or work in the fashion industry as designers, models or fashion writers, suggesting that 'fashionista' conventionally indexes femininity. Given that the fashion industry and femininity are also sometimes associated with male homosexuality, the reader may infer the term 'fashionista' as indirectly indexing a gay male identity if used with male reference. The choice of pre-modifying compound adjective 'woman-hating' also implies a male referent (assuming that it is not intended masochistically!).

In an interview in *Scarlet* magazine, 'Tornado', a professional glad-iator, is categorized as a *pin-up*, which arguably usually names female referents:

> How do you feel about becoming a pin-up?
> I love it.

The term pin-up connotes [+female], as it comes from the notion of the women pin-ups and calendar girls featured in popular magazines in the 1940s and 1950s (Horne 2011), although this was later appro-priated by producers of the 'new women's magazines' like *Cosmopolitan* launched in the early years of the second-wave feminist movement, which included nude male centerfolds ostensibly as a way of 'turning the tables' on the female equivalents in magazines for men (Le Masurier 2011: 226). Examining the co-texts of 'pin-up' as a noun in the BNC revealed that a slight majority (53%) had female referents, and these were most often in the context of war-time, or used as a descriptive term for an 'attractive' woman, whereas the instances of 'pin-up' with a male referent most often referred to celebrities or pop stars in magazines for teenage girls. Additionally, the phrase 'male pin-up' occurred twice in the sample, where the semantic equivalent 'female pin-up' was not present, suggesting that the concept of the female pin-up is more cul-turally recognizable than that of the male.

In the context of women's magazines, however, the reader may likely draw on schematic knowledge of the kinds of nude male pin-ups that populate teenage magazines. Using 'pin-up' to describe Tornado there-fore emphasizes his celebrity status, as someone 'being, or worthy of being, the subject of such a picture; glamorous, attractive' (*OED Online*). 'Tornado' is the stage name given to the actor who plays him in the television game show *Gladiators*, in which 'regular' contestants challenge the gladiators to various duels, tests of strength and endurance modelled on those of the Roman Empire over two millennia ago. It is therefore interesting that the decision to describe Tornado as a 'pin-up' focuses on his identity as a sexual object of desire, rather than on physi-cal strength, as his stage name does.

5.3   Naming: Body Part Nouns

Body part nouns naming parts of the male body serve to either compartmentalize the male body or act as a metonymic reference to a male identity.

In terms of frequency, there are roughly equal numbers of body part nouns with male and female referents in the corpus; a slight but non-significant majority have female referents (641, 55%). There are also roughly equal numbers of gender-exclusive body part nouns: 90 instances of body part nouns only have male referents (7.7%); 103 only co-occur with female identities (8.9%). Whilst it is noteworthy that in terms of pure frequency, men's and women's bodies are afforded roughly equal space in the texts, examining the contexts of these may indicate an underlying gender difference of ideological import, particularly if they reiterate existing discourses of masculinity, because they contribute to the naturalization of hegemonic masculine ideals. Examining what kinds of lexical fields are evident in these two sub-groups will therefore demonstrate what physical differences between the sexes are constructed and indicate how masculinity is conceptualized in relation to femininity in the texts.

Analyzing the lexical fields of both the male-only body parts and female-only body parts revealed the following semantic groupings.

As Table 5.4 indicates, there are shared lexical fields between the male-only and female-only body parts (such as 'face' and 'limbs'), but what is arguably more interesting is the lexical differences in the shared fields. Although this is not intended as a comparative study, examining the kinds of body parts that index femininity will also aid in an analysis of how masculinity is constructed, given that gender is often conceptualized as relational.

Looking at the distribution of body part terms across the corpus shows that the survey reports and true-life stories contain the highest proportion of body part terms, taking into account the relative word counts of the different sub-corpora (Table 5.5).

However, the relative high frequency of body part nouns in the survey reports is most likely an over-representation, since one survey

Table 5.4 Lexical fields of male-only and female-only body parts

Lexical field	Male-only body parts		Female-only body parts	
	Lexis	Frequency	Lexis	Frequency
Genitalia/sex organs	Button mushroom (2); COCK (5); crotch (1); ERECTION (3); li'l guy (1); man garden (1); pencil (3); penis (8); private parts (2); pubic bone (2); sensitive areas (1); shaft (1); sperm (1); testicle (1); todger (1); trouser forest (1); trousersnake (1); WILLY (6); winkle (1)	42	Clitoris (7); labia (1); vulva (1); womb (1)	10
Body	Anatomy (1)	1	Figure (2)	2
Bottom	Ass (1); buns (1)	2	Bottom (1); butt (1); buttocks (1)	3
Chest			Boob (11); BREAST (11); implants (2); tits (1)	25
Face	Buckteeth (1); expression (2); forehead (1); gnashers (1); goatee (1); gob (1); grimace (1); grin (3); jaw (1); lashes (1); moustache (1)	14	Cheekbone (2); chin (1); chompers (1); eye socket (1); eyelashes (1); freckles (2); nostrils (1); WRINKLE (3)	12
Hair	hairs (1); hairstyle (1)	2		0
Head		0	Nape (1); scalp (1); throat (5); tongue (3)	10
Hormones	Testosterone (2)	2	Oestrogen (2)	2
Internal organs/body tissue/fluids	Bone marrow (1); Heart valves (1); pancreas (2); saliva (2); sweat (1); tendons (1); veins (1); vomit (1)	9	bladder (1); kidneys (1); LUMP (3); lungs (1); vomit (1)	7
Limbs	Clutches (1); fingerprint (1); fist (3); THUMB (2)	7	Ankles (2); armpits (1); fingertips (1); foot (1); nails (3); stump (2); TOE (3)	13
Muscles	Biceps (1); brawn (1); pecs (1); six-pack (2)	5	Pelvic-floor muscle (1)	1
Skeleton		0	Pelvis (2); ribs (1)	2
Skin	Complexion (1); scar tissue (1); spots (2)	4	Bruises (2); Cellulite (4); goosebumps (4); ripple (1); scar (1); stitches (3)	15
Stomach	Belly button (1); puppy fat (1)	2	Flab (1)	1
Total		90		103

Table 5.5 Frequencies of body part nouns per text type

Text type	Frequency of body part nouns with male referent (tokens)	Normalized frequencies
True-life stories	163	47.6
Interviews	74	21.1
Fiction	49	33
Features	47	13.3
Survey reports	35	84.1
Columns	24	26.1
Reports	20	24.1
Problem pages	11	7.6
Letters	9	38.9
Profiles	4	29
Advertorials	3	19.5
Lists	3	31
Reviews	1	38.3

article, 'Would You Rather' (*Glamour*), accounts for of 66% of the 35 instances of body part nouns in the survey reports. It would therefore be unwise to claim that the survey report as a text type is prone to representing men in terms of body parts, only that this particular piece does so. However, the high frequency of body part nouns in the true-life stories does appear to be indicative of the text type in general, as they are more evenly distributed across the texts. This may be because true-life stories are fictional narratives, and the representation of body parts and body part agency (as in 'his hand brushed against her cheek') is a well-documented associated stylistic feature (see, for example, Korte 1997).

5.3.1 Button Mushrooms and Trousersnakes: Synonyms for the Penis

By far the largest lexical field in the male-only body parts is that of genitalia, with a total of 42 instances, making up almost half the number of tokens in this category (46%). There are four times more instances of genitalia lexis in the male-only category than in the female-only category, and the items in the female 'genitalia' sub-field mostly denote

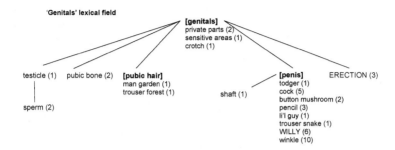

'Genitals' lexical field

Fig. 5.1   Lexical field 'genitals' for the male-only body part terms

internal parts (3 of 4 lexemes). Jeffries (2007: 73) found an implicit distinction made between the 'accessibility' of men's genitalia and 'relative inaccessibility' of female sex organs running throughout her magazine data. She explains how the magazine writers compare female sex organs with everyday objects, as an attempt to reduce the 'mystery' of the female anatomy. In my data, comparisons with everyday objects such as 'pencil' and 'button mushroom' may rather be interpreted as attempts to ridicule male sex organs (Fig. 5.1).

The lexemes in the male-only genitalia lexical field are mostly synonyms for the penis (29 tokens, 69%). Cameron (1992) researched synonyms for the penis in a group of American college students and grouped the terms that the male students listed into the following semantic categories: 'person', 'animals', 'tools', 'weapons', and 'foodstuffs'; terms that the female participants came up with fit into categories including 'names', 'animals', 'tools', 'weapons', 'foodstuff', 'romance', 'size/shape', 'useless things', and 'nonsense terms'. Synonyms for the penis found in the women's magazine corpus can be grouped along similar lines (Table 5.6).

The metaphorical items 'button mushroom' and 'pencil' come from a survey report article entitled 'Would You Rather…', detailing results of a survey garnering (female) public opinion on a series of supposedly oppositional scenarios. The two terms here are in fact constructed opposites (see Chapter 6) in the question 'Would you rather he had a button mushroom or a pencil?':

Table 5.6 Penis terms grouped according to semantic categories

Semantic category	Lexical items	Frequency
Person	Li'l guy	1
	WILLY	6
Animal	Trousersnake	1
Penis	COCK	5
	Penis	8
	Todger	1
Size/shape	Button mushroom	2
	Pencil	3
	Shaft	1
	Winkle	1
Total		29

Unzip him to find a pencil 60%
Unzip him to find a button mushroom 40%
Well, we never. We always thought short and thick would win over long and thin. We stand corrected.

(Glamour)

Here the parallel adjective phrases 'short and thick' and 'long and thin' are glosses for 'button mushroom' and 'pencil', respectively. The scenarios in this survey are intended to entail negative outcomes; respondents are invited to pick the 'best' option from these '"aargh, how to choose" dilemmas' (*Glamour*). The qualities and behaviors discussed in the article are therefore representative of undesirable aspects of masculinity, which are being 'judged' by the people who took part in the survey. Both scenarios here are deemed unconducive to 'satisfying' sexual activity, implied by the idiomatic phrases 'well, we never' and 'we stand corrected'. These negative evaluations of lexis denoting small size ultimately recirculates the notion that 'bigger means better', because, presumably, 'satisfying' sex would necessitate the man possessing a large penis. They can also be seen as euphemistic comparisons with everyday objects that function to reduce the perceived importance of the penis. This differs from the function of such comparisons in Jeffries' study of body part terms for the female body, where they served to reduce the mystery of internal female sex organs (Jeffries 2007: 74).

The term 'winkle' in a report from *Scarlet* magazine also relates to small penis size:

> A 14-year-old boy has been admitted to hospital after a fish 'slipped' up his penis.
> [...]
> While he was having a tinkle the creature apparently escaped his grasp and slid up his **winkle**.
>
> (*Scarlet*)

The word 'winkle' could be interpreted as connoting smallness via the phenomenon of phonetic symbolism. Psychological studies have shown how in pairs of invented words containing /i/ or /a/, (as in 'mil' and 'mal') the /i/ vowel is more often interpreted as symbolizing small size, where /a/ more frequently symbolizes large size (Sapir 1929: 227). It is possible, then, that the short front vowel /ɪ/ is more likely to interpreted by the reader as denoting a small, rather than a large value. Additionally, the reader may infer 'winkle' as an abbreviated form of 'periwinkle', a type of shellfish that is also characterized by smallness. Interestingly, in this interpretation, 'winkle' can be interpreted as another example of the MEN ARE ANIMALS conceptual metaphor discussed in Sects. 5.2.1 and 5.2.3. In this instance, the diminutive connotations of 'winkle' contribute to the infantilization of the teenager, rather than the uselessness of the penis, as in the 'pencil' and 'button mushroom' examples.

The terms 'li'l guy' and 'willy' are personifications of the penis. The instance of 'li'l guy' comes from a column, also in *Scarlet* magazine, by a male writer on his experiences of being a presenter for the adult TV show 'Sexcetera', at a point where he's explaining why he had sex with a married stranger in the middle of an interview with a couple for the program:

> Well, when an attractive naked woman is touching your **li'l guy** at six in the morning, the train has pretty much left the station and you ain't looking for the brake lever.

'Willy' is also a personification, deriving from the name of a cartoon character in *Man's Best Friend*, who was, in fact, a penis. In personifying his penis, the writer draws on the idea that the penis is an 'uncontrollable Other, with a life of its own' (Cameron 1992: 370). The use of a contracted form of *little* arguably connotes fondness and informality, and therefore could be interpreted as non-threatening. However, the decision to use a personal noun rather than a denotative item like 'penis' makes a point of representing the narrator's penis as a separate entity, and thus self-governing. This interpretation is supported by the writer's metaphorical description of the sex act comparing it with the operation of a locomotive, which potentially implies automation, equating sex with a mechanical procedure that is difficult to curtail. This interpretation of male sexuality has serious feminist implications: as Cameron (1992: 370) points out, accepting that male sexuality is 'uncontrollable' gives credence to claims by men in rape cases that they were 'driven' by irresistible sexual urges.

The personifying terms 'li'l guy' and 'willy' connote intimacy rather than heroism, and terms like 'button mushroom', 'pencil' and winkle in the size/shape category arguably all have negative connotations, because they denote small size, focusing on the fallible, rather than powerful, nature of the penis. This echoes the findings of Cameron's sociolinguistic study, where the women informants also produced more terms relating to size/shape, focusing on the penis as non-threatening or 'useless' (Cameron 1992: 375).

5.3.2 Muscles

In the lexical field of muscles, all the words in the male-only category refer to the externally visible; 'pelvic-floor muscle' in the female-only category refers to an internal muscle, which is not visible, and therefore does not index physical strength in the same way that the muscle terms in the male-only category do (see Fig. 5.2). The fact that terms relating to muscularity only have male referents is indicative of their importance for the construction of the ideal male body.

'Muscles' lexical field

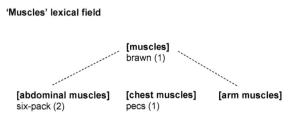

Fig. 5.2   Lexical field of 'muscles' for the male-only body part nouns

The dashed lines in Fig. 5.2 represent a relationship of hyponymy: for example, 'six-pack' is a type of 'abdominal muscle', which in turn is a member of the broader category 'muscle'. While body part lexis relating to muscularity is clearly not significant in any statistical sense, the co-occurrence of these items with male identities suggests that muscles are represented as specific to masculine identity in the texts, and because the muscle terms collocate more frequently with male referents, they may be said to exhibit social gender, functioning as indirect indexes of masculinity. In his study of body part vocabulary in lifestyle magazine advertising, Motschenbacher (2009) found that male bodies were described in terms of muscularity significantly more than female bodies. Interestingly, muscle terms found in the male-targeted magazine *Men's Health* were more likely to be those typical of bodybuilding language such as 'abdominals' and 'quadriceps', which serve to 'desexualize' the male body (2009: 16). The opposite is the case in my data, where the colloquial forms of muscle terms (such as 'six-pack' or 'pecs') contribute to an overall conversational tone, and are positively evaluated as markers of the desirable masculine body, as the following examples indicate:

> Dreamy Daniel was also runner-up on TV show *Top Celebrity Arm Wrestlers*. We'd certainly love to see his **biceps** in action!
>
> (*Woman*)

Here the reader is included as a referent via inclusive pronoun 'we' in the proposition that witnessing this celebrity's arm muscles at work would be desirable. The writer also uses pre-modifying adjective 'dreamy' to describe the owner of the biceps, which conventionally indicates a positive evaluation.

'Pecs' is positively appraised via its constructed opposite 'temper' in the following extract:

> Talent-show judge, Piers Morgan, 43, talks about Simon Cowell's **pecs** and Sharon Osbourne's temper…
>
> *(Woman's Own)*

In this example, the parallel structure of the noun phrases produces oppositional meanings; anger has a negative semantic prosody, foregrounding the positive connotations of 'pecs' (see Chapter 6 on opposition construction).

In addition to the sexual desirability of muscles, the following extract from an interview with boxer Ricky Hatton in *Cosmopolitan* magazine foregrounds discussion of his 'six-pack' as something to be worked at:

> Rickey Hatton tells us he's proud of his **six-pack**.
>
> Wow! It must take a lot of working-out to hone that **six-pack**… " It takes three hours in the gym and a five-mile run every day - I have to be physically ripped for a big fight.

The text is accompanied by a 'pin-up' style photo, immediately visually emphasizing his physical appearance. The idea that he should be 'proud' of his stomach muscles, and that maintaining such an appearance is laborious, triggered by epistemic modal verb 'must', implies that bodybuilding is hard work. Ricky's commitment to maintaining a muscular physique (the fruits of his labor) is appraised here as a positive achievement, which is also signaled by the informal exclamation 'wow!', alongside the choice of verb 'hone', which emphasizes the skill involved in obtaining a six-pack. Searching for collocates of 'hone' in a random sample from BNC shows that 'skill' is the most statistically significant collocate within a three-word span to the left and right of the search term, supporting this interpretation of bodybuilding as associated with skilled labor.

5.3.3 Face

Examining the lexical field 'face' reveals some interesting differences between meronyms with only male referents, and those that are only used with female identities. Meronymy differs from hyponymy in that rather than category membership, it refers to relationships of compartmentalization: for example, 'lashes' are a part of the 'eyes', which in turn are a component of the 'face'. In the female-only terms, meronyms WRINKLE, and 'freckles' are aesthetic features, associated with beauty. WRINKLE is always a beauty flaw; a sign of aging, whereas 'freckles' are sometimes perceived as a positive attribute (Fig. 5.3).

The male-only body part lexis contains hyponyms of facial hair: 'beard', 'moustache' and 'goatee', all indirect indexes of masculinity. The synonyms for teeth, 'chompers' in the female category and 'gnashers' in the male-only group, have interesting differences in their semantic connotations: 'gnashers' has a distinctly violent, animalistic association in comparison with 'chompers', a colloquial term indicating informality.

5.3.4 Limbs

There are also interesting differences in the lexical field 'limbs'. The female-only group contains the items 'nails' and 'fingertips', which

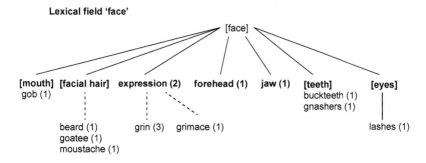

Fig. 5.3 Lexical field 'face' in the male-only body part terms

are not shared by the male-only category. Motschenbacher (2009) observes how the co-occurrence of finger-part terms with female referents in magazine advertising contributes to the social gendering of these words. There is an instance of 'fingerprint' in the male-only category, which in this case belongs to a murderer from true-life story 'Have Sex or Die' (*That's Life*). Also in the male-only group is the nominalization 'clutches', which is used to describe the behavior of a possessive ex-boyfriend in one of the problem pages. The lexeme 'fist' can also be grouped within this field, all three instances of which are the agents of material actions (see Chapter 7) in two true-life stories from *Love It*:

1. Lee pulled his **fist** back again and pummelled my face hard.
2. As his **fist** slammed into my cheek, the room span around me.
3. 'Get out!' I shouted, close to tears. But instead, he pulled back his **fist** and smashed it into my cheek.

The material actions performed by the body parts, 'pummelled', 'slammed' and 'smashed', all have violent connotations. The fact that these aggressive actions are constructed as being performed by the fist reduces agency, and therefore self-control, attributable to the men. The phenomena of male body part agency and its stylistic functions is discussed further in Chapter 7.

5.4   Describing: Adjectives

The kinds of adjectives used to describe an entity or event point to the writer's attitudes towards it; looking at the kinds of adjectives used in descriptions of men in the corpus therefore indicates the kinds of behaviors and attributes that are presented as desirable by the magazine writers. Adjectival descriptions were collected using both quantitative and qualitative methods: I first established statistical collocates of male identities in the corpus, in order to uncover salient words that are repeatedly used to describe men in the data. However, as with nominal labels, just looking at which words are found repeatedly near to male referents does not tell the whole story, as low-frequency but semantically-related words taken together contribute to particular discourses of masculinity that can be said to hold ideological (as opposed to statistical) saliency. For example, 'hot', 'fit' and 'sexy', synonyms relating to physical attractiveness that individually occur infrequently in the corpus, together build up a picture of how physical attractiveness, and certain kinds of attractiveness, are privileged as desirable aspects of masculinity for the reader.

Statistical collocates were calculated in WordSmith Tools using the lemmas MAN and MEN as search terms. In total there were 170 collocates of male referents with a very high statistical strength, but only nine of adjectival collocates serving a modifying function.

The adjectives 'skinny' and 'chubby' in Table 5.7 are descriptions of physical appearance; 'Black', 'British' and 'young' are social classifications; 'single' denotes relationship status and 'gay' describes the sexuality of the referents in question. The collocates are ordered in Table 5.7 according to statistical strength: 'skinny' and MAN has the strongest collocation out of all the pairs listed. 'Skinny' and 'chubby' are lexical opposites, in that they are culturally recognizable as contrasting. Most of the tokens of 'skinny'/'chubby' appear in the same report from *Glamour* magazine, apart from line 4, which is from an opinion column written by a male writer in *Asiana* magazine (Fig. 5.4).

'Skinny' can be interpreted as having positive connotations, which becomes clear when the co-texts are expanded. This reflects the wider cultural context in which a slim appearance is attractive. For example,

Table 5.7 Adjectival collocates of MAN and MEN

Rank	Collocate	Collocates with	Frequency in the corpus	MI score
1	Skinny	MAN	3	7.774
2	Chubby	MAN	3	7.359
3	British	MEN	4	6.778
4	Young	MEN	4	5.852
5	Young	MAN	7	5.333
6	Gay	MEN	4	5.276
7	Single	MEN	3	4.670
8	Gay	MAN	4	3.949
9	Black	MAN	3	3.586

```
1 leep with a chubby  man   or a skinny man? Chubby "It's nice to have som

2  sleep with a chubby man or a skinny  man?  Chubby "It's nice to have so

3   chubby man 42% Sleep with a skinny man  58% You'll take a man with svel

4   unattractive than watching a chubby  man  tighten his belt? 'You won't

5 extremely bendy. Sleep with a chubby  man  42% Sleep with a skinny ma

6 Would you rather sleep with a chubby  man  or a skinny man? Chubby
```

Fig. 5.4 Concordance of 'skinny' and 'chubby'

Table 5.8 Semantic categories of adjectives modifying men

Semantic category	Example lexis	Frequency	% of total frequency of adjectives
Personality and behavior	Shy, romantic	149	31
Physical appearance	Dark, stocky	80	17
Evaluation	Terrible, fabulous	74	16
Social classification	Gay, black, young	71	15
Relationship	Former, new, long-term	51	11
Mental/emotional states	Shocked, ecstatic	47	10
Total		472	

'chubby' is equated with unattractiveness in line 4: 'Is there anything more unattractive than watching a chubby man tighten his belt?' (*Asiana*).

Qualitative analysis of adjectives used to modify male identities in the corpus revealed similar semantic groupings to that of the statistical collocates (Table 5.8).

The majority of adjectives relate to personality and behavior, suggesting that personality traits are deemed more important male qualities than, say, physical appearance or age. We can infer from the relative lack of adjectives concerning mental and emotional states that men are not viewed as emotional or cognitive beings by the magazine producers. This reiterates a broader ideology of men as unemotional, reflected in traditional idioms such as 'boys don't cry'. The idea that men should not express their emotions (other than aggression) is also potentially damaging, and it is this kind of ideology which has led to the need for initiatives like the Campaign Against Living Miserably (2014), dedicated to preventing male suicide.

A small number of adjectives in the personality and behavior category relate to sexual behavior. Some inscribe (heteo)normative sexual behaviors, and some relate to sexual promiscuity, but interestingly they have mostly negative connotations:

> I had this very **experimental** boyfriend, and he was always bringing home sex toys. I thought it was funny, until the night he promised me 'a surprise.' Expecting a new vibrator, I was completely horrified when he produced a strap-on dildo, complete with studs and chains. And no, I didn't wear it. (Casey, 24, Gateshead)

Although being 'experimental' initially seems to be valued positively via the subject complement 'funny' in the following clause, this is then appraised negatively, indicated by the narrator's description of herself as 'completely horrified'. In this example, sexual practices which deviate from what is perceived as 'normal' heterosexual sex are denigrated.

In the following example from *Glamour*, the notions of both sexual repression and experimentation are negatively valued:

> He's a bit of a **prude** 34%
> He's too **kinky** 66%
>
> "Just bend over there, love. Yes that's right. What do you mean the bridle is uncomfortable? Bad horsey." Oh, the mind boggles as to what you've let yourself in for.
>
> *(Glamour)*

Despite the fact that the figures here show that being 'kinky' was the preferred choice in this scenario, this quality is evaluated negatively, by both the pre-modifying adverb 'too', and the commentary provided by the magazine writer underneath ('Oh, the mind boggles...'). The intensifier *too* does much of this evaluative work here, both assuming that men *are* kinky, and also implying that while being kinky is a desirable quality in moderation, it becomes undesirable in excessive quantities (signaled by the conventional meaning of *too* as denoting 'in excess' [*OED Online*]).

The idea that men are 'naturally' sexually promiscuous is evident in representations of men 'behaving badly':

> Together 17 years, I'd trusted Ian completely. He was a great dad and a caring husband, and we still made love twice a week. More to the point, he didn't seem that kind of a guy. He wasn't **lecherous** or **flirty**.

The narrator of this true-life story paints a picture of her husband by describing him in terms of what he is not. The negative connotations attached to the words 'lecherous' and 'flirty' here contribute to the implicature that behaving in an overly-sexual manner is not constitutive of being a good father or husband; the reader might infer from this that the ideal husband behaves asexually towards other women. It also implies that men who commit adultery cannot make good fathers or husbands, because they are driven by their carnal instincts.

The inherent sexual promiscuity of men is also used in descriptions of perpetrators of violence against women, similar to its use in news reporting of sexual violence (see for example Clark 1992; O'Hara 2012). The true-life narrative 'Have Sex or Die' tells the story of Jesse Pratt, who tried to rape, and then murdered one of his female employees. Because this was a sexual crime, Pratt is described in terms of his sexuality:

> Fact 5: Her **lustful** boss Jesse Pratt has been sentenced to death for her murder.
>
> (*That's Life*)

The decision to use a pre-modifying adjective assumes that Pratt is 'lustful', and also presents the quality of lustfulness as a permanent attribute of his character; the reader might infer from this that Pratt committed this crime *because* of his carnal urges.

In another example describing men in terms of what they are not, in this feature from *Asiana* on blind dating, the narrator invokes the concept of sleaziness to assert that her date is *not* 'sleazy'.

When I was feeding him during dinner, he licked my fingers, which was totally unexpected, but it didn't feel too awkward because there's nothing **sleazy** about him.

Rather than using an adjective with an oppositional meaning to 'sleazy' in order to categorize her date, she has chosen to use the negative form. Denying propositions entails an invocation of the positive state, thus her denial of his sleaziness here necessarily implies the concept of sleaziness. The word 'sleazy' usually co-occurs with male referents: For example, out of 50 randomly sampled concordances of 'sleazy' in the English Web 13 corpus using Sketch Engine, only 3 (0.06%) referred to women, but 16 (32%) specified a male referent (Kilgarriff et al. 2004). Therefore the writer's decision to describe this man as such reinforces unwanted sexual behavior as a specifically male quality, reiterating the idea that men are driven by sexual urges. Interestingly, the intensifying adverb *too* in the adjective phrase 'too awkward' presupposes that she *did* feel awkward, reminding the reader of the possible danger of the situation, had he turned out to be 'sleazy', and thus a threat.

5.4.1 'Are You a Romantic or a Bad Boy?': Positive and Negative Descriptions

The items in the 'evaluation' category exhibit explicit positive or negative evaluations of men, meaning that words in this category include the semantic component [+negative] or [+positive] in their denotative meanings, and can be interpreted as hyponyms of *good* or *bad*. Traditionally in linguistics, 'hyponymy' is used to describe hierarchical relationships between nominal areas of vocabulary, but Murphy (2003: 221) points out that scalar adjectives can also be described in hyponymous terms, if we define hyponymy as a relationship of inclusion. For example, 'excellent' is logically a hyponym of *good*, in that 'excellent' entails *good*, which is broader in meaning. Lexical relations like hyponymy also exist irrespective of context; the examples from the magazine data discussed in this section also fulfil this criterion.

The majority of lexis in this category serve as positive appraisals of men (56 tokens, 76%). As the following extracts demonstrate, positively evaluating adjectives are either hyperbolic evaluations (such as 'fantastic', 'amazing', 'fabulous'); assessments of morality (such as 'decent', 'good') or suitability for partnership ('eligible', 'perfect', 'right', 'dream'):

> Sometimes they [women] get weary of what they consider the hassles of romance and dating within the complications of the dwindling supply of **eligible** males and the challenges of juggling love, marriage, parenthood and work outside the home.
>
> *(Ebony)*

The attributive adjective 'eligible' occurs in a post-modifying prepositional phrase to 'supply'. The pre-modifying adjective 'dwindling' implies that there are increasingly fewer suitable partners. Similarly, 'perfect', an evaluative adjective with positive connotations, is used to express negative meaning in this extract from a feature article on celebrity break-ups:

> It happens all the time to Hollywood's most gorgeous, seemingly perfect women: their equally gorgeous and seemingly **perfect** guys humiliate them by fooling around with someone else.
>
> *(Glamour)*

The pre-modifying modal adverb 'seemingly' evaluates the celebrity men in question as *im*perfect, because they are adulterous, reinforcing normative values about heterosexual relationships. This evaluation also presupposes the possibility of 'perfect guys', however hard they are to find.

However, the pre-modifying adjective 'right' does express positive sentiment in this extract from a fictional narrative in *Woman's Weekly*:

> "So how do you feel about being a father again?" she asked, in an attempt to put him in the hot seat.
>
> "In principle, I'd love it, given the right woman."
>
> "You mean Jules isn't?"
>
> "I mean, Jules needs the **right** man, or no man at all. She's no good at compromise."

In this extract, 'right' denotes 'correct', forming part of the 'right/wrong' canonical pair. This implies that suitability for partnership is a binary construct. In this context, being the 'right' partner means being a caring father.

The attributive adjective 'dream' is also used to denote desirable qualities in a man:

> Errol is Cosmo's **dream** man because:
>
> He's a hairdresser who makes celebs - like Kelly Rowland - even more gorgeous, then finds time to help ill, needy or homeless women.
>
> (*Cosmopolitan*)

Here the conjunction 'because' links the positive classification of Errol Douglas in the initial clause with the propositions in the proceeding assertions—the he is both charitable and skilled in beautification processes—which are therefore intended to be read as desirable qualities in a man. We could interpret this as a subversion of gender stereotypes, in that heterosexual masculinity is not usually associated with hairdressing. However, the word 'dream' also conventionally has connotations of fantasy, therefore the reader might infer that for men to be beauty-conscious *and* benevolent is in fact an unrealistic ideal.

Negatively evaluative adjectives are synonyms for incompetence (for example 'hapless', 'daft') and immorality ('depraved', 'bad'), as the following examples illustrate:

> But what stared back at me was pure evil. You see, my face reminded me of one of the most **depraved** men I'd ever met... *My dad.*
>
> (*Real People*)

> 'Who says you can't TAME A **BAD** BOY?' He might play hard men in his movies but, deep down, Danny Dyer loves a woman to take control.
>
> (*Cosmopolitan*)

> **Are you a romantic or a bad boy?** Take your pick. I will be whatever you want me to be.
>
> (*Asiana*)

The first extract comes from a true-life story in which a female narrator tells of how she was sexually abused by her father, and underwent plastic surgery to change her facial appearance in a bid to erase the physical connection between herself and her father. The adjectival choice here focuses on immorality; according to the *Oxford English Dictionary*, 'depraved' denotes "[r]endered morally bad; corrupt, wicked" (*OED Online*). The connotations of this word are perhaps more extreme than others in this semantic field, such as 'good-for-nothing' or 'bad.' The choice of an adjective at the extreme end of the *good/bad* scale reflects a tendency for magazines to employ a "vocabulary of excess", which emphasizes the entertainment value of the texts (McLoughlin 2000: 21).

The second and third examples here contain the alliterative idiomatic phrases *bad boy*, which is associated with 'laddish' masculinity. For instance, a random sample of 50 occurrences of the phrase 'bad boy' in the BNC showed that 12 of these described footballers, often in newspaper headlines: "'FOOTBALL 'bad boy' Ian Jolosa is in trouble again…" (*The Daily Mirror* 1992)'. The behaviors associated with the 'bad boy' image appear to be related to violence and womanizing, staple practices attributed to New Lad masculinity (Attwood 2005; Coy and Horvath 2011). In the second extract, the descriptions 'bad' and 'hard' are treated as synonymous; when used to refer to men, *hard* is usually associated with hegemonic masculine concepts such as violence, which the reader is likely to infer here. The choice of verb 'tame' also connotes animal behavior, as it is often used with reference to wild animals. The concepts of being 'romantic' or a 'bad boy' in the final example are contrasted via co-ordinating conjunction 'or', which suggests that being a 'bad boy' is incompatible with romanticism.

5.5   Summary

Men, then, are most often labelled in these magazines according to social roles and occupations, and most frequently described in terms of behavior and personality, rather than physical appearance or mental attributes. Nominal labels with lexical gender such as 'lad' and 'bloke' can also invoke connotative meanings associated with New Lad masculinity of the kind found in men's magazines and understood as indices of UK 'lad culture' more generally. An analysis of the metaphorical nouns used to define men revealed intertextual references to male characters of fiction, particularly from fairy-tale and romance, presenting idealized images of masculinity. Some terms for male genitalia connote infallibility and small size; these ridiculing techniques seem to function to reduce the prowess of the penis, although the assumption that 'bigger means better' is also present.

Words that function to describe male identities can be interpreted broadly as hyponyms of *good* and *bad*, which suggests that the magazines use adjectival description as a strategy for showing women the kinds of men who are desirable, and who should be avoided. These descriptions are also indicative of a set of stereotypical beliefs about men: that they are incompetent, carnally-driven, and that they have violent tendencies. The negative connotations attached to qualities like being 'filthy', 'kinky' and 'experimental' serve to reinforce normative sexual practices, and adjectives relating to sexual desire and infidelity reinforce an ideology of men as sexually predatory.

References

Attwood, F. (2005). "Tits and Ass and Porn and Fighting": Male Heterosexuality in Magazines for Men. *International Journal of Cultural Studies, 8*(1), 83–100.

Benwell, B. (2003). Ambiguous Masculinities: Heroism and Anti-heroism in the Men's Lifestyle Magazine. In B. Benwell (Ed.), *Masculinity and Men's Lifestyle Magazines* (pp. 151–168). Oxford: Blackwell.

Benwell, B. (2004). Ironic Discourse: Evasive Masculinity in British Men's Lifestyle Magazines. *Men and Masculinities, 7*(1), 3–21.

Butler, J. (1990). *Gender Trouble: Feminism and the Subversion of Identity*. London: Routledge.

Cameron, D. (1992). Naming of Parts: Gender, Culture and Terms for the Penis Among American College Students. *American Speech, 67*(4), 367–382.

Campaign Against Living Miserably. (2014). Available at https://www.the-calmzone.net.

Clark, K. (1992). The Linguistics of Blame: Representations of Women in *The Sun's* Reporting of Crimes of Sexual Violence. In M. Toolan (Ed.), *Language, Text and Context: Essays in Stylistics* (pp. 208–224). London: Routledge.

Coy, M., & Horvath, M. A. H. (2011). Lads Mags, Young Men's Attitudes Towards Women and Acceptance of Myths about Sexual Aggression. *Feminism and Psychology, 21*(1), 144–150.

Fairclough, N. (1989). *Language and Power.* London: Longman.

Gibbs, R. W. (1994). *The Poetics of Mind: Figurative Thought, Language and Understanding.* Cambridge: Cambridge University Press.

Hellinger, M., & Bussmann, H. (2001). Gender Across Languages: The Linguistic Representation of Women and Men. In M. Hellinger & H. Bussmann (Eds.), *Gender Across Languages: The Linguistic Representation of Women and Men* (Vol. 1, pp. 1–25). Amsterdam: John Benjamins.

Horne, S. J. (2011). *Judged by Their Covers: Robert Harrison's Girlie Magazines, 1941–1955* (Unpublished MA thesis). University of Missouri, Columbia.

Jackson, P., Stevenson, N., & Brooks, K. (2001). *Making Sense of Men's Magazines.* Cambridge: Polity Press.

Jeffries, L. (2007). *Textual Construction of the Female Body: A Critical Discourse Approach.* Basingstoke: Palgrave Macmillan.

Kilgarriff, A., Rychlý, P., Smrž, P., & Tugwell, D. (2004). Itri-04-08 the Sketch Engine. *Information Technology.* Available at http://www.sketchengine.co.uk. Accessed September 2018.

Korte, B. (1997). *Body Language in Literature.* Toronto: University of Toronto Press.

Le Masurier, M. (2011). Reading the Flesh. *Feminist Media Studies, 11*(2), 215–229.

McLoughlin, L. (2000). *The Language of Magazines.* London: Routledge.

Merriam-Webster Online. (2013). Available at http://www.merriam-webster.com. Accessed March 2013.

Motschenbacher, H. (2009). Speaking the Gendered Body: The Performative Construction of Commercial Femininities and Masculinities Via Body-Part Vocabulary. *Language in Society, 38*(1), 1–22.

Murphy, L. (2003). *Semantic Relations and the Lexicon.* Cambridge: Cambridge University Press.

Naylor, B. (2001). Reporting Violence in the British Print Media: Gendered Stories. *The Howard Journal of Criminal Justice, 40*(2), 180–194.

O'Hara, S. (2012). Monsters Playboys, Virgins and Whores: Rape Myths in the News Media's Coverage of Sexual Violence. *Language and Literature, 21*(3), 247–259.

Phipps, A., & Young, I. (2015). "Lad Culture" in Higher Education: Agency in the Sexualisation Debates. *Sexualities, 18*(4), 459–479.

Sapir, E. (1929). A Study in Phonetic Symbolism. *Journal of Experimental Psychology, 12,* 225–229.

Soothill, K., & Walby, S. (1991). *Sex Crime in the News.* London: Routledge.

Talbot, M. (1992). The Construction of Gender in a Teenage Magazine. In N. Fairclough (Ed.), *Critical Language Awareness* (pp. 174–199). London: Longman.

Taylor, Y., & Sunderland, J. (2003). "I've Always Loved Women": The Representation of the Male Sex Worker in *Maxim*. In B. Benwell (Ed.), *Masculintiy and Men's Lifestyle Magazines* (pp. 169–187). Oxford: Blackwell.

6

'Good Men' and 'Bad Men': Equating and Contrasting

This chapter examines the kinds of qualities and behaviors that men are equated with: how oppositional constructs contrast 'good' men with 'bad' men; present masculine identity in terms of sets of complementary binaries that treat men as homogeneous (predictable) beings, and promote an overarching 'gender differences' discourse (Sunderland 2004).

The textual-conceptual functions 'equating' and 'contrasting' refer to the way in which concepts are presented as equivalent or oppositional (Jeffries 2010a). Equating and contrasting are linguistically realized through novel synonymous and oppositional meanings, those that rely on their specific context of use in order to be interpreted as synonyms or antonyms. There is a strong tradition of research in the field of lexical semantics that considers sense relations between words, including synonymy and opposition (see, for example, Lyons 1977; Cruse 2004; Murphy 2003). These accounts focus on conventional sense relations, and therefore do not consider how novel synonyms or antonyms can be contextually constructed. Davies (2013) and Jeffries (2010a, b) show how a speaker's knowledge of conventional sense relations can aid the interpretation of novel synonyms and opposites. For example, in a construction like 'this is a university, not a corporation', although

© The Author(s) 2019
L. Coffey-Glover, *Men in Women's Worlds*,
https://doi.org/10.1057/978-1-137-57555-5_6

university and *corporation* are not deemed as conventional opposites in English in the way that, for instance, a pair like *night/day* would be, in this context the syntactic frame 'X not Y' creates a contrast between the two concepts. It is easy to see how the construction of these kinds of novel oppositional or equivalent meanings can be used for ideological purposes: in setting up a contrast between educational establishments and businesses here, for example, I am rejecting the neoliberal ideology that views education as a business transaction between 'service providers' and 'consumers' (see, for instance, Molesworth et al. 2010).

6.1   Equating

Jeffries' (2007) study of the female body in women's magazines found that equivalence mainly functions as a pedagogical device, to explain technical terms relating to the body, or to indicate that two referents are deemed synonymous, as in, for example 'The opening to the womb, the diameter of a thin straw…' (2007: 107). Equivalence works in much the same way in my data, where the writers use equivalent meanings to explain what men are *like*; the use of propositional forms with intensive verbal processes create the idea that these are statements of 'truth', and therefore a reliable source of information about the 'mystery' of man.

The model of equivalence is that put forward by Jeffries (2007, 2010b), which presents three different types of equivalence: appositional, intensive relational and metaphorical. There is by no means a finite set of triggers for equivalence, but some are provided in Table 6.1 with examples from the women's magazine corpus:

Jeffries defines appositional equivalence as 'the juxtaposition of two or more noun phrases in the same syntactic role' (Jeffries 2007: 104), which also therefore have the same referent, for example 'Louis, the fabulous saxaphonist'. Appositional equivalences often serves a pedagogical purpose, to explain or elaborate. This frequently occurs in the interviews, where appositional noun phrases explain who the male interviewee is. For example:

Table 6.1   Different types of equivalence

Type of equivalence	Equivalence triggers	Example
Appositional equivalence	X, Y, (Z); X and Y	As the film develops, we see him mature **and** grow
Intensive relational equivalence	X is Y; X became Y; X seems Y	I've **become** a better husband
Metaphorical equivalence	X is Y; X is like Y; the Y that is X; X looks like Y	the wonder that **is** Gok Wan

I'm a para Olympics Ambassador and HIV activist, along with Ashley Judd and recently performed to handicapped children in Mumbai, I do these things to help others not myself.

(Asiana)

Here the noun phrases 'a para Olympics Ambassador' and 'HIV activist' both have the same referent, 'I', fulfilling the syntactic role of Subject Complement. Their equivalent relationship is triggered syntactically via coordinating conjunction *and*, although as we will see, *and* can also signal oppositional relationships (see below). In this example, the two conjoined noun phrases are taken to form part of the same overarching concept, namely 'good', or more specifically, 'selfless.'

The conjunction *and* can also be used in the creation of lists, as in 'he's gorgeous, kind, gentle and honest' *(Best)*. This example could be interpreted as either a four-part list, fulfilling the textual-conceptual function of enumerating (see Sect. 4.2.1 above), or they can be interpreted as appositional: the adjectives in Complement position ('gorgeous', 'kind', 'gentle' and 'honest') are all semantically related, and all serve the same grammatical function. There is therefore often a fine line between these two functions, which highlights the importance of considering textual function in applying these categories. In my analysis of appositional equivalence using 'and', I had to examine the contexts carefully and discard the more obvious examples of lists.

Appositional equivalences can also be created by the juxtaposition of phrases or clauses with no co-ordination, as in 'Her lustful boss Jesse Pratt has been sentenced to death for her murder' *(That's Life)*. The noun phrases 'her lustful boss' and 'Jesse Pratt' refer to the same referent, constituting different ways of referring to the same male identity (occupational role or given name, respectfully). However, due to limitations in automated parsing, I was unable to capture instances of appositional equivalence that relied on this simple juxtaposition of noun phrases, in other words, those that were not syntactically triggered by the coordinating conjunction *and*. Additionally, appositional equivalence significantly overlaps with processes of naming discussed in Chapter 5; the analysis of equivalence-construction below thus concentrates on intensive relational equivalence, and in particular on forms of metaphorical equivalence.

Intensive relational equivalence refers to equivalent relations constructed between the Subject and Complement of intensive verb clauses, for example 'he's a typical bloke who leaves all his stuff everywhere', where the noun phrases 'he' and 'a typical bloke who leaves all his stuff everywhere' have the same referent. In this case the phrase 'a typical bloke' and relative clause 'who leaves all his stuff everywhere' do not simply refer to the same person, the reader interprets them as equivalent in meaning, taken to be part of the same concept, 'masculinity.' The Complements of the intensive verbs are often either noun phrases or adjective phrases. In the women's magazine corpus, intensive relational equivalence tended to attribute men with labels or descriptions, and therefore mostly served a naming or describing function (see Chapter 5).

Metaphorical equivalence also utilizes intensive relational processes, and involves making metaphorical relations between the Subject and Complement of the verb. For example, in 'But I want you to know he was a real soldier' (*Pick Me Up*), a synonymous relationship is created between the male Subject and the Complement noun phrase ('a real soldier'), but the intended meaning is not that the referent is literally a soldier, but implies that he has been brave, in the way associated with being a member of the armed forces. As far as I am aware, this kind of equivalence is not used in relation to women, because the occupation of soldier is traditionally associated with men, and therefore can be said to indirectly index masculinity. This kind of equivalence seems to be the most interesting ideologically, as it reveals equivalences between male referents and idealized or culturally recognizable metaphors of masculinity.

The list of different possible triggers for intensive relational and metaphorical equivalence is particularly open-ended. The fact that there are so many different kinds of trigger for synonymy is testament to its prevalence in the language, and therefore its importance for meaning making.

6.1.1 Distribution of Equivalence in the Corpus

On the whole, the textual practice of equating was much more prevalent in the data than that of contrasting, with types of synonymy comprising 83% of the total instances of equivalence and opposition recorded. Looking at the distribution of equivalence across the different text types shows that in terms of normalized frequency, the profiles text type is the one most likely to contain instances of equivalence, as Table 6.2 indicates.

Given that profiles are concerned with relaying information about specific people, who they are and what they are like, it is not surprising that these would contain the greatest amount of equivalence, particularly intensive relational equivalence formed using an 'X is Y' frame, such as 'Kayvew is all about mean and moody' (*Asiana*). Indeed, intensive relational equivalence makes up 79% of equivalences in the profiles.

Table 6.2 Frequencies of equivalence according to text type

Text type	Raw frequency of equivalence	Normalized frequency (per 1000 words)	% of total frequency of equivalence in the corpus
Interviews	442	12.6	36
Real life stories	230	6.7	18
Features	180	5.1	14
Problem pages	96	6.6	8
Fiction	89	6.0	7
Columns	60	6.5	45
Survey reports	41	9.9	3
Reports	37	4.5	3
Profiles	24	17.4	2
Letters	23	9.9	2
Listicles	14	14.5	1
Advertorials	7	4.6	1
Reviews	1	3.8	0

There is also generally more intensive relational equivalence than the other types of synonymous relation, as Table 6.3 illustrates:

Table 6.3 Frequencies of equivalence according to type of equivalence

Type of equivalence	Frequency of equivalence	% of total frequency of equivalence in the magazine corpus (%)
Appositional equivalence	112	9
Intensive relational equivalence	892	72
Metaphorical equivalence	240	20

While intensive relational equivalence is by far the most frequent form of synonymy used in descriptions of men, they overlap in many ways with that of the naming strategies discussed in Chapter 5, and do not have as much potential for ideology construction as the metaphorical equivalences. The analysis that follows thus focuses on the role of metaphorical equivalence in constructing ideologies of masculinity.

6.1.2 Themes of Metaphorical Equivalence

Equating men with cultural ideals

A pervasive theme of metaphorical equivalence is the construction of synonymy between a male referent and a cultural ideal of masculinity. These include the form of 'masculine title + proper noun', such as 'Mr Perfect', or a more specific cultural identity such as 'Prince Charming' (a heroic figure from the fairy-tale narrative genre), or personal nouns such as 'dream man' or 'soulmate'. The extracts discussed below demonstrate equivalences with metaphorical personas using proper nouns:

> They are now divorced and Pam believes Max is Jules's Mr Right.
>
> (*Woman's Weekly*)

> 'If you have a bad fight with your boyfriend but you've let your friends believe he's Mr Perfect, you could find yourself without anyone to talk to,' warns Joanna.
>
> (*Cosmopolitan*)

The nouns 'Mr Right' and 'Mr Perfect' are tropes that will probably be familiar to the reader as personifications of abstract concepts, 'right' and 'perfect', which in turn can both be interpreted as synonyms of *good*. I am not aware of any female equivalents, suggesting that the concept of the ideal man is much more prevalent in Western popular culture than that of the ideal woman; for example, 'Mr Right' is listed in the *Oxford English Dictionary*, but 'Mrs Right' is not (*OED Online*). These, and other metaphors for the ideal man, such as 'the love of my life' (*That's Life*) and 'Mark's The One' (*Love It*) reveal the desirability of finding the 'perfect' partner, and not settling for second best. The fact that this kind of ideology doesn't seem to translate to female representation could also point to the idea that men's desires are not perceived by society as being as specific as women's, the assumption being that men are primarily interested in sexual encounters or short-term relationships, where women seek longer-term commitment.

In this final example, the equation of the male first person narrator with 'Prince Charming' is recognizable as the stock protagonist of fairy tales, reinforced by the reference to a 'happy ending':

> I used to be Prince Charming too, but baby, why did you have to change the happy ending?
>
> (*Pride*)

'Prince Charming' is listed in the *Oxford English Dictionary* as a noun referring to 'A fairy-tale hero; an ideal or idealized young male lover; a perfect young man.' (*OED Online*). The codification of the more generalized meaning of this compound as denoting the 'ideal man' is testament to its pervasiveness in the language.

Interestingly, a small number of equivalences involve the metaphorical use of lexical items that directly index male sex, such as 'bloke', 'man' and 'gentleman', which in other contexts would simply have a denotative function, but here imply other connotative meanings, indirectly indexing a specifically hegemonic form of masculinity:

> I'm not usually shocked. Apart from one weird occasion, involving **a guy who seemed like a real gentleman** when we first met... We went

to gourmet restaurants, had intelligent conversations and he kissed me goodbye, rather than pushing for anything more straight away.

(*Company*)

And at the end of the night...?
Well, **I'm a gentleman,** so it would be a kiss and goodbye.

(*Scarlet*)

These first two examples demonstrate an equivalence between male referents and the concept of being a 'gentleman'. In both cases, it is implied that being a 'gentleman' involves resisting sexual activity beyond kissing, the assumption being that the men have to consciously curtail their sexual desires. This of course feeds into the 'male sexual drive' discourse that assumes men are motivated by the pursuit of sexual relations with women (Holloway 1984).

In the following extract, the reader testimony contains a tautology with an equivalence that equates being a man to being in charge of pursuing romantic relations with women:

Should a girl ever make the first move? [...] Yes, but only subtly. They should still let **the man be a man**.

(*More*)

The ideology that men are (hetero)sexually driven evident in these examples is discussed in more depth in the analysis on assuming and implying below (see Chapter 8). What's clear is that all three extracts, the tautological equivalences result in lexically gendered items 'man' and 'gentleman' taking on additional connotative meanings linked to hegemonic masculinity.

Men as sexually predatory

While the metaphorical equivalences in the examples above are intended to have positive connotations as facets of the 'ideal man', equating men with sexual relations can also take on more negative associations, reflecting the idea that men are sexually predatory:

The other day, I found a pair of knickers in his drawer. Could **he be a pervert**, or even a transvestite?
[...]

If **he's a Lothario** who's working his way through as many women as possible, make sure he's having safe sex. If he likes putting on women's pants,
although you both might be embarrassed, it's not the end of the world.

(*Best*)

In this example, the two proposed scenarios, that the man (the reader's
son) is a 'Lothario', or that he is a 'transvestite', are opposed via coordinating conjunction *or*, where the second scenario is evaluated as com-
paratively more negative than the first, implied by the conventional
meaning of *even*. The terms 'pervert' and 'Lothario' are treated as synonymous, which is supported by both their negative connotations and
the kinds of lexis they usually collocate with. As discussed in the naming analysis of metaphorical nouns in Chapter 5, 'Lothario' is a fictional
male character who seduces women in Nicholas Rowe's *The Fair Penitent*,
but is often used as a colloquial term for a sexually promiscuous man.
A quick glance at a random sample of the noun 'pervert' in the BNC
confirms that it is most frequently used to refer to a male identity in sexual contexts. The agony aunt's answer to the possibility that the second
scenario is true, that he is a 'transvestite', indicates that this would be
undesirable, in that it is assumed the mother may be 'embarrassed'; the
possibility that he is a 'pervert' or 'Lothario' is not imbued with the same
negativity, as the advice is simply that if her son is going to seduce lots of
women, he should do it safely. Male sexual promiscuity is therefore not
chastised, but implicitly promoted, something that has been well documented in the literature on the semantic asymmetry of terms denoting
women's and men's sexual behavior (Baker 2008; Pearce 2008).

Equating men with food and animals

Another low-frequency but ideologically interesting set of metaphorical equivalences are those that relate to the conceptual metaphors MEN
ARE FOOD and MEN ARE ANIMALS. In my analysis of metaphorical naming strategies in Chapter 5, I referred to conceptual metaphors
as higher-level cognitive structures that underpin metaphorical uses of
language (see Lakoff and Johnson 1980; Crisp 2002; Semino and Short
2004). In the following example, we could argue that the metaphor

'Jesse's a treat' is underpinned by the conceptual metaphor MEN ARE FOOD:

> With his phenomenally hot body and puppy dog eyes, **Jesse's a treat for any woman.**
>
> *(Love It)*

Analyzing a random sample of 'treat' as a noun in the BNC showed that where it is used in reference to food, in 67% of cases, it denotes sweet foods, twice as often as savory foods. The concept 'Jesse' is therefore being understood in terms of (sweet) 'food'. Feminist scholars have discussed the practice of representing women's physical attractiveness via sweet food terms, noting their trivializing effects (Schulz 1975; Mills 1995; Hines 1999). 'Treat' can be understood as a kind of male equivalent to the WOMEN AS DESSERT metaphor if we consider that 'Jesse' and 'a treat' are constructed here as equivalent, referring to the same concept, namely 'attractive male.' The reader will likely infer this from the physical descriptions 'hot body' and 'puppy dog eyes', which conventionally have positive connotations. The equation of actor Jesse Metcalf with a generic term for sweet foods therefore emphasizes his attractiveness, implying that he is 'good enough to eat.' One could argue, in a similar vein to the example of the male pin-up discussed earlier, that representations of men focusing explicitly on their desirability to women is liberating, representing female sexual empowerment. However, one might also question the progressiveness of this kind of 'reverse sexism,' as it could also serve to validate the presence of the female pin-up in men's magazines.

The conceptual metaphor MEN ARE ANIMALS is also produced via the conceptual-textual function of equivalence. The animal metaphors equate men with both positive and negative attributes, concerning physical appearance or behavior:

> Many 'traditional' women prefer the men to ask, but if **he's a good catch,** get in there before someone else does!
> *(Ebony)*

This example actually seems to cross over both MEN ARE ANIMALS and MEN ARE FOOD metaphors, because this use of 'catch' derives from the practice of catching fish, which are caught to be eaten. This kind of meaning is roughly equivalent to the 'women-as-sex-objects are food' metaphor (Hines 1999) represented by terms like *cheesecake, cherry pie*, and *crumpet*. However, unlike other such metaphors for women, there seems to be an implication that the woman's role here is predatory ('get in there before someone else does!'), which may reinforce an ideology of women as hunters. Other metaphorical equivalences align with this interpretation, such as 'I was so love-struck' (*Woman & Home*), and 'he'll be hooked' (*Cosmopolitan*), both with male subjects, in which the adjectival Complements of the verbs imply that a female agent has 'charmed' or 'caught' her prey.

Less positively, metaphorical equivalence is made between men and dogs:

> When you think you're ready to get back out there, drop the stereotypical thinking that '**men are all dogs.**'
>
> (*Ebony*)

The animal metaphor here implies sexual promiscuity, feeding into the broader ideology of men as sexually predatory. Although the reader is urged not to tar all men with the same negative brush, it is assumed the reader will be familiar with the animal trope which it reinforces. The metaphorical association is therefore taken to be part of a common-sense ideology about men's sexual behavior.

6.2   Contrasting

My analysis of 'contrasting' is concerned with how the texts use oversimplified binaries in both the way that they talk about men, and gender relations more generally. Linguists have acknowledged the universal nature of opposition (Murphy 2003: 215) and its importance for the organization of language; as Lyons claims: 'binary opposition is one of the most important principles governing the structure of languages' (1977: 271). Research in CDA often investigates how social actors or events are polarized 'in dichotomous ways that oppose good and evil forces' (Achugar 2004: 291), or establish the construction of 'in-groups' and 'out-groups'. Davies (2013) points out further that while the role of opposition in ideology construction has been acknowledged in CDA, little attention is often paid to the specifically *linguistic* realizations of oppositional meaning.

6.2.1 Gradable and 'Non-Gradable' Opposition

Studies on lexical semantics have identified different categories of opposition (Lyons 1977; Cruse 2004; Murphy 2003; Davies 2013; Jeffries 2010a). In particular, Lyons (1977: 271) makes a distinction between 'gradable' and 'non-gradable' opposition, after Sapir (1944): gradable opposites are those which have measurable and comparative qualities; non-gradable or 'complementary' (Jeffries 2010a) opposites are mutually exclusive, binary opposites. For example, *masculine/feminine* is an example of gradable opposition, because it is possible to assert that there are different degrees of femininity and masculinity; *male/female* have conventionally been considered as complementary opposites, because of an assumption that the properties of 'male' and 'female' are ungradable (in other words, that one is either male or female). The increased visibility of trans identities means that this assumption needs some rethinking, since biological sex, as well as gender, may in fact be considered as a scalar concept, and it is therefore more accurate to perceive lexical categories of both sex and gender as gradable antonyms (see, for example, Zimman 2014). However, the idea of sex differences is so ingrained in our culture that the complementarity of gendered items like *male/female* is often taken for granted in public discourse. Women's magazines are no exception, and the very fact that there are magazines dedicated to men on the one hand and women on the other demonstrates just how pervasive the (perceived) gender binary is.

6.2.2 Constructing Opposites

I have used the models for contrasting put forward by Davies (2013) and Jeffries (2007, 2010a, b) in my analysis of opposition construction in the corpus. The categories of opposition, with their syntactic triggers, textual functions and examples from the women's magazine corpus, are outlined in Table 6.4.

The model of contrasting outlined here shows how fixed syntactic frames or parallel syntactic structures can create novel oppositions with predictable in-text functions; these can produce ideological effects to be interpreted by the reader. For example, Davies' (2013) study of opposition in newspaper reports of anti-war protest marches demonstrates how novel constructed opposites produce mutually exclusive 'us'/'them' identities, such as 'extremists' in contrast with 'Joe public', which encourages the reader to view anti-war protestors in a negative light. He also shows how the gradable concept of *good/bad* is constructed as a non-gradable binary in order to represent social actors as exclusively 'good' or 'bad', encouraging readers 'to construe the world as made up of "goodies" and "baddies"' (Davies 2013: 26). In my own data, opposition construction emphasizes the binary nature of gender differences, and the constructed complementarity of *good/bad* produces exclusive choice in men, encouraging a similarly reductive view of men as desirable or threatening to women (see Sects. 6.2.4–6.2.6).

6.2.3 Distribution of Opposition in the Corpus

In the women's magazine corpus, the vast majority of instances of opposition were found in the glossy genre (80%). This suggests that the glossies are more likely to represent men as behaving or appearing exclusively one way or another, constructing masculine identity as a binary and denying the possibility of different ways of being. However, as the analysis below shows, both genres exploit oppositional lexical relations in their representations of masculinity. However, the resulting oppositions are different, and largely dependent on the text types involved.

Table 6.4 Types of opposition with examples from the women's magazine corpus

Category	Syntactic Frames	Example	Functions
Contrastive opposition	X or Y X but Y X and Y	Would you rather he's a bit of a prude **or** a bit too kinky? nice **but** broke an ambulance man, all muscles **and** manners	Presents exclusive choices Creates 'additional rhetorical emphasis' (Jones 2002: 90)
Negated opposition	Not X, Y X not Y Not X, just Y	The likelihood is that he is **not** repulsed by you, just hurt and confused [...]	Indicates change of state
Transitional opposition	X became Y X turns into Y	However, with my Martini goggles on, he **became** Mr. Darcy	Presents comparisons
Comparative opposition	Rather X than Y More X than Y	He'd **rather** be anywhere else in the world **than** perched awkwardly on a sofa with your golf-obsessed dad	Indicates preferred states
Replacive opposition	X over Y X rather than Y X instead of Y	You'll take a man with svelter thighs than you **over** a human trampoline any day	Indicates surprising state of affairs
Concessive opposition	Despite X, Y In spite of X, Y	Pratt usually kept his darker side well hidden and **despite** his grungy exterior, he had the gift of the gab	Highlight the contrastive meaning of a pair
Explicit opposition	Difference between X and Y X contrasted with Y	There is a **difference between** making a baby and being a father	Often used for rhetorical emphasis
Parallelism		When it comes to men, he's old enough to know better—and gay enough to give it to you straight!	

Table 6.5 Frequencies of opposition in the women's magazine corpus according to text type

Text type	Raw frequency of opposition	Normalized frequency (per 1000 words)	% of total frequency of opposition
Interviews	81	2.3	31
Features	44	1.2	17
Survey reports	39	9.1	15
Columns	27	2.9	10
Real life stories	26	0.8	10
Problem pages	18	1.3	7
Letters	8	3.5	3
Listicles	5	5.2	2
Fiction	4	0.3	2
Reports	4	0.5	2
Advertorials	3	2	1
Profiles	2	1.5	1
Reviews	0	0	0

The normalized frequencies in Table 6.5 suggest that the survey reports show the most opposition, once the differences in word length between text types are taken into account. However, almost all the instances of opposition in the survey reports (38 of 39 instances) were found in one article from *Glamour*, 'Would you rather…', a questionnaire surveying responses to various relationship-related dilemmas posed to selected readers. As a result, the article is concerned with constructing polarized images of men in the presentation of exclusive choices, and I discuss this in more detail below (Sect. 6.2.6).

Superordinate oppositions
Understanding new, non-canonical opposites often relies on an understanding of superordinate canonical opposites that serve as culturally recognizable 'planes' of difference (Davies 2013). For example, to interpret 'nice' and 'broke' in 'the nice but broke guy' (*Glamour*) as opposites, the reader may well draw on the conventional oppositional pairing *good/bad* (due to the positive value placed on courtesy and altruism, and negative associations of lacking wealth in capitalist societies). I therefore found it helpful to note the higher-level oppositional concepts present in the textually constructed examples. These could be

Table 6.6 Semantic categories of superordinate oppositions

Superordinate category	Frequency (tokens)	Percentage of total frequency (%)
Sex, gender and relationships	57	31
Behavior	9	5
Morality and evaluation	58	31
States of being	14	7
Actions	12	6
Physical appearance	26	14
Deixis	9	5
Total	188	

categorized into six broad semantic fields: sex, gender and relationships, behavior, states of being, actions, physical appearance and deixis.

Table 6.6 shows that the superordinate opposites most frequently drawn on relate to the fields of sex, gender and relationships, and morality and evaluation. In fact, the most frequent superordinate opposite is GOOD/BAD, comprising 31% (58 tokens) of the total number of superordinate opposites. In her study of ideology construction in women's magazines, Jeffries (2007: 109) also found that 'good versus bad' was the most salient category of constructed opposites relating to representations of the female body, and that hyponyms of good/bad opposition, such as 'normal/abnormal', 'natural/unnatural' and 'healthy/unhealthy', worked to tell the reader what are (or should be) desirable or undesirable bodily practices and appearances, indicating 'a hugely normative drive [...] towards an ideal, youthful and unchanging body shape' (Jeffries 2007: 128). In my data, *good/bad* opposition also functions to present an idealized gender identity, polarizing men as desirable or undesirable.

6.2.4 Good Men Versus Bad Men

There are cases of GOOD/BAD opposition most frequently in the glossy magazines (37 instances, 64%), again suggesting that this genre is more concerned with polarizing men, here in terms of positive or negative value. The text type with the greatest number of examples of GOOD/BAD opposition, once the raw frequencies are normalized, is the listicles. The following extracts from these illustrate oppositional pairs that rely on the higher-level GOOD/BAD hyponym in order for the reader to interpret them as complimentary opposites:

1. CONDOMS We all want a guy who's happy to practise safe sex, but does carrying a condom make him **sensible or presumptuous?** Overall, it indicates a degree of maturity and personal responsibility.
   (*Cosmopolitan*)

2. RECEIPTS 'If receipts keep his wallet from closing, it's likely he has a **laid-back approach to life, but he's probably disorganised**,' says David.
   (*Cosmopolitan*)

3. [14 things you should never ask a bloke to do…] Carry your handbag. Ever. This is **not** chivalry, it's the best way to make a man look instantly ridiculous.
   (*More*)

The first two examples from *Cosmopolitan* are of contrastive opposition, the primary function of which is to present exclusive choices to the reader (Mettinger 1994). It is often triggered syntactically by coordinating conjunctions *and, or,* or *but.* In these examples, contrastive triggers 'or' and 'but' signal complementary opposition between 'sensible' and 'presumptuous' in the first extract, and the concepts of 'having a laid-back approach to life' and being 'disorganised' in the second. These are not canonical opposites, therefore the reader relies on both the syntactic frames 'X or Y' and 'X but Y', as well as schematic knowledge about the respective positive and negative connotations of each pair. The use of 'presumptuous' in the first example draws on the assumption that men are carnally driven (in contrast to women), and that they presume women will want to sleep with them. An interpretation of the two adjectives as opposites also relies on the superordinate antonyms GOOD/BAD, where the notion of presumption is evaluated as negative, and sensibility as positive.

Example (3) utilizes negated opposition, defined by Jones as 'the co-occurrence of an antonymous pair within a framework that negates one antonym as a device to augment the other' (2002: 88). Here the negator *not* emphasizes the writer's negative evaluation of asking a man to carry a woman's handbag, where the concepts of chivalry (evaluated as positive) and looking ridiculous (negative) are opposed in a 'X not Y' syntactic frame.

While the listicles contain the highest normalized frequency of GOOD/BAD opposition, the true-life stories have the highest in terms of raw frequency. As with other text types, being a 'bad' man in the true-life stories often involves being morally corrupt, where being a 'good' man entails physical attractiveness and a caring nature, as these examples demonstrate:

> David was so kind and gentle… *Could he really be a murderer?*
> (*Real People*)

> One was a popular big-hearted man adored by hundreds on his estate. The other was jealous, spiteful and hell bent on getting revenge.
> (*Pick Me Up*)

These extracts contain examples of opposition constructed via parallelism: repeated structures at phrase, clause or sentence level, which results in particular words or concepts being foregrounded, and often in oppositional meanings becoming apparent (Leech 1969: 67). Davies (2013) found that parallel structures were the most frequent syntactic trigger for opposition in his study of opposition in news discourse, and Jeffries' (2010a) acknowledges the ubiquity of parallelism in literary genres such as poetry and political speeches creating new non-conventional opposition for rhetorical effect. True-life narratives are then additional prolific sites for this kind of opposition.

In the first example, the parallel structure of the clauses 'X BE Y' separated by ellipsis triggers oppositional meaning between the synonyms 'kind' and 'gentle', and the noun phrase 'a murderer'. Unlike a lot of the GOOD/BAD opposition in the other text types, the concepts being opposed in these examples appear more extreme: in other words, there is a notably high degree of difference in meaning between the contrasted concepts in these narratives. In this example, the aspect of meaning that the two opposed items share, what Davies (2013) calls 'plane of equivalence', could be called something like MORALITY; the 'plane of difference' (Davies 2013) being the degree of morality involved. In the second extract, oppositional meanings are constructed via the parallel structure of the sentences 'X was Y', combined with the positive connotations of the adjectives 'popular', and 'big-hearted', and negative associations of 'jealous', 'spiteful' and being vengeful, evoking the conventional GOOD/BAD oppositional pair. The writer thus highlights the monstrous behavior of the male antagonist of the story as a dramatic deviation from the positive behavior of the protagonist.

The contrast between 'good' and 'bad' men can also involve a transition from one state to the other, as in the following extract from a true-life story about a woman who began dating a man she met after placing an ad in a lonely-hearts column, only to discover he was not what he seemed:

> Lynn loved her flash new man. But behind his fake tan and dazzling smile lurked cold, hard, evil…
>
> *(Real People)*

Here the contrastive conjunction *but* triggers a contrastive opposition between the positively valued qualities in the initial clause, and the propositions in the second. The preposition 'behind' creates a relationship of equivalence between the adjectives 'flash', 'new' and the qualities in the adverbial 'fake tan' and 'dazzling smile', implying that these are desirable attributes. These attributes are contrasted with 'cold', 'hard' and 'evil' because of their opposing negative connotations, again relying on a superordinate GOOD/BAD pairing.

In the same text, opposition is again used to imply a transitional contrast from the appearance of a good to a bad man, reminiscent of Jekyll and Hyde: 'I put that ad in the paper looking for love. But all I found was a monster.' Here coordinating conjunction *but* signals contrastive opposition between the noun phrases 'love' and 'a Monster'. The respective positive and negative associations of these concepts again confirm this unconventional opposition. These are metaphorical meanings: 'love' is used metonymically for 'a partner'; 'monster' is a familiar (mythical) cultural trope that personifies unattractive or violent qualities.

These examples imply that physical attractiveness is an important aspect of what makes a man 'good' or 'bad', which is also evident across other text types in the corpus:

> I once met a man who had more teeth than Mr Ed, and was barely bigger
> than a hamster. However, with my Martini goggles on, he became Mr
> Darcy.
>
> (*Woman & Home*)
>
> Skint and sexy 92% Loaded and ugly 8% To the 8% - thank you for your
> honesty, but a Miu Miu bag can't hug you at night, y'know…
>
> (*Glamour*)

In this *Woman & Home* example, the syntactic frame 'X became Y'
constructs the noun phrases 'a man who…' and 'Mr Darcy' as opposites. This is an example of transitional opposition, indicating a change
in state (Jones 2002). Transitional opposition is often signaled by verbs
such as *turn* and *become*; here 'became' denotes that the same man
turned from ugly (bad) to attractive (good). In utilizing opposition,
the narrator presents attractiveness as a binary construct. The same
technique is employed in the *Glamour* extract, where the parallel structures create oppositional meaning between 'skint' and 'loaded', and
'sexy' and 'ugly'. The opposed noun phrases in the 'Mr Darcy' example are novel opposites that rely on a superordinate ATTRACTIVE/
UNATTRACTIVE opposition, as well as cultural knowledge of Jane
Austen's romance novel *Pride & Prejudice*, of which Mr. Darcy is the
central love interest; the opposed lexical items from the *Glamour* listicle
are semi-canonical opposites in themselves.

The idea that women must choose between physical attraction and
material wealth (and the assumption that the two are mutually exclusive) is also reflected elsewhere in the corpus:

> If I had a penny for every time I've seen a beautiful woman pick the **nice
> but broke guy** over **the ugly but rich one**, I'd be penniless.
>
> (*Asiana*)

This extract comes from an opinion column written from the perspective of a male columnist. The contrastive conjunction *but* produces
oppositional meaning between the words 'nice' and 'broke', and 'ugly'
and 'rich'. The parallel structures of the noun phrases also create a contrast between the concepts 'nice'/'ugly' and 'broke'/'rich', which the

reader is likely to infer from their knowledge of superordinate conventional pairs RICH/POOR and ATTRACTIVE/UNATTRACTIVE. Given that being rich and attractive are usually seen as positive attributes, and being poor and unattractive negative, these oppositions are also hyponyms of the canonical oppositional pair GOOD/BAD. Opposition construction thus functions here to polarize men as either good-looking or ugly, and rich or poor; and consequently as either good or bad.

As well as attractiveness and wealth, morality is also treated as a desirable attribute that comes with mutually exclusive choices:

> You need to get to know him better - and if he then reveals that his true desires involve duct tape and a herd of goats, that's the time to make your excuses and leave. Before that, he's **innocent until proven filthy**.
>
> (*Company*)

This problem page from *Company* magazine draws on a discourse of morality in order to position the male subject of the letter as a 'good' man until proved a 'bad' man, done in part via transitional opposition. Here the adjectives 'innocent' and 'filthy' are constructed as transitional opposites using syntactic frame 'X until Y'. The phonological similarities between the lexemes *guilty* and *filthy* will also likely prime the reader to interpret 'filthy' as synonymous with 'guilty', via recognition of the superordinate canonical oppositional pair INNOCENT/GUILTY. This allusion to 'innocence' as a constructed binary opposite of 'filthy' indexes morality, associating 'orthodox' sexual practices with normative heterosexuality, and being 'filthy' with sexual deviancy, emphasized further by the parallel syntactic structure of the familiar idiom 'innocent until proven guilty'. The allusion to the more canonical pair INNOCENT/GUILTY, which can also be interpreted as hyponyms of the GOOD/BAD dichotomy, equates 'filthy' with the same connotations of immorality, and is therefore negatively evaluative.

The following extract also contains an example of transitional opposition, where the narrator uses a 'from X to Y' frame to indicate changes to men's level of commitment in relationships:

It takes more than a pork chop and a Kawasaki 750 to get a man to change his ways **from** playa to staya **or from** bachelor boy to married man.

(Pride)

There are two layers of opposition present here: the first is actually contrastive, where the coordinating conjunction *or* triggers oppositional meaning between the two prepositional phrases, aided by the parallel structure of the prepositional phrases 'from X to Y', which produces complementary oppositional meaning between 'playa' and 'bachelor boy', and 'staya' and 'married man'. The syntactic frames also create transitional oppositions between these. The phonological similarity of 'playa' and 'staya' will help the reader to infer these as opposites, and potentially knowledge of *player* as a colloquial term for someone who is:

a known love offender, known also as a notorious heartbreaker, one who engages in flirtatious, seductive and/or scandalous liasons [sic] of little to no meaning and/or feeling, with the opposite sex.

(Urban Dictionary 2009)

What is implied is that bachelors are promiscuous and uncommitted, unlike married men who are monogamous and committed.

6.2.5 Gender Differences

As Table 6.6 (Sect. 6.2.3) showed, oppositions relating to 'sex, gender and relationships' are the most frequent semantic category of superordinate oppositions drawn upon in the construction of opposites in the corpus. This semantic category contains the following canonical opposites:

Table 6.7 shows that words serving as classifications of sex or gender are the most frequent type of superordinate opposite in the 'sex, gender and relationships' category. These are mostly instances of the superordinate pairs MALE/FEMALE and MASCULINE/FEMININE, and serve to emphasize the construction of binary gender differences in the corpus. The advertorials and feature articles contained the highest

Table 6.7 Canonical opposites relating to 'sex, gender and relationships' in the magazine corpus

Name of sub-category	Canonical opposite members	Total frequency in sub-category	% of total number of canonical opposites
Sex/gender classifications	MALE/FEMALE (31); MASCULINE/FEMININE (3)	34	58
Sexual relationships	SINGLE/MARRIED (5); MARRIED/DIVORCED (2); HUSBAND/WIFE (2); MR/MRS (1); FAITHFUL/ UNFAITHFUL (1)	11	19
Sexual desire	STRAIGHT/GAY (7); SEXUAL/NONSEXUAL (2)	9	15
Kinship and personal relationships	PARENT/CHILD (2); FRIEND/RELATIVE (2); FRIEND/ STRANGER (1)	5	8

proportions of opposition relating to sex/gender differences, and so are the focus of analysis here.

The following example is from an advertorial in *Easy Living*, where the higher-level MASCULINE/FEMININE oppositional pair contributes to the construction of gender differences:

> They look **more like** members of an indie band, but these male movers and shakers are responsible for the way we cut our hair and wear our make-up...
>
> (*Easy Living*)

In this example, a comparative syntactic frame 'more like X than Y' opposes the concepts of being in an indie band with being a hairdresser. The 'Y' element of the frame is 'auto-evoked' (Jones 2002), something the reader will likely infer from an intuitive knowledge of how opposition is formed syntactically, as well as cultural knowledge about how occupational domains are socially gendered: hairdressing is traditionally female-oriented; rock music is conventionally a male-dominated domain. Therefore, the reader might rely on a superordinate MASCULINE/FEMININE pairing in order to interpret being in a rock band and being a hairdresser as opposites.

In the following example, from an advice feature on sex and relationships, knowledge of conventional comparative structures and the conceptual MALE/FEMALE oppositional pair is required to understand the notions of gender differences drawn on:

> Women are more creative and most men will be happy to go along with what you suggest.
>
> (*Cosmopolitan*)

A comparison between men and women is again 'auto-evoked' (Jones 2002), where comparative 'more' implies 'than men'. The auto-evocation works because of the codified status of *man/woman* as conventional complementary opposites in English. The idea that men are 'happy to go along with' suggestions could also be interpreted as indicating passivity, with female creativity implying proactive behavior, underpinned by a superordinate ACTIVE/PASSIVE oppositional binary. This can be seen as evidence for the idea that in women's magazines, as elsewhere, women are presented as responsible for relationship maintenance (Eggins and Iedema 1997: 169; Litosseliti 2006: 100–101).

> I'm an extrovert, she's an introvert. I'm open, she's private, I never see her cry.
>
> (*Easy Living*)

In this final example, from an article on what makes a successful marriage in *Easy Living*, parallel structures reinforce opposition between the conventional gradable opposites 'extrovert' and 'introvert', 'open' and 'private', as well as the complementary pronouns 'I' and 'she', because the first-person narrator is male, this also draw on the superordinate pair MALE/FEMALE. Here the writer uses more conventional opposites to emphasize gender differences between the couple; within the context of the article, this also reinforces the heteronormativity of marriage, since it is assumed that marital unions are exclusively the reserve of opposite-sex couples.

6.2.6 'Would You Rather...': Exclusive Choice in Men

Earlier in this chapter I noted that one article in particular from the corpus contained 38 examples of opposition (18% of the total frequency of recorded oppositions), and that these functioned to construct the notion of exclusive choice in men. The text in question is a survey report entitled 'Would you rather', from *Glamour* magazine, presenting the results of a questionnaire surveying responses to various relationship-related dilemmas that were posed to a sample of readers. The dilemmas constitute exclusive choices constructed via parallelism and contrastive opposition pertaining to desired physical appearance (20), behavior (11), attributes (3) and choice between different individual men (5). The majority of opposition in this article is therefore related to physical appearance, the magazine writers thus suggesting that this is the most important aspect of a potential partner, although there is only one lexical opposite concerning physical attractiveness, 'sexy'/'ugly'. The rest concern the appearance of body parts (8), skin color (3), overall body appearance (5) and size (3).

The extracts below show how parallelism is used to construct exclusive choices concerning body parts:

> Bald below 49%
> Trouser forest 51%
> Almost half of you would prefer Ken-doll baldness? It's just a bit wrong.

> Unzip him to find a pencil 60%
> Unzip him to find a button mushroom 40%
> Well, we never. We always thought short and thick would win over long and thin.

In the first example, the parallel lexical structure 'physical attribute + statistic', and the higher-level opposition BALD/HAIRY, help the reader to interpret 'bald' and 'trouser forest' as opposites. Metaphorical meanings are also exploited in the second extract: interpreting 'pencil' and 'button mushroom' as opposites relies on the more conventional oppositional pairs SHORT/LONG, and THICK/THIN, which are referred to by the magazine writers in the commentary underneath. It seems more likely that men and women will be concerned about the size of body parts if they are polarized like this, rather than acknowledging the variability of physical appearance. The inclusion of this particular choice in the article also emphasizes the importance of penis size, reifying the idea that a man's penis is symbolic of his status as a 'real' man, and therefore a successful display of masculinity. Given that these representations of penis size are made in the context of discussion about sexual relations, the reader will likely infer that penis size is treated here as an important indicator of a man's potency and success as a lover, reinforcing the notion that virility is an essential component of masculinity. A critical reader may well view these lexical choices as ironic (the modifier 'ken-doll' in the first example is potentially infantilizing, for example), but whether or not the reader 'resists' the assumption that the penis is an important symbol of virility, the point is that this text does nothing to challenge such assumptions.

The article also includes instances of opposition related to behavior. Of particular interest are those concerning sexual behavior, such as:

Too hard a thrust during sex 65%
Too soft a thrust during sex 35%
In a tussle of 'youch!' vs 'is it in yet?', most of you were on Team Hard rather than Team Gentle.

The juxtaposed clauses 'too hard...' and 'too soft...' are both syntactically and lexically parallel, with only the choice of adjectives providing a point of deviation (readers will be familiar with the canonical gradable opposites HARD/SOFT). The 'too X, too Y' syntactic frame is reminiscent of what Jones (2002: 101) terms 'extreme antonymy'. *Hard* and *soft* are placed at opposite ends of a scale, but are not treated as gradable, since the reader is not offered the option of any midway point on the scale, and are in fact presented as complementary. Both options are presented as negative, via the conventional negative prosody of *too*, implying that neither option would be enjoyable. What is disturbing about this example is that it effectively tells women that it is normal to not enjoy sex, which could be interpreted as blurring the boundaries between consent and resistance.

In this next extract, the lexical items 'sister' and 'best friend' are constructed as opposites, achieved via the parallel lexical structure of the clauses, and the relationships of equivalence and difference which underpin the two concepts:

Your boyfriend fantasises about your sister 46%
Your boyfriend fantasises about your best friend 54%
How to choose? A true divider.

Given the heterosexual context (provided via the use of second person pronoun 'your' which presupposes the reader having a male partner), we can assume that 'best friend' also has a female referent. 'Sister' and 'best friend' both usually denote close personal relationships; they differ in terms of kinship. Expressing the object of the man's desires as a binary choice excludes the possibility of other options, and, importantly, implies the possibility of one of these scenarios: the idea that the reader's boyfriend may fantasize about either her sister or best friend reflects the ideology that men are driven by their sexual urges.

The final example concerns choices in appearance but is underpinned by an assumption of hegemonic masculinity:

> He dressed up as a policeman 25%
> He dressed up as a fireman 75%
> Forget being cuffed and chastised - you want to be thrown over a shoulder 'n' rescued.

These parallel clause structures construct the lexically gendered nouns 'policeman' and 'fireman' as contrasting concepts, rather than co-hyponyms of the superordinate category 'emergency services'. Both figures are traditionally viewed in Western cultures as heroic, and exemplary of hegemonic masculinity. This is compounded by the comment underneath which presents women as enjoying domination (note also that the idea of being 'rescued' implies that women are physically weaker than men and in need of 'saving'). The fact that these are the only choices presented to the reader is indicative of the saliency imbued in these cultural ideals.

6.3   Summary

This chapter has considered the function of equating and contrasting in constructing desirable and undesirable facets of masculinity. Metaphorical equivalences liken men to cultural ideals of masculinity in these texts, which present the search for the 'ideal man' as an intrinsically important endeavor. Equivalent metaphors for the ideal woman appear less evident, given that female equivalents of cultural tropes such as 'Mr Right' and 'Mr Perfect' are not codified in English.

Superordinate opposites aid the interpretation of novel opposites in the data, the most prevalent being the GOOD/BAD canonical pair. 'Good' men, for example, are presented as kind, attractive and not sexually driven; 'bad' men are morally corrupt, unattractive and promiscuous. The superordinate MALE/FEMALE also works to emphasize gender differences in the magazine corpus, encouraging an interpretation of gender as binary.

The following two chapters focus on how ideologies of male behavior are constructed through processes more closely tied to grammatical structure, rather than lexis.

References

Achugar, M. (2004). The Events and Actors of 11 September 2011 as Seen from Uruguay: Analysis of Daily Newspaper Editorials. *Discourse and Society, 15*(2–3), 291–320.

Baker, P. (2008). "Eligible" Bachelors and "Frustrated" Spinsters: Corpus Linguistics, Gender and Language. In J. Sunderland, K. Harrington, & H. Saunston (Eds.), *Gender and Language Research Methodologies*. London: Palgrave Macmillan.

Crisp, P. (2002). Metaphorical Propositions: A Rationale. *Language and Literature, 11*(1), 7–16.

Cruse, A. (2004). *Meaning in Language: An Introduction to Semantics and Pragmatics*. Oxford: Oxford University Press.

Davies, M. (2013). *Oppositions and Ideology in News Discourse*. London: Bloomsbury.

Eggins, S., & Iedema, R. (1997). Difference Without Diversity: Semantic Orientation and Ideology in Competing Women's Magazines. In R. Wodak (Ed.), *Gender and Discourse* (pp. 165–196). London: Sage.

Hines, C. (1999). Rebaking the Pie: The WOMAN AS DESSERT Metaphor. In M. Bucholtz, A. C. Liang, & L. Sutton (Eds.), *Reinventing Identities: The Gendered Self in Discourse* (pp. 145–162). Oxford: Oxford University Press.

Holloway, W. (1984). Gender Difference and the Production of Subjectivity. In J. Henriques, W. Holloway, C. Urwin, C. Venn, & V. Walkerdine (Eds.), *Changing the Subject: Psychology, Social Regulation and Subjectivity* (pp. 227–339). London: Methuen.

Jeffries, L. (2007). *Textual Construction of the Female Body: A Critical Discourse Approach*. Basingstoke: Palgrave Macmillan.

Jeffries, L. (2010a). *Opposition in Discourse*. London: Continuum.

Jeffries, L. (2010b). *Critical Stylistics*. Basingstoke: Palgrave Macmillan.

Jones, S. (2002). *Antonymy: A Corpus-Based Perspective*. London: Routledge.

Lakoff, G., & Johnson, M. (1980). *Metaphors We Live By*. Chicago: University of Chicago Press.

Leech, G. (1969). *A Linguistic Guide to English Poetry*. London: Longman.

Litosseliti, L. (2006). *Gender and Language: Theory and Practice*. London: Hodder Arnold.

Lyons, J. (1977). *Semantics* (Vol. 1). Cambridge: Cambridge University Press.

Mettinger, A. (1994). *Aspects of Semantic Opposition in English*. Oxford: Clarendon Press.

Mills, S. (1995). *Feminist Stylistics*. London: Routledge.

Molesworth, M., Nixon, E., & Scullon, R. (2010). *The Marketisation of Higher Education and the Student as Consumer*. London: Routledge.

Murphy, L. (2003). *Semantic Relations and the Lexicon*. Cambridge: Cambridge University Press.

Pearce, M. (2008). Investigating the Collocational Behaviour of MAN and WOMAN in the BNC Using Sketch Engine. *Corpora, 3*(1), 1–29.

Sapir, E. (1944). On Grading: A Study in Semantics. *Philosophy of Science, 2*, 93–116.

Schulz, M. (1975). The Semantic Derogation of Women. In B. Thorne & N. Henley (Eds.), *Language and Sex: Difference and Dominance* (pp. 64–75). Rowley, MA: Newbury House.

Semino, E., & Short, M. (2004). *Corpus Stylistics: Speech, Writing and Thought Presentation in a Corpus of English Writing*. London: Routledge.

Sunderland, J. (2004). *Gendered Discourses*. Basingstoke: Palgrave Macmillan.

Zimman, L. (2014). The Discursive Construction of Sex: Remaking and Reclaiming the Gendered Body in Talk About Genitals Among Trans Men. In L. Zimman, J. Raclaw, & J. Davis (Eds.), *Queer Excursions: Retheorizing Binaries in Language, Gender, and Sexuality* (pp. 13–34). Oxford: Oxford University Press.

7

Representing Processes

Aside from labels, descriptions and evaluations, the magazine writers also make choices in representing men's actions and states of being that reveal gender ideologies. Critical linguistic approaches to ideology construction (including CDA) frequently draw on Halliday's system of 'transitivity' from Systemic Functional Grammar, where transitivity refers to the manner in which speakers encode their experiences of the real world via processes: "'goings-on': of doing, happening, feeling, being' (Halliday 1985: 101). Decisions about what kind of action is performed by an individual can create impressions about the character of that person. For example, a participant who is represented with more stative verbs (such as *is* or *was*) than those of action (*kicked* or *punched*), can produce an effect of passivity; an individual attributed more verbs of speech may give the impression of loquacity. Choices made in the verbal element of the clause, for example by choosing to construct the clause in active or passive voice, can also make people more or less connected with actions.

© The Author(s) 2019
L. Coffey-Glover, *Men in Women's Worlds*,
https://doi.org/10.1057/978-1-137-57555-5_7

7.1 Transitivity Analysis

I have used Simpson's (1993, 2004) model of transitivity, which is derived from Halliday and informed by a symbiosis of stylistic and CDA approaches to text analysis, and therefore aligns with my own approach. According to Simpson, transitivity 'shows how speakers encode in language their mental picture of reality and how they account for their experience of the world around them' (1993: 88).

Transitivity is an attempt to encode semantic meaning into the grammar of the clause, in a way which traditional grammars do not. This is perhaps best illustrated by the way in which participant labels can make a distinction between grammatical roles and semantic roles in active and passive clauses:

1. Richard played the trumpet
2. The trumpet was played by Richard

In both of these examples, the semantic meaning is the same: 'Richard' is the entity performing the action of playing, and the trumpet is the affected participant in each case. If we assign semantic roles to these clause elements, meaning is reflected in the grammar of the clause: we can say that in both of these examples, 'Richard' is the agent, or Actor of a material action process, and 'the trumpet' is the affected participant, or Goal. In (1), 'Richard' is the grammatical Subject of the verb phrase 'played', but in (2), 'the trumpet' is the Subject and 'by Richard' is an adjunct.

The transitivity system is based on the verbal element of the clause, or *process*. The processes expressed by the clause have three potential components:

- The process itself, expressed by a verb phrase (such as 'played').
- Participants involved in the process, usually realized by noun phrases (for example 'the blue piano').
- Any circumstances involved in the process, which usually comprise of adverbial and prepositional phrases (such as 'yesterday, she played the blue piano in the drawing room').

Processes can be categorized according to their semantic meaning: whether they represent actions, states of mind or states of being. Participants have different labels depending on the type of process they are associated with, which express their relationships to the process. Circumstances are optional elements that provide information such as time, place and manner, and are usually realized by prepositional or adverb phrases. There are five broad categories of process: material, behavioral, mental,[1] verbalization[2] and relational. The processes, their sub-types and associated participants used in this study are discussed below.

Halliday's transitivity model has been utilized in a number of feminist linguistic studies to demonstrate how choice of process type and agency patterns contribute to gender inequality in literary texts (Burton 1982; Talbot 1997; Wareing 1994) and mass media publications (Attenborough 2011; Jeffries 2007; Mills 1994).

Material processes

Material processes are processes of 'doing'. They can be subdivided into material actions of intention, unintentional actions or 'supervention' (Simpson 1993) processes, and material events, which are performed by an inanimate agent. The participants associated with material processes are the Actor and the Goal. For example:

1. Richard played the piano (Material action-intention)
2. Richard fell onto the piano (Material action-supervention)
3. The piano slammed shut (Material event)

---

[1]Mental processes express mental perceptions, such as *see, hear*; mental reactions, such as *love, hate*; and mental cognitions, for example *understand, think*. These were less prominent than material and relational processes, therefore I have not discussed the function of mental processes here.

[2]Verbalization processes are verbs of speech, such as *said* or *announced*, although there is often a cross-over with behavioural processes: a process such as *grinned* in '"Morning", he grinned.' Out of context, *grinned* can be interpreted as a behavioural verb. However, in this instance, 'grinned' is a reporting verb; it is therefore intended as a categorization of speech, and is more accurately coded as a verbalization process. This kind of choice is interesting for an analysis of speech and thought representation, as it gives an indication of point of view (see, for example, Semino and Short 2004). However, I have not given space here to an analysis of verbalization processes, because other transitivity choices, mainly types of material and relational processes, were more prevalent.

In (1), Richard is an animate Actor of an intentional material action process; 'the piano' is the Goal of the process; the affected 'participant'. In (2), the process 'fell' is arguably an unintentional action, and in (3), the Actor is in fact an inanimate process, and is therefore termed an 'event' rather than 'action'.

Feminist linguists have commented on the gendered distribution of material action processes in texts. Deirdre Burton's (1982) influential analysis of Sylvia Plath's *The Bell Jar* demonstrated how the female protagonist is assigned a passive role, where other (male) characters act upon her, indicating her subordinate role in the text. Critics writing about romance fiction (Talbot 1997; Wareing 1994) have also shown how men are constructed as active in romantic encounters, where women are acted upon, and often presented in terms of their constituent body parts. This is interpreted by feminist analysts as indicating women's lack of control, and men's dominance over women. In her analysis of the female body in women's magazines, Jeffries (2007) identified a significant number of material intention processes with female participants fulfilling the role of Actor, but that these mostly came from instructions of what women can do to please men, particularly in articles concerning sex (2007: 170). This suggests that the women in the texts are not as in control of their actions as a transitivity analysis alone might suggest.

Since I only captured processes with male agents, the analysis of transitivity patterns presented below primarily focuses on male agency and the actions and behaviors associated with men. However, the examples discussed below show that the active/passive dichotomy is relevant to gender construction more widely.

Behavioral processes

Behavioral processes can be thought of as occupying a realm somewhere between material actions and mental processes, and usually denote physiological processes, such as *cough* or *smile* (Simpson 2004: 23). The participant roles associated with behavioral processes are that of Behaver and occasionally a Behavior, as in the following: 'he [Behaver] smiled [Process] a smile [Behavior].'

The behavioral category was useful for coding verbs that were not adequately described by mental, material or relational categories, such as the following:

Lee appeared in the doorway.

(Love It)

In this clause, the verb 'appeared' suggests an action, but there is no affected participant, only a circumstance adverbial of place, and *appear* is not a dynamic verb. It could be coded as a 'relational circumstantial' process (see Sect. 7.4.3 below), but at the same time, *appear* feels less static than *was*; some kind of action is implied. It therefore seems to sit somewhere between 'material action-intention' and 'relational circumstantial'.

Relational processes

Relational processes are processes of being. In Simpson's (1993) account, relational processes can be further categorized into three different sub-types: 'intensive', 'possessive', or 'circumstantial'. Intensive relations usually involve a form of BE, as in, for example, 'he is kind.' Possessive processes express a relationship of ownership, such as 'he has long hair.' Circumstantial processes relate to the time or place of the state, as in 'he was at the bar.'

While the account of the different process types outlined here is on the surface logical, there are often problems with applicability. Some verbs can be assigned more than one category, depending on context of use. In this study, in a number of cases, verbs could belong to different categories depending on who is the 'focalizer': 'the consciousness through which a fictional event is presented in any text' (Wareing 1994: 127). For example, in the clause 'he wowed me', the action is performed by a male persona, but seems to represent the point of view of the female participant: I have coded 'wowed' as a material action process following grammatical criteria, but it could be interpreted as implying that the female participant *felt* 'wowed' as a result of the male agent's actions. The magazine writer's decision to construct her as the recipient of a material action process, rather than the agent of a mental process, as in 'I felt wowed', subordinates her participation, focusing on the man's active role in the process.

Other issues with the relationship between form and function include mismatches between the surface form of the process and pragmatic meaning. For example, in a process like 'he's having an affair', the use of the verb HAVE presents this as a relational possessive process, and therefore a state of being, but really it is an action, meaning 'he is committing adultery.' The decision to present this as a state of being, where the action becomes nominalized as 'an affair', has the effect of reifying the act, because it is being presented as a tangible object. Paying attention to transitivity choices can therefore be very revealing in terms of how linguistic structure interacts with discourse-level meaning.

7.2   Distribution of Transitivity Processes

Looking at the overall distribution of transitivity process types across the corpus shows that the magazine writers are mostly engaged in presenting men's actions and states of being, rather than their speech or thoughts. This is reflected in the relative high proportion of material actions and relational processes (Table 7.1):

Table 7.1   Total frequencies of process types in the magazine corpus

Process type	Raw frequency	Proportion of total number of processes (%)
Material actions	1954	30
Relational processes	1759	27
Behavioral processes	969	15
Mental processes	994	15
Verbalization processes	810	12
Total	6486	

Looking at the distribution of different process types across the different text types shows whether this pattern is observable across the corpus, or whether the kinds of actions and states men are seen to be engaged in differs according to kind of text in which they appear.

Table 7.2 shows the distribution of processes across the corpus, taking the size of each sub-corpus into account. The listicles contain the highest frequency of both material and mental processes, where the profiles contain the highest number of both behavioral and relational processes. The profiles are thus more likely to represent men in terms of states of being and behaviors than actions, where the listicles are concerned with how men act and think, but not what they are *like*. The letters text type contains the highest relative frequency of verbalization processes, which would be expected given their communicative function.

Looking at which processes are most prominent within particular text types also tells us something about how the texts characterize male behavior, as shown in Table 7.3.

The text types containing mostly material processes, such as the advertorials, feature articles and reports, tell the reader what men 'do'. We might expect that material processes would constitute the highest proportion of processes in the fiction and true-life story text types, because as narratives they are centered on one or more 'complicating actions' (Labov and Waletzky 1967), involving male characters.

The features and reports are informative articles that tell the reader about particular issues, and the majority are concerned with sex and relationships (21 articles, 68%), some of which are explicit guides on how to improve relationships (13 articles, 42%). The material processes in these text types are mainly related to how men behave in relationships or sexual encounters, or what women should ask men to do, in order to satisfy their sexual or emotional needs.

Examining the distributional frequencies of the different process types across the corpus demonstrates that for each text type, the processes containing the highest frequencies are either material actions or relational processes. Across the corpus, then, the most frequent ways of representing men are in terms of the actions they perform, or how they appear, either physically or in terms of personality. For this reason, material actions and relational processes form the focus of the thematic analysis in the remainder of this chapter.

Table 7.2 Normalized frequencies of transitivity process types across text types

	Material actions	Behavioral processes	Verbalization processes	Mental processes	Relational processes
Advertorials	97.7	58.6	19.5	19.5	32.6
Columns	85.8	84.8	50	80.4	100
Features	75	32.2	32.2	40.1	69.7
Fiction	112.4	68.6	61.2	51.8	98.3
Interviews	182.3	64.2	40.2	90	180.3
Letters	116.6	82.1	112.3	64.8	168.5
Listicle	351.6	103.4	72.4	113.8	237.9
Problem pages	100	49.8	52.6	81	92.1
Profiles	224.8	166.8	72.5	29	261.1
Survey reports	101	98.6	24	101	173.1
True-life stories	122.1	72.5	76	46.2	81.5
Reports	112.1	33.7	31.3	43.4	65.1
Reviews	0	0	0	0	38.3

Table 7.3 The distribution of transitivity process types within each text type

Text type	Process type Material actions (%)	Behavioral processes (%)	Verbalization processes (%)	Mental processes (%)	Relational processes (%)
Advertorials	43	26	9	9	14
Columns	21	21	12	20	25
Features	30	13	13	16	28
Fiction	29	17	15	13	25
Interviews	33	12	7	16	32
Letters	21	15	20	15	30
Listicles	40	12	8	13	27
Problem pages	26	13	14	22	25
Profiles	30	22	10	4	35
Survey reports	20	20	5	20	35
True-life stories	31	18	19	12	20
Reports	38	11	11	15	25
Reviews	0	0	0	0	100

7.3   Material Processes

7.3.1   Sexual Activity

The feature articles are an important text type in the representation of men's behavior, since they are 'ideational' in function: their primary purpose is to offer information to the reader, often backed up with 'expert' opinion. Examining the kinds of behavior women are told to expect from men, in editorial features, as well as how in control of their actions men are seen to be in these texts, is therefore imperative for assessing their potential influence on the reader. The actions that men perform in the features text type most frequently relate to sexual activity, such as those highlighted in the following extract from an instructional article on sexual technique in *Cosmopolitan* entitled 'The Nice Girl's Guide to Naughty Sex':

> Get him to **massage** your pubic area with the palm of one hand, before **sliding** two fingers inside. Next, get him to **rub** the upper and lower parts of the inside of your vagina, before **moving** up to the G-spot, which is the focal area. Encourage him to gently **squeeze** the clitoris and **circle** it between his fingers.

The fact that the reader is instructed to guide her partner in performing these actions indicates that women's magazines do not always simply tell the reader how to please men, as is purported in much of the literature (such as Farvid and Braun 2006; McLoughlin 2008), and also suggests that men are not simply in control of their own actions.

In the example below, while the text producer initially instructs women to actively engage in sexual activity, their passivity is however ultimately implied by the representation of male action:

> Kiss him! "A scientific study showed that a man's saliva fills up with testosterone when he sees a woman he considers sexy. Simply **kissing** her can pass on some of those hormones, making her feel more in the mood for lust," says Sarah Hedley.
>
> (*Best*)

Although the excerpt from this instructional feature begins with an implied female agent of the action 'kiss', male agency is the focus of the actual advice: men are the agent of the actions 'sees', 'considers', 'kissing' and 'making'; there are no female agented processes apart from the opening gambit. The text here also implies that women need men to initiate sexual activity, because they would not ordinarily be 'in the mood for lust.'

Material processes also make up the largest proportion of processes with male agents in the listicles. The majority relate to sexual activity and attracting women more generally, and, as in the example from *Best* above, men are often presented as in control of sexual activity, women's role being passivized:

> Cash, not cards, is an easy way to **impress** women. It says, 'I'm beating the credit crunch - I buy things with real money!' But don't be fooled - It could be a ploy to **make** you fancy him, or even a sign he can no longer get credit.
>
> *(Cosmopolitan)*

The choice of verb 'impress' in the initial subordinate clause is interesting, as it could imply agency on the part of the woman, but the syntactic structure of the clause represents 'women' as an affected participant: the clause means 'women are impressed', and thus expresses women's alleged point of view. However, positioning men as the agent of the action has a foregrounding effect, backgrounding the role of 'women.' The male agent is elided, but it is clear from the context that 'men' is the intended Actor here. 'Make' implies coercion or reluctance; that some kind of force would be required for women to be sexually attracted to men. The lack of modalization in the verb phrase, for example with a verb that does not imply success such as 'try to make you fancy him', indicates that wealth is indeed an attractive quality in a man, since the implication is that if men carrying cash is a ploy to attract the reader, it would indeed prove successful.

Male sexual agency is also ascribed in the following example from an article in *Company* magazine, in which five 'sexperts' tell the story of their most embarrassing sexual encounters:

> Then, when he **freed** his erection and rubbed it against my clothed body,
> I was happy to go along with the frisky teenage role-play.

The choice of verb 'freed' here also implies agency on the part of the penis; that his penis is in some way 'struggling' to escape (ordinarily it is *people* that are 'freed'). The reader could also interpret this agency as the man having reduced control over his penis, reiterating representations of male sexuality as an 'uncontrollable other' (Cameron 1992: 370), discussed in the naming of male sex organs above (see Chapter 5). However, the fact that this example is in the context of an article on sexual blunders suggests that the 'power' of his erection is not to be taken seriously here.

In the reports, seven processes are a form of HAVE + 'sex', an idiomatic phrase in English which appears to present a material action as a possessive process, as in '63% of men have thought about another woman while **having** sex' (*More*). Using HAVE in this way focuses on 'sex' as an object, or experience, rather than a straightforward action, as a more prototypical material process like *do* might, although the reader will clearly infer 'have sex' to be metaphorical. It is also clear from the co-texts of examples like this that the other participants involved in the processes are female, again reiterating heteronormative sexual relations.

7.3.2 Physical Strength

Male agented material actions also often serve to highlight the physical strength of male Actors, as in the following examples from true-life story 'I Dumped my Hubby to Marry a Killer' (*That's Life*):

1. Kelly stayed back as I ran into his arms and he **scooped** me up, **swinging** me round.
2. 'I'm so glad you're here,' Rickey said, **stroking** my dark hair.
3. He stood up, his chair crashing to the floor as he **wrapped** me in his arms.
4. 'I love you more, wifey,' he said, **kissing** me hard.

It is notable that the female narrator does not perform these types of material actions; she is the affected participant in these romantic encounters, which reflects findings of other feminist research on female representation in fiction (Talbot 1997; Wareing 1994). In example (1), material actions 'scooped' and 'swinging' have connotations of ease and free movement: a random sample of 50 instances of 'scooped up' from the BNC showed that 43 (86%) of these precede noun phrase objects denoting small, light items. By implying that the actions are easy to perform, the first-person (female) narrator is diminutized, which consequently foregrounds Rickey's strength. Her hair is the affected participant in (2), which has the similarly diminutive effect of compartmentalizing her as a body part. The paratactic clause 'his chair crashing to the floor' in (3) implies that the force of behavioral action 'stood up' caused this material event; the reader may infer from this and 'wrapped' that Rickey is big, physically strong and domineering. Manner adverbial 'hard' in (4) indicates the force of the action, again evoking a sense of physical strength and domination.

7.3.3 Women as Affected Participants

An analysis of female-affect participants demonstrates to what extent, and in what contexts, women are affected by male actions in the data. Table 7.4 shows frequencies of female-affected participants in processes with male agents across the corpus.

Table 7.4 shows the text type in which female-affected participants make up the largest proportion of processes with male agents to be the reader survey. The text types with no female-affected participants are the profiles and reviews. This is because the profiles are solely intended to showcase men and their achievements, not to describe men's behavior towards women. Similarly, the review text type is intended to evaluate products, not behavior.

Initiating romantic relationships with women
Processes with female-affected participants in the surveys mostly concern initiating romantic relationships with women, including verbs such as:

Table 7.4 Frequencies of female affected participants in clauses with male agents across the corpus

Text type	Frequency of female affected participants	% of total affected participants
Advertorials	3	10
Columns	21	18
Features	98	29
Fiction	52	27
Interviews	65	13
Letters	2	5
Listicles	4	9
Problem pages	77	35
Profiles	0	0
Surveys	30	43
Reports	31	29
Reviews	0	0
True-life stories	174	41

'dating', 'approach', 'meet/ing' and 'invited'. The co-texts of 'approach' and 'dating' are interesting in that they form part of an assumption that it is normally men's responsibility to instigate relationships:

'Definitely. I'm way too scared of rejection to **approach** a girl.' *Craig, 21, Essex*

'It's how I met my girlfriend, I didn't have the balls to **approach** her.' *Mathew, 24, Oxford*

(*More*)

These quotations are 'real-life' responses to the question 'Should a girl ever make the first move?'. The implication of course is that it is men who usually initiate relationships. These are actually examples of men *not* approaching women. This is expressed here in terms of men's fallibility: assessments that the man was 'too scared' in the first response and 'didn't have the balls' in the second. The latter is an interesting idiom, which directly links male biological sex with the concept of masculinity: 'balls' is a metaphor for something like *courage*, a staple characteristic of hegemonic masculinity.

This pattern of male agency in romantic relationship is also evident in the fictional texts, as the following concordance lines demonstrate (Fig. 7.1):

1. no good at compromise." "Did you	dump	her? Is that what all this is ab
2. all this is about?" "I didn't dump	her.	If you remember, I'd arranged
3. the problem? Was Max refusing to	leave	his wife? Jules wouldn't have m
4. comment. Justin telling me he was	leaving	me for someone else came as a h
5. ... "As Fay's love of eight years	leaves	her for someone else, we share
6. as his owner. "Are you going to	marry	her?" she asked impulsively. She
7. 'm not surprised he simply had to	marry	one." And in private... in priv
8. roposal - he said: "But I've only	met	you a few minutes ago... and I
9. thing of the sort, of course. "I	met	my ex-wife at art school. She h

Fig. 7.1 Concordance of processes relating to dating in fiction with female as affected participant

Lines 1–3, 7 and 9 come from a story called 'Step by Step' in *Woman's Weekly*. Line 6 is from a story in *My Weekly* called 'His Girl Friday', described as a 'romance' narrative centering on the relationship of a male boss and his female secretary. Lines 4–5 come from another story from *My Weekly*, called 'Obsession', which tells the story of an obsessive man who leaves his partner for another woman. Line 8 features in a story from *Woman & Home*, 'The Christmas Ring', about a wealthy divorced couple; after leaving his wife for another woman, the man tells his ex-wife that he wishes to buy back her engagement ring to give to his new partner. All the fictional narratives in the corpus, apart from 'Village Secret' (*Best*) are focused on romantic relationships between men and women. Unlike the processes from the survey reports, the verbs relating to relationships in the fiction texts mostly involve marriage or married participants; this reflects the distinction between the glossy magazines as engaged in depicting a world full of single people, and the domestic weeklies as one in which marriage is a given.

Violence towards women

As shown in Table 7.4, the true-life stories contain the second highest proportion of processes with female-affected participants (174 tokens,

41% of total processes with affected participants). The most prominent theme in these was that of violent actions (38 tokens, 22%). The vast majority of these (30 tokens, 79%) come from what I have termed the 'monster' narratives, stories about men who have committed criminal or adulterous actions. In most cases, the male perpetrators were known to the female victims, and the majority are told from the first-person perspective of the female victim-narrator. These violent actions are either related to sexual violence (for example, 'raped', 'sexually assaulted'), murder ('killed', 'murdered'), grievous bodily harm ('stabbing', 'punched'), or, less emotively, verbs that highlight physical dominance ('forced', 'pulled', 'overpowered'). This last set of processes is interesting in that they imply the helplessness of the female victims, as in the following examples:

1. 'We're going,' he snarled, **pulling** me from the bed, still naked. 'Let me get dressed,' I begged, laying Sophia on the sheets. But he just **pulled** me <u>into the hall and down the stairs</u>.

2. 'Why have you done this to me?' Nabil said as he suddenly **picked** me up and **threw** me <u>over a fence</u>.

   (*That's Life*)

3. 'Get off!' I yelled at him, fear pounding through me as Lee **pulled** me <u>towards my bedroom</u>.

   (*Love It*)

In all three extracts, the female participant is the helpless recipient of the verbs 'PULL', 'picked' and 'threw'. The circumstantial phrases (underlined) are also an important part of this construction of dominance, as they imply that a good degree of physical force is involved in carrying out these actions.

In 'Have Sex or Die' (*That's Life*), a third person narrator uses material actions with violent connotations to describe convicted murderer Jesse Pratt's actions towards female victim Carrie, to present him as dominating and sexually violent:

When she refused, he **overpowered** her, **covering** her nose and mouth with paper towels. He then tried to **rape** her, before **stabbing** her to death.

Pratt then **drove over** his victim's body before **burying** her 15 miles away under some loose gravel.

Pratt is the Actor of the material verbs 'overpowered,' 'rape,' 'stabbing' and phrasal verb 'drove over', which all have semantic connotations of domination, and are exemplary of the evaluative lexis attributed to tabloid reporting and women's magazine fiction (Fowler 1991: 45; Nash 1990: 48; Talbot 1997). Additionally, the unmodalized, categorical nature of the propositions means they are represented as irrefutable 'facts'. As well as these 'facts', underneath the main text of the article there is a linear sequence of more explicitly labelled 'facts' about the case, which also describe Pratt's crimes and represent him as violent and sexually driven:

Fact 1: A trucker found a sleeping bag containing Carrie's **blood-spattered** handbag.
Fact 2: Her **battered** body lay 15 miles away under a mound of gravel.
Fact 3: She'd been **stabbed** and **asphyxiated**, as revealed by hemorrhaging to her eyes.
Fact 4: Paper towels with pieces of duct tape attached were strewn close to her body.

Unlike those above, these sentences are all written in passive voice, hiding the agents of the actions, Pratt, the implied Actor of these material actions. In Facts 1 and 2, the violent actions are implied by the adjectival modifications 'blood-spattered' and 'battered' in the noun phrases 'Carrie's blood-spattered handbag' and '[H]er battered body'. These nominalizations foreground the cause and recipient of the violence, which arguably has the effect of evoking sympathy from the reader. Lexical verb 'strewn' in Fact 4 has connotations of chaos or disorganization, which contributes to the construction of Pratt as out of control.

Gendered practices
As well as sexual behavior and violence towards women, some material processes with female recipients serve to (re)construct stereotypically gendered practices. For example, in a report from *Scarlet* magazine

entitled 'Boys Talk', practices associated with stereotypical femininity occur with male agents:

1. "The first thing I'd do is **fondle** my breasts, then I'd get pampered and **do** girly things." SCOTT, 37
2. "**Go shopping**, then **look** for a nice, good-looking man." NANDO, 30
3. "I'd **put on** a dress, **make** myself look beautiful, **walk** my dog and then have lunch in a restaurant. If I had sex, I'd **sleep with** another woman or have an orgy." ALEXANDER, 32
4. "I'd **spend** a day at the spa - something I don't do enough as a man. If I had sex I'd **sleep with** a man because, as a woman it would be the right thing to do." MARTIN, 34

'Boys Talk' is a regular section of *Scarlet* in which every month selected men answer a different question. The question in this issue is 'If you were a woman for the day, what would you do?' The men's responses mostly reveal behaviors stereotypically associated with women, such as: shopping, engaging in beautification processes (wearing make-up, going to a spa) and wearing dresses. A number of these are also sexual actions, which reinforces the idea that men are sexually driven beings.

What is interesting is the way in which sex and gender are seen to uncomplicatedly map onto one another; that the prospect of changing biological sex would necessarily entail changing the kinds of activities the men would ordinarily engage in. Butler's theory of performativity can usefully highlight the mechanisms at work here: 'there is no body prior to its marking', thus there is no inner 'essence' that is masculine or feminine: the gendered identities that we produce are made to seem real because they are 'citations' of gender norms (Butler 1990: 98).

These examples from 'Boys Talk' also illustrate the workings of Butler's 'heterosexual matrix', through which identities cohere if they adhere to 'a stable sex expressed through a stable gender [...] that is oppositionally and hierarchically defined through the compulsory practice of heterosexuality' (Butler 1990: 206). The heterosexual matrix dictates that to be normative requires a male/female dichotomy, that gender performances match biological sex, and that individuals desire the opposite sex. So, in order for the male participants in this hypothetical situation to 'qualify' as female, they must normatively ensure that their gendered behavior is in alignment with their newfound sex, which also entails adhering to heteronorms. One could argue that the respondent in example (3) subverts the heterosexual matrix by stating that as a female he would want to have sex with a woman. However, it is equally likely that his motivation for saying this is that he imagines he would retain some 'essence' of being a man, and therefore would desire women in adherence to heteronormativity. Ultimately, then, these examples serve to reinforce normative heterosexuality.

Table 7.2 (Sect. 7.2 above) showed the listicles to be the text type with the highest normalized frequency of material actions. In these texts, there are a number of examples of material action processes concerning stereotypically gendered practices. The following, from *More* magazine, is a list of actions that men should not be asked to perform, the implication being that this would compromise their identity as men:

1. To **buy** and **wrap** your friend/mum's birthday present.
2. **Put up** some shelves. You'll either never hear the end of how brilliant he is or you'll have to re-plaster an entire wall.
3. To **get rid of** his porn collection. It'll just become a porn collection in a better hiding place.
4. **Carry** your handbag. Ever. This is not chivalry, it's the best way to make a man look instantly ridiculous.
5. **Cut down** on his beer drinking, because, 'It's giving you a bit of a belly, babe'.

(More)

In (1), the instruction that men should not be asked to 'buy and wrap' presents can be interpreted as an assumption that men are no good at buying presents, reflecting the gender ideologies that shopping is the domain of women, and that women are better at managing social relationships. The humor of (2) relies on the reader's schematic knowledge of DIY as a stereotypically male endeavor: the reader is advised not to ask men to carry out DIY projects because the assumed outcome would be either failure or boasting, relying on the reader's knowledge of the folklinguistic stereotype that men boast more than women.

The existence of men's porn collections is assumed uncritically in example (3), which also draws on the ideology that men's libidos are stronger than women's. Men are advised not to carry women's handbags in example (4) because this would index femininity; this is negatively evaluated via the adjectival Attribute 'ridiculous', implying that this action would not be consistent with heterosexual masculinity. Example (5) assumes that men drink beer, a drink stereotypically associated with men, and particularly 'lad culture' (Edwards 2003). It is interesting that women are advised not to tell men to curb their beer drinking here because of its potential weight-gaining effects, implying that diet and fitness should be the preserve of women, not men. As well as presenting stereotypically gendered behaviors, these examples are also heteronormative, assuming the reader's heterosexuality, and that she is currently in a relationship.

7.4 Relational Processes

Looking at which text types use different types of relational processes tells us which are most likely to present men in terms of Attributes, Possessions or Circumstances. Table 7.5 shows frequencies of different types of relational processes with male agents across the corpus:

Table 7.5 shows that intensive processes such as 'is' or 'was' make up the largest proportion of relational processes across the corpus. Out of the three different ways of representing men's state of being, the text producers are thus most concerned with expressing what men are like, as opposed to where they are or what they have.

Jeffries (2007: 178) notes that the decision to use an intensive process, rather than a possessive process, can have the effect of making the participant feel closer to the description. For example, in 'Lee's eyes were bloodshot' (*Love* It), the decision to represent the affected participant 'bloodshot' as an Attribute in an intensive structure represents this description as a state; a possessive verb, as in 'Lee had bloodshot eyes' would construct the affected participant ('eyes') as a separate object, and therefore not as intrinsic to the agent ('Lee'). The fact that the majority of relational processes are intensive suggests that the text producers

Table 7.5 Frequencies of the different relational processes with male Carriers according to text type

Text type	Intensive processes		Possessive processes		Circumstantial processes	
	Raw frequency	% of relational processes	Raw frequency	% of relational processes	Raw frequency	% of relational processes
Advertorials	5	100	0	0	0	0
Columns	67	71	18	19	10	11
Features	182	73	51	20	17	7
Fiction	93	63	29	20	29	20
Interviews	397	63	161	26	74	12
Letters	30	73	7	17	4	10
Listicles	17	74	6	26	0	0
Problem pages	97	71	32	24	7	5
Profiles	27	73	7	19	3	8
True-life stories	220	78	22	8	39	14
Reports	36	58	21	34	5	8
Reviews	1	100	0	0	0	0
Surveys	48	65	23	31	3	4

are more concerned to present Attributes as inherent aspects of male Carriers, and therefore more permanent aspects of male identity.

The advertorials and reviews contain the highest proportion of relational intensive processes, although the raw frequencies are very low. The text type containing the next highest proportion of intensive processes is the true-life story; the analysis of relational processes that follows focuses on these.

7.4.1 Intensive Processes

All the instances of intensive processes describing male Carriers in the advertorials come from an article in *Easy Living* magazine called 'The Men who Make you Look Good', is a piece on male hair and make-up artists, showcasing their services and the cosmetic products they use on women. For example:

1. They **look** more like members of an indie band, but these male movers and shakers **are** responsible for the way we cut our hair and wear our make-up…

2. Now spending as much time at fashion shows as on rock tours, Woods **is** as known for his classic cutting skills ("I just love cutting people's hair off," he says) as his big, sexy styles created with velcro rollers and broken up with surf styling spray (see right).

3. His unique retro sets **continue to look** modern and glamorous on his current celeb clients, such as Gwen Stefani.

The Attributes following the intensive process here are positive, and concern the men's abilities and success. Some of the pre-modifying adjectives in the Attributes of these intensive verbs can be said to indirectly index femininity: 'glamorous' in (3) and 'sexy' in (2) usually collocate with female referents (Caldas-Coulthard and Moon 2010: 109). We can interpret this as due to the fact that hairdressing and related beauty industries are stereotypically associated with women and gay men; in order for the idea of men operating in female-dominated industries to cohere, they have to be described using language that performs normative gender identities.

In the true-life stories, Attributes of intensive verbs with male agents are most frequently noun phrases that have a naming function (59, 26.5%). For example, in a clause like 'he **was** a joiner', or 'he **is** a brilliant dad', the Attributes describe the male agent in terms of his occupation or relationship role. These noun phrase Attributes with a naming function can be categorized into different semantic themes.

Kinship relations is the most prominent theme of noun phrase Attributes with a naming function in the true-life stories. These terms mostly denote fatherhood: 'daddy', 'father', 'dad' and 'stepdad'. This is indicative of the tendency for the true-life stories to revolve around family relations. Some of the noun Attributes in Table 7.6 can also be interpreted as hyponyms of *good/bad*, suggesting that men are presented in terms of positive and negative states: as well as the negatively modified nouns, the Attributes in the 'criminal' category could also arguably denote negative representations, as could some of the metaphorical Attributes:

Table 7.6 Noun phrase attributes of relational intensive processes in the true-life stories grouped into semantic fields

Category of attribute	Example lexis	Frequency	Proportion of total attributes (%)
Kinship relations	A brilliant dad	13	22
Proper nouns	Keith Todd	9	15.3
Metaphorical	A monster	7	11.9
Positively modified nouns	Such a nice guy	7	11.9
Criminal	A killer	5	8.5
Neutral nouns	The first man	4	6.8
Friendship	My confidant	3	5.1
Negatively modified nouns	A weak, controlling man	3	5.1
Occupation	A joiner	3	5.1
Romantic relationship	Husband	3	5.1
Body part	His stomach	2	3.4
Total		59	

1. I put that ad in the paper looking for love. But all I found **was** <u>a monster</u>

   (*Real People*)

2. Giovanni Cruz **is** <u>a contender</u> in our latest competition, Britain's Got Love Rats.

   (*Take a Break*)

3. David was so kind and gentle… *Could he really **be** <u>a murderer</u>?*

   (*Real People*)

The first two examples here contain metaphorical Attributes with negative connotations. In (1), the decision to use a relational construct 'was a monster', where the antagonist is an Attribute of a process indicating his state of being, as opposed to, say, a manner adverbial modifying a material process, such as 'he acted monstrously', is arguably more dramatic, and means that the reader is more likely to interpret his actions as attributable to his 'monster' status, rather than human folly. In (2), the male antagonist Giovanni is not literally a 'contender' in a competition; this label serves to emphasize a negative evaluation of him as a cheat. In (3), the negative connotations of the criminal Attribute 'murderer' are foregrounded by the juxtaposition with the positive evaluative adjectives 'kind' and 'gentle', again for dramatic effect.

7.4.2 Possessive Processes

The survey is the text type containing the greatest proportion of possessive relational processes (see Table 7.5), which indicates that men are presented mostly in terms of what they have rather than what they are like. An analysis of the kinds of Attributes related to these processes showed that they are mainly personal attributes, and the processes often occur in a sexual context. The decision to use possessive, rather than intensive processes creates distance between the Carrier and the Attribute. For example:

Should a girl ever make the first move? [...] 'It s how I met my girlfriend,
I didn't **have** the balls to approach her.' *Mathew, 24, Oxford*

(More)

The attribute 'balls' is a metaphor for 'courage' (discussed in Sect.
7.3.3). By treating bravery as a separate entity to his identity, rather
than using an intensive process, such as 'I wasn't brave enough to
approach her', the reader can interpret courage as a quality that can be
acquired, rather than forming an innate part of male identity. Similarly,
there are instances where Attributes of the process 'has' are represented
as objects, as in:

Would you rather [...]

> He **has** years of experience in bed 40%
> He **has** a willingness to learn in bed 60%

(Glamour)

As discussed in Chapter 5, male body part nouns reduce men to their
constituent parts; talking about personal attributes as separate entities
using possessive processes could also be interpreted as having a similar
compartmentalizing effect.

7.4.3   Circumstantial Processes

The fiction text type is shown to contain the highest frequency of circumstantial processes (see Table 7.5); these texts are therefore most
concerned with where men are in the fictional world. The majority of
Attributes involved in circumstantial processes in the fiction texts are
introduced by deictic adverbs, as in 'he's here waiting for you.' In the
true-life stories, which also have a higher proportion of circumstantial
relational processes, the majority of Attributes of Circumstantial processes denote domestic settings. As the true-life stories frequently feature
representations of criminal men, some Attributes are connected to judi-
cial settings, as in: 'David was in custody awaiting trial' (*Real People*).

There are also some metaphorical examples of this, for instance, the prepositional phrase 'on the edge of legality' in 'He's lived on the edge of legality for years' (*That's Life*), presenting legality as a tangible object. Similarly, 'bars' in the alliterative prepositional phrase 'behind bars' acts as a metonym for 'prison'.

A small number of Attributes denote a connection between the male Carrier and romantic relationships with female participants presented as circumstances:

1. I thought I **was** <u>in love</u>, behaving more like a teenager than a middle-aged father-of-two.

   (*Best*)

2. 'I want to **be** <u>with you</u>,' he said, clamping his lips on mine.

   (*That's Life*)

The prepositional phrase 'in love' could be interpreted as an example of the conceptual metaphor LOVE IS A PLACE. This has the effect of presenting *love* as a tangible object, which arguably makes it easier to conceptualize than non-metaphorical expressions, with 'love' as a material action process, such as 'I thought I loved her'. The prepositional phrase 'with you' in (2) presents the relationship in terms of deictic proximity, focusing on the physical, as opposed to emotional connection. As with the 'in love' example, this decision also presents the abstract notion of a romantic relationship in more concrete terms, reifying its importance for a successful performance of (heterosexual) masculinity.

7.5   Body Part Agency

In addition to men as holonymic (complete body) agents of actions (Nash 1990: 139), men are also represented with agency meronymically, in terms of body parts. While there is only a small number of instances

Table 7.7   Frequencies of processes with body part agency across the corpus

Text type	Frequency of processes with male agents	Frequency of processes with male body part agency	% of total processes
Advertorials	35	0	0
Columns	371	4	1
Features	886	6	1
Fiction	586	17	3
Interviews	1952	2	0
Letters	132	3	2
Listicles	88	0	0
Problem pages	544	3	1
Profiles	105	0	0
True-life stories	1380	25	2
Reports	238	3	1
Reviews	1	0	0
Surveys	207	6	3

of male body part agency in the corpus, body part agency is an interesting stylistic phenomenon with implications for ideology construction.

Table 7.7 shows that the text types with the highest proportion of male body part agency are those based on a narrative structure, namely the fictional texts and the true-life stories. This is not surprising, given that body part agency is a well-documented stylistic feature of fictional genres (see, for example, Burton 1982; Mills 1994; Wareing 1994), but what is interesting is the ways in which, as with holonymic processes, the *kinds* of processes with body part agency differ according to text type.

7.5.1   Meronymic Violence

The raw figures in Table 7.7 show the true-life story text type to contain the highest number of tokens of male body part agency, and these frequently present actions with violent connotations. The most frequent body part in the role of agent is the eyes, as demonstrated by the concordance lines in Fig 7.2:

1. I shook hands with Lee, his brown	eyes	lingered on mine. 'Nice to meet
2. thought. I opened the door. Lee's	eyes	were bloodshot. He looked as if
3. ed? ' I asked. But instead of his	eyes	welling up with tears, they bega
4. Throwing me on the bed, his brown	eyes	danced with hate. 'I want to be
5. cried, backing away from him. His	eyes	glazed with tears. 'I 'm so so
6. was lying in a wooden coffin. His	eyes	shut as if he was sleeping peac
7. t. John 's face was white and his	eyes	were wide with horror . Suddenly
8. look at him, but I could feel his	eyes	bore into me. I was flabbergast
9. locked the doors. As his soulless	eyes	bore into me, I felt like a vuln
10. ht when Ryan stormed round. His	eyes	were glazed, his speech slurred
11. his eyes welling up with tears,	they	began roving over my body. 'You

Fig. 7.2 Concordance of 'eyes' as agent of process in the true-life stories

The processes performed by men's eyes in the true-life stories are either intensive relational, material action or behavioral processes. They are therefore either described in terms of their state of being, or how they are acting. The material action 'bore' and behavioral actions 'twisted', 'glazed' and 'danced' arguably have violent connotations, while behavioral actions 'began roving' and 'lingered' have sexual implications ('they' refers to 'eyes' anaphorically here). These intensive processes present the Attributes associated with eyes as static, rather than dynamic qualities. This corresponds to Jeffries' assertion that descriptions using intensive as opposed to possessive processes in women's magazines create a closer connection between the participant and the Attribute in constructions of female agency (2007: 178).

Other violent actions in the true-life stories are attributed to meronyms of the hand and face:

1. He raped me, his sausage fingers **choking** my throat...

(*Real People*)

2. As his fist **slammed** into my cheek, the room span around me.

(Love It)

3. Spit **trickled** down his jaw and his cheeks **flushed** red with anger

(Love It)

Presenting these actions meronymically has the effect of reducing the distance between the Actor and the process; the first example reformulated as 'he choked me with his sausage fingers', using a holonymic agent, appears to increase the proximity of the participant to the process, and consequently the amount of responsibility attributed to the Actor. In the second example, the process in the main clause is a material event, performed by an inanimate Actor, 'the room'. The decision to present the room as the active participant rather than the narrator further subordinates her role here. In example (3) from the same text, the agency of saliva also arguably connotes animalistic behavior.

In his analysis of women's magazine fiction, Nash interprets the agency afforded to male body parts as representing the totality of men's activity: 'the man vibrates in all his parts' (1990: 43). However, meronymic representations of male violence in the true-life stories have a dehumanizing effect, and imply that the antagonist is *not* in control of his actions. This is similar to the kinds of stylistic techniques used in newspaper coverage of male sexual violence, where offenders are named using terms with animalistic connotations, such as *beast* and *monster* as a way of dehumanizing them and making them appear abnormal (see, for example, Clark 1992; O'Hara 2012; Soothill and Walby 1991).

7.5.2 Physical Attractiveness

In the fiction text type, material processes and intensive relational processes also make up the largest proportion of processes with male agency. Body part agency functions not to present violent images of male behavior, but more positive actions and appearances, as the following examples from 'Just Passing Through' in *My Weekly* demonstrate:

1. The silence between them stretched and stretched, his warm, honey-brown eyes **searching** her profile, willing her to look at him.
2. His eyes **twinkled** mischievously, and she could feel herself blushing.
3. Joe blinked, long dark lashes **feathering** momentarily against ivory skin,
4. the corners of his elegant lips **twitching** mischievously.

In these examples, the actions performed by the body parts have more positive connotations, and there is evidence that the male holonyms are evaluated as attractive to the female recipients, which the reader may infer from the pre-modifying adjectival descriptions in (1) and (3), the manner adverbial 'mischievously' in (4) and the female participant's reaction in (2). Examples (2) and (4) are coded as behavioral processes, in that they are intransitive physiological processes, where (1) is coded as a material action intention process, as there is an affected participant. In this example, the female participant is the passive recipient of 'his' gaze, which is not explicitly encoded in the clause in (2), as the verb is an intransitive process, but implied by her reaction ('she could feel herself blushing').

7.6   Summary

On the whole, the magazine writers are most concerned with presenting the men in these texts as acting or being, rather than speaking or thinking. Analysis of material action processes showed that these mostly relate to sexual activity, and that women are most frequently the affected participants of material actions in the surveys and true-life stories. In the surveys, these were mostly actions regarding men's romantic relationships with women; in the true-life stories, these mainly expressed violence towards women. In the listicles and reports, a higher proportion of material actions expressed stereotypically gendered practices, such as the rejection of beautification processes and other practices associated with femininity such as shopping, practicing DIY, and drinking. These are all practices associated with the New Lad discussed in the literature on men's magazines (see Edwards 2003; Attwood 2005).

The most frequent type of relational process was intensive processes, suggesting that the magazine writers were more likely to present men in terms of what they are like, depicting Attributes of physical appearance or personality, rather than in terms of their possessions or circumstances. As well as instances of holonymic agency, the kinds of processes performed by male body parts were mostly present in the texts based on narrative form, the true-life stories and the fiction text types. In the true-life stories, processes performed by body parts were mostly violent actions; in the fiction texts, they usually depicted physical attractiveness. This indicates that the true-life stories are on the whole more interested in presenting men as doing 'bad things'; the fiction texts are more likely to depict the more desirable facets of masculinity.

The overall picture of how men behave in the texts is therefore contradictory: on the one hand men are objects of desire for women, but they are simultaneously a threat. This confirms Ballaster et al.'s (1991: 9) assertion that: 'there is an evident tension between the need to confirm the centrality and desirability of men in all women's lives and the equally insistent recognition of men as a problem for and threat to women.' The actions that men perform in the texts are both attractive to and problematic for women, reflecting this overall tension between men as both desirable and threatening.

References

Attenborough, F. T. (2011). Complicating the Sexualisation Thesis: The Media, Gender and 'Sci-Candy'. *Discourse & Society, 22*(6), 659–676.

Attwood, F. (2005). "Tits and Ass and Porn and Fighting": Male Heterosexuality in Magazines for Men. *International Journal of Cultural Studies, 8*(1), 83–100.

Ballaster, R., Beetham, M., Frazer, E., & Hebron, S. (1991). *Women's Worlds: Ideology, Femininity and Women's Magazines*. Basingstoke: Palgrave Macmillan.

Burton, D. (1982). Through Glass Darkly: Through Dark Glasses: On Stylistics and Political Commitment. In R. Carter (Ed.), *Language and Literature* (pp. 195–214). London: Allen & Unwin.

Butler, J. (1990). *Gender Trouble: Feminism and the Subversion of Identity.* London: Routledge.

Caldas-Coulthard, C. R., & Moon, R. (2010). 'Curvy, Hunky, Kinky': Using Corpora as Tools for Critical Analysis. *Discourse and Society, 21*(2), 99–133.

Cameron, D. (1992). Naming of Parts: Gender, Culture and Terms for the Penis Among American College Students. *American Speech, 67*(4), 367–382.

Clark, K. (1992). The Linguistics of Blame: Representations of Women in *The Sun's* Reporting of Crimes of Sexual Violence. In M. Toolan (Ed.), *Language, Text and Context: Essays in Stylistics* (pp. 208–224). London: Routledge.

Edwards, T. (2003). Sex, Booze and Fags: Masculinity, Style and Men's Magazines. In B. Benwell (Ed.), *Masculinity and Men's Lifestyle Magazines* (pp. 132–146). Oxford: Blackwell.

Farvid, P., & Braun, V. (2006). "Most of Us Guys Are Raring to Go Anytime, Anyplace, Anywhere": Male and Female Sexuality in *Cleo* and *Cosmo. Sex Roles, 55*, 295–310.

Fowler, R. (1991). *Language in the News: Discourse and Ideology in the Press.* London: Routledge.

Halliday, M. (1985). *An Introduction to Functional Grammar.* London: Arnold.

Jeffries, L. (2007). *Textual Construction of the Female Body: A Critical Discourse Approach.* Basingstoke: Palgrave Macmillan.

Labov, W., & Waletzky, J. (1967). Narrative Analysis. In J. Helm (Ed.), *Essays on the Verbal and Visual Arts* (pp. 12–44). Seattle: University of Washington Press.

McLoughlin, L. (2008). The Construction of Female Sexuality in the "Sex Special": Transgression or Containment in Magazines' Information on Sexuality for Girls? *Gender and Language, 2*(2), 171–195.

Mills, S. (1994). Close Encounters of a Feminist Kind: Transitivity Analysis of Pop Lyrics. In K. Wales (Ed.), *Feminist Linguistics in Literary Criticism* (pp. 137–156). Cambridge: D.S. Brewer.

Nash, W. (1990). *Language in Popular Fiction.* London: Routledge.

O'Hara, S. (2012). Monsters Playboys, Virgins and Whores: Rape Myths in the News Media's Coverage of Sexual Violence. *Language and Literature, 21*(3), 247–259.

Semino, E., & Short, M. (2004). *Corpus Stylistics: Speech, Writing and Thought Presentation in a Corpus of English Writing.* London: Routledge.

Simpson, P. (1993). *Language, Ideology and Point of View.* London: Routledge.

Simpson, P. (2004). *Stylistics: A Resource Book for Students*. London: Routledge.

Soothill, K., & Walby, S. (1991). *Sex Crime in the News*. London: Routledge.

Talbot, M. M. (1997). An Explosion Deep Inside Her: Women's Desire and Popular Romance Fiction. In K. Harvey & C. Shalom (Eds.), *Language and Desire: Encoding Sex, Romance and Intimacy* (pp. 106–122). London: Routledge.

Wareing, S. (1994). And Then He Kissed Her.... In K. Wales (Ed.), *Feminist Linguistics in Literary Criticism* (pp. 117–136). Cambridge: D.S. Brewer.

8

Implicit Masculinity: Assuming and Implying

Assumed and implied meanings are forms of implicit language, those that operate at the discourse-level of a text. Assuming and implying meanings are powerful ways a text can influence a reader's viewpoint, because presupposing or implying ideas can make them appear to be common sense (see Jeffries 2010: 93). In some ways, then, processes of assuming and implying have the greatest potential for constructing ideologies of masculinity in women's magazines, because they involve implicitly drawing on the reader's background assumptions about gender to make notions of how men do or should behave appear 'common sense', and therefore naturalized.

Assuming and implying are achieved via the linguistic processes of presupposition and implicature (see Sect. 8.1 below). As with the other textual-conceptual tools, 'assuming' and 'implying' are not simply less technical names for 'presupposition' and 'implicature', rather, the two sets of terms reflect the idea that presupposition is one way in which texts can assume meanings; implicature is one way in which texts imply meanings. The functions of assuming and implying are therefore part of the 'ideational metafunction' of language (Halliday 1985), in that they are ways of creating world-views. In reality, the distinction between

© The Author(s) 2019
L. Coffey-Glover, *Men in Women's Worlds*,
https://doi.org/10.1057/978-1-137-57555-5_8

'assuming' and 'implying' is a subtle one, and one which non-linguists often do not make when they talk about the 'underlying meaning' of texts. The technical categories help us to make a broad distinction between background information that the reader brings to the text (presupposition) and meanings which the reader infers from reading the text (implicature).

8.1 Presupposition and Implicature

8.1.1 Presupposition

Presupposition refers to assumptions that are triggered by grammatical structures, and is thus a type of pragmatic inference (Levinson 1983: 167). Unlike implicature (see Sect. 8.1.2), presupposition can be can textually located specific lexical triggers. There are two main types of presupposition: existential and logical. Existential presuppositions assume the existence of a particular individual or object, and are most commonly triggered using definite articles, demonstratives or possessive pronouns (such as 'the', 'those' or 'their'). Logical presuppositions, on the other hand, assume the occurrence of an action. The possible set of triggers for logical presuppositions is much more open-ended than that for existential presuppositions. However, Levinson (1983: 181–184) provides a (by no means exhaustive) list of possible triggers, which I used as a guide for identifying logical presuppositions in the corpus. These include:

- Change of state verbs ('Peter **stopped** smoking' presupposes *Peter smoked previously*)
- Factive verbs ('can I **remind** you that you are under oath' presupposes *you are under oath*)
- Iterative words ('he kissed her **again**' presupposes *he kissed her*)
- Comparative constructions ('Louise is **bigger** than Molly' presupposes *Molly is big*)
- Cleft constructions ('it was Sara that stole the money' presupposes *the money was stolen*)

Given the open-ended nature of presupposition triggers, it is unlikely that I will have managed to capture *all* instances of presupposition that would be relevant to the question of masculinity construction, but it made the search much more manageable. The analysis provided ample evidence for patterns of gendered discourses constructed via presupposition.

8.1.2 Implicature

Conventional implicatures are implied meanings that are associated with particular lexical items by convention (Grice 1975). For example, the coordinating conjunction *but* always implies that there is some kind of contrast between the propositions or entities on either side of it:

1. Louis likes jazz music, but he also listens to electronica.

2. Louis likes jazz music, and he also listens to electronica.

If we compare the effects of the different coordinating conjunctions in (1) and (2), 'but' in (1) implies some kind of contrast between the noun phrases 'jazz music' and 'electronica', whereas we might infer from (2) that these noun phrases are being treated as equivalents (see Chapter 6). Therefore, the implied meaning of contrast in (1) can be gleaned from the conventional meaning of the word *but*.

The above examples show that conventional implicatures are textually triggered in a similar manner to presupposition. Conversational implicatures, on the other hand, are implied meanings that cannot be inferred from individual lexical items, but are generated as a result of a 'flout' of one or more of Grice's four maxims of conversation. Together, these form the Co-Operative Principle: 'make your contribution such as it is required, at the stage at which it occurs, by the accepted purpose or direction of the talk exchange in which you are engaged' (1989: 26). Grice's maxims express expectations of behavior in conversation, as follows:

Maxim of Quality
Do not say what you believe to be false.
Do not say that for which you lack evidence.

Maxim of Quantity
Make your contribution as informative as is required for the purposes of the exchange.
Do not make your contribution more informative than is required.

Maxim of Relation
Be relevant.

Maxim of Manner
Avoid obscurity of expression.
Avoid ambiguity.
Be brief.
Be orderly.

Implicature works on the basis that, as hearers, we seek out meaning in interaction with our interlocutors; when confronted with an utterance that does not adhere to our expectations, we nevertheless attempt to glean meaning from it.

Conversational implicatures are defeasible: they can be cancelled by adding additional premises to the original ones (Levinson 1983: 114). For example, if I say to a friend 'I'm really skint at the moment', this could be interpreted as a request for money. If my friend treats this as a request but I do not wish my friend to feel imposed upon, I can defease the situation by asserting that 'I'm not asking for money, I was merely stating a fact'. Conversational implicatures are also context-dependent and non-detachable: they are tied to the semantic content of what is said rather than to linguistic form (Levinson 1983: 116). This means that they need the 'right' circumstances to take effect, often involving access to appropriate cultural knowledge.

While implicatures are usually examined as an aspect of spoken interaction, I argue that the same principles of inference can also be applied to a written genre like women's magazines, since, as in ordinary conversation, the reader is required to 'read between the lines'. This idea is also particularly relevant to women's magazines as a 'tissue of voices' (Talbot

1992: 176) that attempts to set up an interpersonal relationship with the reader through, for example, representations of dialogue and rhetorical questions.

Given that implicatures are generally not tied to specific linguistic triggers, I searched manually for these using the list of sentences I had compiled for the analysis of transitivity (see Chapter 7), looking at the co-texts of sentences where necessary. As I was only interested in the creation of implicatures relating to men and masculinity, restricting the search parameters to sentences containing male subjects was the most sensible way of accessing this type of pragmatic meaning.

8.2 Assumed and Implied Discourses of Masculinity

The thematic categories of gendered discourses set out in Table 8.1 are those constructed via presupposition and implicature in the women's magazine corpus; while assumed and implied meanings have different formal realizations, they both work to produce implicit ideologies that are uncovered by the reader, therefore the two processes are considered together in the analysis of presupposition and implicature.

Table 8.1 shows that around a quarter of the assumed and implied meanings concerning men construct discourses about men's sexuality and behavior in relationships, and also reflect stereotypical ideas about gendered practices. The specific interests evident here conform to some of those associated with hegemonic masculinity, such as an interest in sport and cars. The ideas that 'beautification processes are for women', and 'men hate shopping' are interesting in that they rely on the notion that behaving 'like women' is perceived as negative. The idea that men are naturally violent or aggressive is the most frequent discourse relating to non-desirable qualities, while the most frequently assumed or implied desirable quality is that of physical attractiveness.

The 'non-normative' category contains implications of men's non-conformity to expected behavior, which are also often imbued with negative evaluation. For example, the following 'man fact' (*More*), implies that watching TV soap drama is a deviation from expected male behavior:

Table 8.1 Frequencies of assumed and implied discourses of masculinity in the women's magazine corpus

Thematic category	Gendered discourses	Frequency	Total frequency in category	% of total frequency
Sexuality and relationships	Men are carnally driven	36	72	26
	Men are promiscuous	8		
	Men are commitmentphobes	8		
	Men are naturally visual	6		
	Men shouldn't be afraid of commitment	1		
Stereotypically gendered practices	Beautification processes are for women	29	68	24
	Men are excessive drinkers	11		
	Men hate shopping	10		
	Technology is for men	7		
	Sport is a male pastime	6		
	Men are obsessed with cars	5		
Non-desirable qualities	Men are violent/aggressive	14	39	14
	Men are stupid	10		
	Men are unhygienic	6		
	Men behave badly	4		
	Bad men are ugly	4		
	Men are hypochondriacs	1		

(continued)

Table 8.1 (continued)

Thematic category	Gendered discourses	Frequency	Total frequency in category	% of total frequency
Desirable qualities	Men should be sexually attractive	16	36	13
	Men should be successful	6		
	Men should be generous	4		
	Men should be kind	3		
	Men should be charming	2		
	Men should be romantic	2		
	Authority figures are attractive	1		
	Men should be confident	1		
	Men should be modest	1		
Heteronormativity	Heterosexuality is normative	14	26	9
	Homosexuality is bad	12		
Gender and sexuality	Men and women are different	7	16	6
	The gendered division of labor	6		
	Men are all the same	2		
	Gay people are different to straight people	1		
Non-normative behavior			14	5

12% of men can't live without their favourite TV programme. *Virgin Media*, September 2008

This small percentage of the male population represents minority behavior. The declarative statement could be said to flout the maxim of quantity, in that it does not explain why this is noteworthy information. The low percentage, and schematic knowledge of society's gendered assumptions about viewing habits, may cause the reader to infer that this is presented as significant because television soaps are conventionally perceived as attracting female viewers. In the analysis that follows I do not discuss examples from this category, as some of the implicatures generated can also be discussed in terms of the other themes; some express non-normative behavior that also relate to the promotion of heteronormative sexual practices, or the idea that men should dominate in relationships, for example. The main discourses of masculinity I explore in this chapter are those relating to the idea that men are carnally driven; that beautification processes index femininity, not masculinity; that men are naturally aggressive; that heterosexuality is normative, and that men are the dominant partner in relationships.

8.2.1 'Men as Carnally Driven'

The most prominent ideological discourse of masculinity constructed via assuming and implying is the notion that men are driven by their carnal instincts. The majority of these come from feature articles, which frequently represent men as having a high sexual drive, promiscuous and driven by sexual urges.

'Tough Love' is a feature article from *Pride* magazine, which provides dating advice from Gerry Stergiopoulos, author of dating guidebook *Treat Them Mean, Keep Them Keen* (2008). The 'dating tips' advise women to refrain from sexual contact with men during the first three dates of a new relationship, because men will 'lose interest'. This idea is clearly predicated on the notion that men are primarily motivated by sex, and that women are not:

1. No kissing: The aim is to create intrigue and make him wait, no matter how attracted you are to him. Unfold gradually without handing yourself over to him on a plate.

2. Make him wait: If you like him after the first three meetings, then continue seeing him. However, don't jump straight into bed with him - it's better to make him wait.

3. If you give too much too soon, he will quickly lose interest.

The imperative 'make him wait' in extracts (1) and (2) implies that men are naturally keen to engage in sexual activity with women. This works via conventional implicature, rather than a flout of the maxims, as the implied meaning is triggered by the conventional use of *wait*, meaning 'to defer action' (*OED Online*). The idea that men are keen to engage in sexual activity is also evident in (3), where the implication is that men will lose interest because they have already got what they want, namely sex. The reader is likely to infer this because of prior knowledge of assumptions about men's behavior in the context of dating rituals. The first instance of adverb *too* in this example implies that to have sex with a man at this stage is a bad idea, while the second implies that there is an appropriate time to do so. This is also due to the conventional meaning of *too* with its negative connotations.

As well as advice on dating, feature articles giving advice on sex are also reveal the taken-for-grantedness of the 'male sexual drive' discourse (Holloway 1984). This is evident in the following examples from an instructional article in *Cosmopolitan* called 'The Nice Girl's Guide to Naughty Sex':

1. Whispering in his ear is a fail-safe method of planting your fantasy - describe it and he'll be hooked.

2. Women are more creative and most men will be happy to go along with what you suggest...

3. 'Some men 'pester' their partners into trying sexual acts, so be firm and state simply what you want or don't want,' says Rachel. And if he still pushes? 'Make sure your 'no' was clear.

In example (1), the proposition 'he'll be hooked' appears to flout the maxim of quantity, as it is not clear *why* describing a sexual fantasy would get a man's attention (note also that the existence of such a desire is presupposed via possessive pronoun 'your'). This is contextual information the reader might expect for the text to be fully co-operative. The reader could infer from this the implicature that he will be 'hooked' whatever the fantasy is because, ultimately, he will just be pleased that sex is a possibility, because all men are driven by their sexual urges. The choice of adjectival metaphorical adjective 'hooked' also flouts the maxim of quality, in that he will not literally be 'hooked'; men are therefore framed here in terms of food (fish are caught on hooks), which could be interpreted as equivalent to the 'women-as-sex-objects-are-food' metaphor (Hines 1999) represented by terms such as *honey* or *crumpet*. However, unlike other such metaphors for women (discussed in Chapter 6), there is an implication that the woman's role here is predatory, which may reinforce an ideology of women as temptresses.

Men's inherent carnality is also taken for granted in extract (2), triggered via premodifying adjective 'most': the reader can only make sense of this text if she takes as uncontroversial truth the proposition that the majority of men are happy to accept women's (sexual) suggestions. The resulting implicature is that men will go along with the woman's suggestions because they are being given the opportunity to have sex, which is ultimately all men care about. In extract (3), the hypothetical clause 'and if he still pushes?' presents persistence as a possibility in this situation; this implies that men are sexually aggressive and domineering in relationships, and therefore the reader can expect to encounter this behavior herself. The advice given to the reader to refuse male pestering is also reminiscent of rape prevention programs that instruct women to 'just say no' to male sexual advances (Cameron 2007: 92). This is likely to evoke the reader's schema for rape and sexual assault, which may well include the notion of men as predatory sexual beings.

Features articles like those from *Cosmopolitan* and *Pride* discussed above have a 'pedagogical' function, in that their role is to teach the reader how to be a woman (Jeffries 2007), through relaying information, and often relying on testimony from 'expert' voices. This makes them susceptible to ideology construction. In the case of instructional features on the topic of sexuality and relationships, this involves making assumptions and implying what a (heterosexual) relationship should be like, and in turn how men do and should behave. These themes are evident in a feature article from *Best* magazine, which lists 18 things women should do in order to improve their sex lives:

> **4 Go solo** Female masturbation is still quite taboo, with one study revealing that only 62 per cent of women, versus 92 per cent of men, masturbate.

The idea that female masturbation is relatively unusual is propounded by these statistics; adverb 'only' generates the conventional implicature that 62 is a low percentage. The reader may infer that the reason for this gender difference is that men have higher sex drives than women, underlined by the notion that female masturbation is 'taboo': the reader could conclude from this that men are given license to masturbate *because* of the fact that they are assumed to have stronger libidos than women.

One report article from *More* magazine, 'Man Facts', provides several statistics about male behaviors, collected from various commercial sources. These are presented in the form of unmodalized, declarative statements, often followed by some kind of evaluative comment from the magazine writers. The 'facts' listed below all reiterate the idea that men are carnally driven, via processes of presupposition and/or implicature:

1. 1.7 million British men admitted they would lie about their sexual past in order to get a girl into bed. *www.benaughty.com survey, July 2008*

2. 6% of men spend meetings imagining what it would be like to have sex with their female colleagues. *VisitBritain, September 2008*

3. Men are likelier to ask out a woman who's wearing red because the colour makes them think of sex. *Journal of Personal and Social Psychology, October 2008*

In example (1) the factive verb 'admitted' presupposes the clausal complement, that men *do* lie about their pasts in order persuade women to sleep with them (albeit guiltily!). While in extract (2) the figure is small (logically 94% of men therefore *don't* spend meetings thinking about sleeping with their colleagues), the fact that this is the statistic the magazine writers have decided to focus on means that these propositions are those being foregrounded. This arguably flouts the maxim of quantity, in that it neglects the reverse statistic, generating an implicature that men are constantly thinking about sex. In example (3), the superlative form of the adjective *likelier* creates a logical presupposition, assuming that men are likely to ask out any woman, regardless of the color they're wearing. This potentially flouts the maxim of relevance: for the reader to accept this 'Man Fact' as relevant, noteworthy information, she must infer that sex is a primary motivation for pursuing a woman, and that therefore men are motivated by sex. The fact that the last statistic comes from an academic, peer reviewed journal could also make the reader more trusting of its scientific 'truth': for example, Cameron (2007, 2010) shows how the findings of scientific studies of sex differences are often (mis)used by the media to perpetuate gender stereotypes.

Like the instructional features, reports have a pedagogical function, in that they are intended to relay factual information to the reader about a particular topic, often including statistics. Because reports are arguably intended to present the 'truth' about a topic, the reader is perhaps less likely to challenge or even recognize the ideologies in them.

Also featured in *More* magazine is the listicle entitled '14 things you should never ask a man to do', in which two items contribute to the idea that men are driven by their sexual urges:

11. To get rid of his porn collection.

13. Prove he loves you by punching that bloke who pinched your bum.

The masculine pronouns 'his' and 'he' refer to the male population as a whole in the first example, and the reader's (assumed) partner in the second. The possessive pronoun *his* in the first extract presupposes that men do indeed have porn collections. The text flouts the maxim of quantity, because it does not provide an explanation of why one should never ask a man to get rid of his porn collection, the implication being that a man's porn collection is 'natural' and a highly valued item, because all men are sex obsessed. The reader can only access this implicature if her schema for men includes the idea that men have a high sex drive, and/or that they are driven by their sexual urges, and that being interested in pornography is indicative of these attributes. More subtly, the relative clause post-modifying 'bloke' produces the logical presupposition that a man has indeed committed this sexual assault. The fact that the writers directly address the reader using second person pronouns *you* and *your* also contributes to the idea that the reader should expect this behavior, particularly because of the existential presuppositions created by possessive pronoun *your*. To assume the occurrence of such sexist behavior like this is problematic, because it could result in women expecting to encounter this kind of behavior, or at least perceiving it as a common occurrence, and normative.

Problem pages are intended to provide advice and guidance to women, and the problems featured are often related to men, sex and relationships. In the following problem page from *Company*, the advice is to exploit men's natural virility for her own gain:

DRIVING ME CRAZY!
My boyfriend has an unhealthy obsession with his car. He spends every weekend washing it, driving it, talking about it, talking to it. There are definitely three of us in this relationship. What can I do?
Emily, 22, Reading

Put your foot down on his clutch, grab his gear stick and show him who's boss. If he persists in giving his motor preferential treatment over you, might I suggest you take up knitting in bed until he realizes the error of his ways…

The propositions expressed in the *if*-clause of the agony aunt's answer appear to flout the maxim of quantity: it is not explained what the consequences of the reader knitting in bed would be; this negligence of information is denoted graphologically here via ellipsis, a writing convention that signals to the reader that she must 'fill in the gaps'.

To reach the conclusion that the man would react negatively (rather than positively) to her knitting in bed, the reader must infer that he would rather be having sex than watching her knit; and is likely to reach this interpretation because of her schematic associations of beds and what people do in them, and perhaps also the traditional notion of knitting as a solitary pastime for older women, with its negative semantic prosody. The woman's refusal to have sex can only serve as punishment for the man's behavior if it is assumed that he would be distressed by the situation. The fact that the agony aunt does not know the man in question means that she is assuming that because he is a man, he will be aggrieved, given that all men have a high sex drive. It is assumed the woman would *not* suffer similarly for being deprived of sexual activity, drawing on the conventional stereotype that women have lower libidos than men.

The idea that women can use men's sexual urges to their advantage is expressed in another problem page from *Scarlet*, called 'Pleasure Aunts':

> My bloke's flat is so filthy that it's actually putting me off having sex with him - how can I get him to change his ways?
>
> Tell him his Stig of the Dump routine is seriously dampening your sexual urges towards him and he'll soon sit up and listen.

The proposition expressed in 'and he'll soon sit up and listen' arguably flouts the maxim of quantity, because it does not provide an explanation why this would help. The implicature arising from this is that the man would view his partner's reduced libido as negative because sex is important to him, again because it is assumed that as a man he will have a high sex drive.

The following text, from *Cosmopolitan*, is in answer to a reader concerned that her cellulite is discouraging her boyfriend from having sex with her:

> We take microscopes to our bodies, but men see us in soft focus - at least during sex. I assure you, when he's busy behind you, it's not your cellulite he's looking at.

The cleft sentence 'it's not your...' presupposes the proposition that he *is* looking at something. The decision to highlight the negative proposition that the man is not looking the woman's cellulite does not provide the reader with sufficient information to be fully co-operative, because we have not been told what the man *is* looking at, with the writer flouting the maxim of quantity. The reader is likely to infer that he is focused on her bottom; reaching this interpretation relies on the assumption that men are preoccupied by sexual desires, one way or another.

8.2.2 'Beautification Processes Are for Women'

The second most prominent theme of discourses constructed via presupposition and implicature are those relating to stereotypically gendered practices, and most prevalent is the idea that paying attention to personal appearance should be a specifically feminine pursuit (see Table 8.1). Examples of this idea were mostly found in the glossy sub-corpus. One particular feature article from *Company*, 'The New Man Make-up' explores these stereotypical ideas about make-up as directly indexing femininity. An article dedicated to the topic of male cosmetics suggests that it is interesting or unusual in some way—a deviation from the expected norm. A number of points suggest that the idea of men wearing make-up is deemed unusual behavior. The article begins with:

> There's a new breed of young men who are comfortable with face scrubs, masks and moisturisers - now they simply want to take it one step further.

The decision to postmodify 'men' with the relative clause 'who are comfortable...' arguably flouts the maxim of quantity in that it provides too much information; the implicature arising from this might be that this information is in contrast to an assumption that men would *not* be comfortable with beautification processes, because it is not seen as normative male behavior. The pre-modifier 'new' here also creates an existential presupposition that there is a 'new breed' of men who are different to 'old men' who are not comfortable with these practices. While the existence of this 'new breed' of men implies a challenge to conventional definitions of masculinity, it simultaneously demonstrates that a rejection of beautification practices indexes hegemonic masculinity. Further claims can be inferred as emphasizing the markedness of men wearing make-up:

1. This rise in the boy-next-door using make-up (Clinique found that more than one in ten men admit to borrowing their partner's beauty products) has prompted the big beauty brands to launch make-up lines aimed at British men, who want to enhance what God gave them.

2. Most men just want to look healthier, without it obvious they're wearing make-up. Then there are the men who are fully embracing their guyliner.

In extract (1), the negative prosody of verb 'admit' produces the conventional implicature that a man borrowing make-up is shameful, or at least unusual. In extract (2), the definite article 'the' in 'the men who…' presupposes the existence of men who wear 'guyliner', but intensifying adverb 'fully' highlights this behavior as a deviation from the norm. Subordinating conjunction 'then' also implies that these men are in contrast to, and therefore a deviation from, the men in the previous sentence who 'just want to look healthier'. The sense of 'just' meaning 'simply' usually carries a positive semantic prosody, and here contributes to the implicature that the majority of men who wear make-up don't want it to be obvious because it is associated with femininity. So while on the surface, this article appears to be in favor of men wearing make-up—the tagline asks 'Why should women have the monopoly on beauty tricks?'—and therefore to some extent challenges traditional gender stereotypes, an analysis of assumed and implied meanings reveals that the article can also be read as recirculating the idea of beautification as a *feminine* practice.

The examples below also demonstrate the idea that beautification processes point to prototypical femininity, and therefore should not be undertaken by men:

1. Bald private parts would look too feminine and no man should be neater than me!

(Glamour)

2. 14 things you should never ask a man to do [...]
   1. Wear 'just a tiny bit of mascara because it'll make your eyelashes look sooo long'.
   2. To give an opinion on anything that involves the phrase 'colour scheme.'

(More)

3. Only 35% of men said they'd be embarrassed to wear make-up. House of Fraser, October 2008

(More)

The adverb 'too' in example (1) creates the conventional implicature that a man having hairless genitals is undesirable, due to the negative prosody of *too* as a premodifier; the implication is that men should be masculine. Here, gender is a binary construct, despite the construction of gradable opposition: 'too' indicates that there are degrees of femininity and masculinity, but the fact that 'male femininity' is negatively evaluated serves to maintain the boundary between what are considered acceptable or unacceptable performances of (hegemonic) masculinity.

Extract (2), from the listicle '14 Things You Should Never Ask a Man to Do' in *More* magazine, specifies a series of actions that men should not be asked to perform, the implication being that these would compromise their identity as men. The dispreferred practices here are wearing make-up and having knowledge of color terminology. The first flouts the maxim of quantity, in that it does not explain why having the appearance of long eyelashes would be negative for a man. The arising implicature is that men shouldn't wear mascara because long eyelashes are considered feminine, and wearing make-up is a feminine practice. Also notable is the mock feminine speech style signaled by intensifier 'soooo'. The non-standard spelling mimics the use of an elongated vowel sound; this arguably flouts the maxim of manner, in that it could be deemed an obscure expression. However, if the reader is familiar with folklinguistic stereotypes of women's speech as involving intensifiers and evaluative adjectives like 'tiny', she will recognize this as an imitation of an exaggerated feminine speech style (see Lakoff 1975; Tannen 1990). The implication is that if a man were to wear mascara, he would become feminine, a negative state of affairs. Additionally, the reader may interpret this feminine speech style as simultaneously indexing a 'camp' male persona, given that a common folklinguistic stereotype of gay men is that they talk like women (Cameron and Kulick 2003: 74).

The second part of example (2) also flouts the maxim of quantity, generating the implicature that asking men to have an input on color schemes would be futile, because interior design is the natural domain of women. In order to reach this implicature, the reader has to access her schematic knowledge of the folklinguistic stereotype that women use more color terms than men (Lakoff 1975), or at least that men are less concerned with aesthetics.

The incompatibility of (hetero)normative masculinity and beautification is exemplified in (3), where the adverb 'only' creates the conventional implicature that more men *should* be embarrassed to wear make-up, since propositions introduced by *only* usually carry a negative prosody. To reach this implicature the reader has to draw on the assumption that the practice of wearing make-up should be a solely feminine pursuit.

8.2.3 'Men Are Aggressive'

The idea that men are naturally aggressive is also reiterated in the corpus, and has been discussed in Chapters 5 and 7 in relation to naming and transitivity strategies. It is however also expressed more implicitly via presupposition and implicature. Earlier, I discussed the predilection for true-life stories to present men as having violent tendencies in infotainment-style narratives intended as having 'shock' value. The following examples of male violence in these stories involve assuming the criminal status of the male referents in question:

1. I was allowed home from hospital in September, just in time to be at Monroe County Circuit Court to watch Stephen plead guilty to

driving with a suspended licence while **causing serious injury**, and **driving while under the influence of alcohol or drugs**.

(Pick Me Up)

2. Three months later, at the High Court in Edinburgh, Ryan pleaded guilty to **'assaulting you** to the danger of your life.'

(That's Life)

3. In October 1999, he was found guilty of **inflicting serious bodily harm on me**. He was also convicted of **robbing John, the barman and the waitress**.

(Real People)

In all three excerpts, the reader will most likely infer that the offender is guilty of the proposed charges. This is achieved linguistically via logical presupposition in the subordinate finite clauses (in bold); this syntactic structure has the effect of presupposing that the defendant did indeed commit the proposed offences. These stories are all told from the point of view of a female first person narrator, and are all stories of the violent actions of male antagonists. Given that the true-life story text type, whilst presented in narrative form, is intended to describe 'real life' events, their representations of men are likely intended to reflect how men are in the real world. Of course, as stories they are also intended to be read for entertainment, therefore their stereotyping of men as violent and aggressive could be interpreted by readers as constructed purely for the purpose of amusement. Whichever way the texts are read, though, women are being confronted with images of masculinity that accord with the dominant ideology of men as dangerous and a physical threat. This is emphasized in these examples by their specific framing as violent criminals, also achieved via references to legal discourse; these excerpts all appear at the end of the articles, and therefore act as 'sentencing statements' for the men concerned.

The following examples from interviews also demonstrate how male aggression is normalized as an inherently male attribute, regardless of celebrity or 'real-life' status:

1. Do you not prefer being muscular?
   The director Apoorva Lakhia, was insistent that we have the right physique for our role. I don't like my muscles to be too big. It gives you a sense of too much power and brings your violent streak to the fore.

   (*Asiana*)

2. Tornado is described as being 'violently destructive' and 'full of unstoppable energy'. How would you describe the real you?
   Maybe not as bad, but I'm in the Marines so obviously I've got that controlled aggression.

   (*Scarlet*)

In the first extract, from an interview with male actor Zayed Khan, possessive pronoun 'your' produces the existential presupposition that the addressee has a violent streak. 'Your' can be read as a collective pronoun to refer to all men and the interviewee as presupposing that all men are intrinsically violent. In example (2), the interviewee uses definite determiner 'that' to introduce the noun phrase 'that controlled aggression', which presupposes the existence of aggression in members of the Marines (the majority of whom are male). Tornado evaluates this as epistemically certain via modal adverb 'obviously', further contributing to the naturalization of male violence. What's interesting about this example is that since being a Marine is a marker of institutional hegemonic masculinity, Tornado's violent descriptions (note also his metaphorical stage name) acquire a level of veneration, even though on the face of it, he negatively appraises violence as 'bad'.

8.2.4 'Heterosexuality Is Normative'

Research on women's magazines has identified the prominence of heteronormativity in mainstream women's magazines (see Chapter 3), and heterosexuality is constructed as an assumed norm in the corpus in part via logical presupposition and implicature. The construction of heteronormativity often depends on invoking the notion of virility:

While men definitely enjoy watching two (or more) girls playing together, the icing on the cake is when the repairman turns up only to be invited to join in.

(*Scarlet*)

This extract comes from a report in *Scarlet* on men's and women's pornography viewing habits, which brands itself as 'the only magazine dedicated to celebrating sex and relationships from the female perspective'. The conjunction *while* generates the conventional implicature that the propositions expressed in the main clause constitute noteworthy information: conventionally this meaning of *while* as a conjunction denoting 'it being granted that' (*OED Online*) implies a contrast between the content of the subordinate clause and the main clause. This contrast is perhaps more obvious if we also talk about it in terms of concessive opposition (Chapter 6), in which the syntactic frame *while X, Y* indicates that in light of the propositions in the subordinate clause, those in the main clause are surprising. The implication here is that this is unexpected behavior for heterosexual men, because straight men should not enjoy seeing another man in a sexual context, thereby upholding heteronormative values. The reader may be directed to this interpretation because this article lists 'facts' about men and women's porn viewing habits, and the information conveyed is therefore intended to be shocking or surprising in some way. It is also significant that 'men' is not pre-modified by any adjective specifying that the noun is intended to refer to heterosexual men, which effectively hides the possibility of a gay referent, and also therefore normalizes heterosexuality.

Heteronormativity is implied in the following example, also from *Scarlet*,

17% of men have fantasised about another man.

This statistic comes from a report article intended to provide the reader with a roundup of 'the latest gossip from around the globe' ('Full Frontal', *Scarlet*), and appears in a small section entitled 'Stats: kinky sex'. The adjective *kinky* has connotations of deviancy: in a random sample of 50 concordances of *kinky* as the node word in the BNC, in that majority of cases, 'kinky' was used to modify concepts being negatively evaluated (57%), and 59% were related specifically to sexual activity. In their study on the representation of male and female social actors in tabloid and broadsheet newspapers, Caldas-Coulthard and Moon (2010) also found that *kinky* is used in relation to sexual practices, and is mainly associated with men (2010: 106–108). The decision to use 'kinky' as a descriptive term implies that fantasizing about other men is being evaluated as unusual or deviant. The negative prosody of *kinky* therefore creates the conventional implicature that homosexuality is deviant, and therefore negative; heterosexuality is normative and positive.

Related to the idea of heterosexuality as normative, is the presence of what Cameron refers to as the 'dread spectre of homosexuality' (Cameron 1997: 51). A particularly interesting example appears in a survey report from *More* called 'Men Overheard', intended to highlight the 'silly' things men say:

> Me: You've got a double bed—why doesn't he just sleep with you?
> Him: Because I don't have enough pillows to build a wall of heterosexuality down the middle.

The man's response to the female contributor's question flouts the maxims of quantity and relation: he does not seem to adequately explain the reasons for his proposed action, and this statement also seems irrelevant to the question of having enough room to accommodate his friend. The implicature generated is that the man is afraid of coming into physical contact with his friend, because for him this would constitute a threat to his heterosexual status.

Feature article 'The Nice Girl's Guide to Naughty Sex' in *Cosmopolitan* is an instructional article on how to 'indulge your saucy side', and contains a section on threesomes. Such a section constructs a threesome as 'naughty', and therefore a deviation from conventional (hetero)sexual practice:

> '[…] If you fancy it as a couple, it's less of an emotional minefield to talk about it as a shared fantasy.' If your man wants the real deal? Rachel says, 'Suggest the third party is a mate of his. He'll soon rethink!'

The implication here is that the man would rethink having a threesome because he wouldn't want to be involved in a sexual encounter with a male friend ('threesome' is seen as 'one man plus two women'), which the reader can only infer if 'mate' is interpreted as having a male referent. This is implicitly homophobic, since the idea of two men in the context of sexual activity is being evaluated negatively.

The following extract from an interview with Bollywood actor Harman Baweja in *Asiana* magazine, expressing a more explicitly homophobic ideology:

> People think that when you do Kathak [a classical north Indian dance] you sort of get all (gestures effeminately) but that's not the case with me. I'm as much a man as I was before.

The paralinguistic gesture is intended to index the connotations associated with the Kathak dance. The word *effeminately* is defined in the *Oxford English Dictionary* as '[i]n an effeminate or unmanly manner or style' (*OED Online*), and the adjectival attribute *effeminate* is often associated with gay male identities (Baker 2003: 250; Baker 2014: 117). From this perspective, the reader is likely to infer that homosexuality is not compatible with masculinity, consequently implying that homosexuality corresponds with femininity. The implied meanings rely on an assumption that this traditional style of dancing is effeminate, and that masculinity directly maps onto maleness. Even though this example comes from a celebrity interview, and therefore we could argue that the magazine is not directly responsible for the content, the choice of lexis in the gloss of the paralinguistic gesture is still an editorial choice, and shapes the range of possible readings of the text.

Less explicitly homophobic, 'Man Facts' in *More* also contains statements that warn against potentially effeminate practices:

12. Dance to anything by Take That.

14. Carry your handbag. Ever. This is not chivalry, it's the best way to make a man look instantly ridiculous.

Point 12 flouts the maxim of quantity, in that it does not provide the reader with an explanation as to why men shouldn't dance to this popular boy band; the heterosexual male reader may infer this would constitute effeminate behavior, which is associated with homosexuality. The reader also has to use the background cultural knowledge that Take That are a successful boy band, the assumption that boy bands often contain gay members, and the association of boy bands with gay culture (see, for example, Doty and Gove 1997; Jamieson 2007).

The second assertion flouts the maxim of quantity, as it's not made clear why a man carrying a handbag would be 'ridiculous'. The reader is likely to infer from her schematic knowledge of handbags as accessories that are conventionally marketed for women, that they are therefore not suitable for men. As with point 12, the reader may also infer that a man wearing a handbag would constitute effeminate behavior, indexing a stereotypical 'camp' gay male identity. This is negatively evaluated here ('ridiculous') because it does not conform to hegemonic ideals.

8.2.5 'Men Are the Dominant Partner in Relationships'

The idea that women are responsible for managing relationships with men is acknowledged in the feminist literature on women's magazines (Eggins and Iedema 1997: 169; Litosseliti 2006: 100–101). However, whilst women are similarly shown to be responsible for relationship maintenance in the women's magazine corpus, a focus on men's roles in the texts shows that it is often expected that men are responsible for 'making the first move' in relationships. The examples below demonstrate how this is manifested through assumed and implied meanings:

1. Many 'traditional' women prefer the man to ask, but if he's a good catch, get in there before someone else does! In fact, many men find a woman who will make the first move attractive and confident.

    (*Pride*)

2. Reached the 'Marry me or I'm outta here' point? 'Say, "I have to figure out what's going on with my life,"' says Parrott. Give him a definite time frame. It could be his best wake-up call.

    (*Glamour*)

3. National Statistics states that men are, on average, 32 years old when they pop the question, with 29 being the average age at which women say, 'I do'.

(*Scarlet*)

The first extract comes from a feature in *Pride* on how women should and should not behave in the world of dating. While the message appears to be that women *can* make the first move when pursuing a male partner, it relies on the implication that it is usually men who initiate dates, and adverbial 'in fact' implies via conventional implicature that women asking men out is usually perceived as *un*attractive by men. Therefore, for women to actively pursue a man is treated as a deviation from the expected norm.

Men's responsibility for initiating romantic relationships also extends to marriage proposals. In the second example, the question 'Reached the 'marry me or I'm outta here' point?' is what Levinson terms a 'yes/no question' (Levinson 1983: 184), presupposing an answer of either 'yes' or 'no'. For the proceeding utterance to accord with the Co-Operative Principle, the reader must answer 'yes', therefore there is an assumption that the reader wants to get married. There is also an assumption that marriage is the end goal of a relationship, achieved via the use of implicative verb 'reached', which presupposes a journey towards this point. Whilst the reader is clearly being constructed as invested in marriage, it is also clear that initiating wedlock is perceived as the man's responsibility: the imperative to '[g]ive him a definite time frame...' flouts the maxims of quantity and relation, as it is not stated what the timeframe is for, or what the purpose of such a 'wake-up call' would be, implying that he needs encouragement to propose, drawing on the stereotype that men are commitmentphobes.

Extract (3) is from an opinion column in *Scarlet* intended to highlight the drawbacks of getting married. This is not in itself surprising, given that *Scarlet* is one of the more 'feminist-friendly' magazines, and focuses much more on the sexual liberation of women than other more traditional women's magazines, it contains numerous articles about sex: the 'pleasure aunts' who advise readers focus explicitly on problems relating to sex and sexual health, and the monthly horoscope is relexicalized as 'sextrology'. However even here the notion of marriage proposals is treated specifically as a man's responsibility: temporal adverb 'when' creates the logical presupposition that men *do* propose to women, women's role being to accept. Rejection is not an option here, with the non-restrictive relative clause 'at which...' presupposing women's (universal) acceptance of marriage proposals.

8.3   Summary

Assumed and implied meanings reiterate five key discourses of (hegemonic) masculinity in the texts: that men are primarily motivated by sexual desires; that beautification processes are not compatible with heterosexual masculine performance; that men are naturally aggressive; that heterosexuality is normative; and that men are the dominant partner in relationships.

Many of the examples discussed rely on readers' existing schemata, and therefore serve to reinforce them. The ideology that men are driven by a biological need for sex is well documented by previous research on women's magazines (see, for example, Farvid and Braun 2006; Hasinoff 2009; Litosseliti 2006), and corresponds with what Holloway (1984) refers to as a 'male sexual drive' discourse: the idea that men cannot help having a high sex drive. Implicitly assuming this kind of ideology about male sexuality can have serious consequences. For example, Cameron notes that a man's 'irresistible physical urges' are sometimes used as justification in cases of sexual assault and rape (1992: 370). If women are continually confronted with the idea that men are primarily motivated by sex, this could influence their own sexual conduct, especially considering the amount of editorial space dedicated to instructing women on how to increase men's pleasure in sexual encounters (Gill 2007; Litosseliti 2006: 100; McLoughlin 2008).

On the surface, one might argue that some of the examples of male beautification processes and other aesthetic pursuits are evidence of a greater understanding of gender as performative and a deconstruction of traditional gender practices; for example that cosmetics and beauty products do not automatically index a female identity, or necessitate the feminization of male identity. However, the writers still imply that for heterosexual men to wear make-up is unexpected behavior, and therefore outside of normative gender practices. The texts assume a universal heterosexuality, which also contributes to the maintenance of traditional gender roles and associated sexuality as sets of binary opposites, thereby upholding the 'heterosexual matrix' (Butler 1990), and precluding the possibility of subversion.

References

Baker, P. (2003). No Effeminates Please: A Corpus-Based Analysis of Masculinity via Personal Adverts in Gay News/Times 1973–2000. In B. Benwell (Ed.), *Masculinity in Men's Lifestyle Magazines* (pp. 243–260). Oxford: Blackwell.

Baker, P. (2014). *Using Corpora to Analyze Gender*. London: Bloomsbury.

Butler, J. (1990). *Gender Trouble: Feminism and the Subversion of Identity*. London: Routledge.

Caldas-Coulthard, C. R., & Moon, R. (2010). 'Curvy, Hunky, Kinky': Using Corpora as Tools for Critical Analysis. *Discourse and Society, 21*(2), 99–133.

Cameron, D. (1992). Naming of Parts: Gender, Culture and Terms for the Penis Among American College Students. *American Speech, 67*(4), 367–382.

Cameron, D. (1997). Performing Gender Identity: Young Men's Talk and the Construction of Heterosexual Masculinity. In S. Johnson & U. H. Meinhoff (Eds.), *Language and Masculinity* (pp. 47–64). Oxford: Blackwell.

Cameron, D. (2007). *The Myth of Mars and Venus: Do Men and Women Really Speak Different Languages?* Oxford: Oxford University Press.

Cameron, D. (2010, November 23). *Gendered Behaviour: What Can Science Tell Us?* Public Debate in Association with the University of Cambridge Centre for Gender Studies, King's Place. Available at http://www.guardian.co.uk/commentisfree/audio/2010/nov/24/gendered-behaviour-science-forum?popup=true. Accessed March 2018.

Cameron, D., & Kulick, D. (2003). *Language and Sexuality*. Cambridge: Cambridge University Press.

Doty, A., & Gove, B. (1997). Queer Representation in the Mass Media. In A. Medhurst & S. R. Munt (Eds.), *Lesbian and Gay Studies: A Critical Introduction* (pp. 84–98). London: Continuum.

Eggins, S., & Iedema, R. (1997). Difference Without Diversity: Semantic Orientation and Ideology in Competing Women's Magazines. In R. Wodak (Ed.), *Gender and Discourse* (pp. 165–196). London: Sage.

Farvid, P., & Braun, V. (2006). "Most of Us Guys Are Raring to Go Anytime, Anyplace, Anywhere": Male and Female Sexuality in *Cleo* and *Cosmo*. *Sex Roles, 55*, 295–310.

Gill, R. (2007). *Gender and the Media*. Cambridge: Polity Press.

Grice, P. (1975). Logic and Conversation. In P. Cole & J. L. Morgan (Eds.), *Syntax and Semantics 3: Speech Acts* (pp. 41–58). New York: Academic.

Grice, P. (1989). *Studies in the Way of Words*. Cambridge, MA: Harvard University Press.

Halliday, M. (1985). *An Introduction to Functional Grammar*. London: Arnold.

Hasinoff, A. (2009). It's Sociobiology, Hon! Genetic Gender Determinism in *Cosmopolitan* Magazine. *Feminist Media Studies, 9*(3), 267–283.

Hines, C. (1999). Rebaking the Pie: The WOMAN AS DESSERT Metaphor. In M. Bucholtz, A. C. Liang, & L. Sutton (Eds.), *Reinventing Identities: The Gendered Self in Discourse* (pp. 145–162). Oxford: Oxford University Press.

Holloway, W. (1984). Gender Difference and the Production of Subjectivity. In J. Henriques, W. Holloway, C. Urwin, C. Venn, & V. Walkerdine (Eds.), *Changing the Subject: Psychology, Social Regulation and Subjectivity* (pp. 227–339). London: Methuen.

Jamieson, D. (2007). Marketing Androgyny: The Evolution of the Backstreet Boys. *Popular Music, 26*(2), 245–258.

Jeffries, L. (2007). *Textual Construction of the Female Body: A Critical Discourse Approach*. Basingstoke: Palgrave Macmillan.

Jeffries, L. (2010). *Critical Stylistics*. Basingstoke: Palgrave Macmillan.

Lakoff, R. T. (1975). *Language and Woman's Place*. New York: Harper & Row.

Levinson, S. C. (1983). *Pragmatics*. Cambridge: Cambridge University Press.

Litosseliti, L. (2006). *Gender and Language: Theory and Practice*. London: Hodder Arnold.

McLoughlin, L. (2008). The Construction of Female Sexuality in the "Sex Special": Transgression or Containment in Magazines' Information on Sexuality for Girls? *Gender and Language, 2*(2), 171–195.

Stergiopoulos, G. (2008). *Treat Them Mean, Keep Them Keen*. London: Square Peg.

Talbot, M. (1992). The Construction of Gender in a Teenage Magazine. In N. Fairclough (Ed.), *Critical Language Awareness* (pp. 174–199). London: Longman.

Tannen, D. (1990). *You Just Don't Understand*. London: Virago.

9

Conclusion: The Men in 'Women's Worlds'

In embarking on this project, examining the textual construction of men for female readers of women's magazines, I aimed to uncover the stylistic techniques used to represent male identities in a corpus of women's magazines, and to consider their potential effects on heterosexual women: how women readers may perceive themselves and the role of men in their lives, in the wake of ongoing feminist debates about sexism and 'lad culture'. I have also considered the magazines' treatment of the relationship between maleness and masculinity, and how the texts' constructions of masculinity can be said to also constitute gender performance.

Men are most frequently named using nouns relating to social role, particularly occupational roles (see Chapter 5). The presence of traditionally male-dominated occupations such as the emergency services and armed forces serve as indirect indices of hegemonic masculinity. Less frequent but ideologically salient metaphorical nouns such as 'Mr Darcy' and 'Romeo' are intertextual references to stereotypical masculine figures from romantic fiction, promoting discourses of the 'ideal man' that entail heterosexual prowess and fairy-tale happy endings. This kind of linguistic repertoire helps to solidify a broad 'gender differences'

© The Author(s) 2019
L. Coffey-Glover, *Men in Women's Worlds*,
https://doi.org/10.1057/978-1-137-57555-5_9

discourse (Sunderland 2004), ultimately underpinned by an expectation that men and women have very different roles in heterosexual relationships.

Body part nouns were an important device for representing men and their actions: the lexical field of genitalia show that terms for the penis simultaneously indicate both fallibility and power. Adjectival descriptions of men most frequently denote personality traits or behavioral qualities, rather than physical appearance. Positively evaluative adjectives describe men's suitability as potential partners; adjectives providing negative appraisals denote bad behavior in relationships, such as infidelity and promiscuity, as well as morally corrupt behavior (again, see Chapter 5).

Men are sometimes equated with cultural ideals of masculinity, or direct indices of masculinity that take on connotative meanings, such as the use of 'man' as a metaphor to mean 'heterosexual' (Chapter 6). I also showed how men are equated with concepts expressed in conceptual metaphors like MEN ARE FOOD and MEN ARE ANIMALS, which serve to challenge similar conceptual metaphors equated with women. While these metaphors can be viewed as in some ways as a kind of 'postfeminist' subversion of indirect sexism, the extent to which these framings truly equate to a critique of the gender order is debatable. Oppositional meanings often rely on the reader's schematic knowledge of conventional oppositional pairs, such as GOOD/BAD, MALE/FEMALE, upholding the notion of gender as a binary construct. Differences between men are treated in exclusive terms, rather than as scaler concepts, which also prohibits heterogeneity in favor of portraying 'ideal' versus 'monstrous' male identities (Chapter 6).

In terms of how the texts represent men's actions and states of being, men are most frequently seen to perform material action intention processes or relational processes. In the features, these were mostly sexual actions; in the true-life stories, mostly actions indicating physical strength. Women were most frequently the affected participants of violent or sexual actions, and material actions also presented men as performing stereotypically gendered behaviors and practices. Intensive relational processes were the most frequent type of relational process used to denote states of being, with Attributes serving a naming function, such as 'he is a brilliant dad'.

The most frequently assumed or implied idea about male behavior was that men are motivated by sexual urges. The text producers also reiterate normative gender ideologies such as the idea that beautification processes index femininity, not masculinity, and that heterosexuality is normative. Men are also constructed as naturally aggressive, and it is assumed that while relationship maintenance is primarily women's responsibility, relationship instigation should be done by men.

9.1 Ideologies of Masculinity in Women's Magazines

The magazine data showed a number of central ideologies of masculinity that cut across the different Critical Stylistics tools: the text producers often present men as either 'good' or 'bad'; as driven by their carnal instincts; and as naturally aggressive. In terms of gender more broadly, the texts rely heavily on a binary conceptualization of gender, and the notion of heteronormativity.

9.1.1 'There Are 'Good' Men and 'Bad' Men'

Men are often presented dichotomously as 'good' or 'bad' men. In Chapter 5, I demonstrated how this is achieved though naming strategies, by which men are labelled and described using nouns and adjectives with positive or negative connotations, such as 'hero' or 'monster'. Through a construction of oppositional meanings (see Chapter 6) the reader's schematic knowledge of the superordinate GOOD/BAD pairing aids an interpretation of novel opposites such as 'innocent'/'filthy' as hyponyms of *good/bad*. The notion of physical strength, indicated by the kinds of actions performed by men in the data, is seen as desirable where women are the affected participants of material actions in romantic contexts, but negative where the processes denote violent actions (see Sect. 7.3).

9.1.2 'Men Are Driven by Sexual Desires'

In a study of how the texts assume and imply meanings, the assumption that men are driven by sexual urges is a prominent theme, and this idea also cuts across the other tools: men's assumed carnality is embedded in naming strategies, including metaphorical nouns such as 'Lothario' (see Chapter 5), and in the kinds of actions they are seen to perform: men act upon women most often in sexual contexts (see Chapter 7). The assumption that all men are heterosexual is also integral to these representations; women have male partners, and are the objects of men's sexual desires.

9.1.3 'Men Are Naturally Aggressive'

The idea that men are naturally aggressive, another salient thematic thread, appears most obviously in the analysis of transitivity, which demonstrated how the true-life story text type represents men as the Actors of violent material action processes (see Chapter 7). Male aggression is also often normalized through assumed and implied meanings (Chapter 8). Metaphorical naming strategies such as 'beast', 'monster' and 'Tornado' also contribute to the construction of this ideology of masculinity (Chapter 5). Patterns of body part agency presents men as lacking control over their own actions, unlike the kinds of male meronymic agency reported in other genres, such as romance fiction (see Nash 1990).

9.1.4 'Gender Is a Binary Construct'

The notion of inherent gender differences is an overarching theme. In the lexical and social gendering of body part terms (Chapter 5), hyponyms of 'muscle' only co-occur with male referents and hyponyms of 'chest' only co-occur with female referents. The reliance on superordinate oppositional pairs such as MALE/FEMALE and MASCULINE/ FEMININE as underpinning contrasted concepts shows how oppositional meanings are exploited to emphasize gender differences (see Chapter 6). A discourse of gender differences is also assumed and implied with reference to contrasting behaviors and practices (such as make-up as a feminine pursuit and excessive drinking as a male pastime) (Chapter 8). These dichotomies are underpinned by a 'two cultures' approach to gender which views men and women as occupying entirely different worlds (Tannen 1990). This is also evident in the presence of articles with titles such as 'Man Facts' (*More*) or 'Man Talk' (*Love It*), which seem to treat men as alien life-forms that need explaining, analogous to the 'Mars and Venus' model of gender roles (Gray 1992).

9.1.5 'Heterosexuality Is Normative'

Heterosexual desire is presented as an integral part of hegemonic masculine performance: the heterosexuality of the reader is always assumed (the one exception to this being *Diva* magazine). This is often realized linguistically through existential presupposition, for example through male pronouns. There is also evidence for behaviors associated with homosexuality being treated as negative and inconsistent with hegemonic masculinity, achieved via conversational implicatures (see Chapter 8). The analysis of equivalent meanings showed how some nouns with lexical gender, which ordinarily function as direct indices of masculinity, such as 'man' and 'bloke', may signal a specifically heterosexual male identity (see Chapter 5).

9.2   Women's Magazines as Sites of 'Lad Culture'

This book is a contribution to feminist studies of women's magazines: the ideologies of masculinity uncovered are interpreted in terms of their implications for how they might contribute to harmful gender stereotyping, specifically in the context of debates about sexism and 'lad culture'. One of the most pertinent findings of this study, both in terms of statistical and cultural salience, is the texts' contributions to the 'male sexual drive' discourse (Holloway 1984), which asserts that men are motivated by sexual desires, and have a higher sex drive than women. The ideology that men are driven by sexual instincts is reiterated consistently across the corpus, and, I argue, it is this ideology of male behavior that is in most need of feminist critique. If women are repeatedly presented with the idea that men are principally motivated by sexual desire, this may then come to appear as if it were a natural 'essence' of masculinity, something that women can expect from men, and could lead to women changing their own behavior in response to men's (assumed) sexual desires. For example, young women may feel pressurizeded to engage in sexual relationships earlier, or more frequently, and so on. The uncritical reader of women's magazines may be particularly susceptible to this, as she is continuously told that her role in relationships is to keep abreast of the various ways that she can increase men's pleasure. More serious still, any assumption that men are not only driven by their sexual urges, but also that they are not in control of them, may be used as justification for sexual crimes against women (Cameron 2006: 153). Presenting male violence as taken for granted decreases our ability to challenge this stereotype and to instigate change.

The conceptual metaphor MEN ARE FOOD can be interpreted as a kind of male equivalent of the 'women-as-sexual-object as food' metaphors discussed in the feminist literature on gender and semantic meaning (Hines 1999) (see Chapters 5 and 6). Constructions of men as useless, via negatively evaluative descriptions like 'daft,' and lexis indicating the fallibility of the penis, can also be interpreted as attempts to challenge the kind of 'ironic' sexism that critics have observed in men's magazines (see Benwell 2004; Mills 2008). However, the usefulness of directing insults at, or sexually objectifying, men as an effective feminist response to female-targeted sexism is questionable. The representations of men and masculinity discussed in this book are often intended to be humorous, and therein lies the problem: although there are elements of critique of some of the more 'laddish' aspects of male behavior, such as an obsession with sport or heavy drinking, ultimately, from a feminist perspective, these texts proliferate potentially dangerous stereotypes about men's behavior.

9.2.1 The Relationship Between 'Men' and 'Masculinity'

I began this study with the rather uncomfortable concession that in order to examine how the concept of masculinity is constructed by the texts, the only way to do this that would not necessitate having to manually read all the texts would be to search for direct indices of maleness. This seemed enormously counterintuitive for an approach to gender construction which is grounded in feminist post-structuralist thinking. However, distinguishing between lexical, social and referentially gendered lexis, and language which can be said to directly or indirectly index gender, were very useful tools for untangling 'sex' from 'gender'. For example, the instances of lexis which are ordinarily socially gendered with a female bias but that occur with male referents, such as 'pin-up' and 'diva', are (albeit infrequent) subversions of this binary, and therefore can be interpreted as examples of language which begin to unpick the 'rigid, regulatory frame' (Butler 1990: 33) upholding the equation that 'male equals masculine'.

Despite examples like this, though, on the whole, the sex-gender equation remains largely untouched in this data. While there is some evidence for the idea that gender roles are changing, for example in depictions of men wearing make-up, the relationship between maleness and masculinity is largely represented as uncomplicated: 'sex' is seen as equating with 'gender'. Even where there are examples of men wearing make-up or engaging in other beautification processes, this is treated as a deviation from the expected norm, which ultimately reaffirms hegemonic ideologies of masculinity. These subversions are far from normative, because the 'heterosexual matrix' (Butler 1990) dictates that men must act masculine; women should be feminine.

In the opening to this book I argued that 'sex' and 'gender' are best conceived of as gradable, rather than binary, constructs, as not only are *masculine/feminine* scalar concepts, so are *male* and *female*. However, women's magazines treat gender as a binary construct; even where there are potential subversions of this, such as using *too* to pre-modify 'feminine': although this creates a gradable opposite, it ultimately serves to maintain the sex/gender binary, in an assertion that men should *not* be feminine.

9.2.2 Text as Performance

While performativity theory has traditionally been used to analyze the construction of gendered subjects in verbal interaction, gender performativity can also be applied to textual representation: texts' constructions of gender can also be interpreted as performances of masculinity or femininity by their writers/narrators. If gender is 'the repeated stylization of the body' (Butler 1990: 33), then coherent repeated representations can be considered performances of gender, because they form part of our everyday understanding of 'masculinity' or 'femininity'. Sunderland (2004: 23–24) makes a distinction between the 'representation' 'of some*thing* or some*one*', and 'performance' as constitutive. However, we can see representations as performances if we interpret 'representation' as also denoting the practices that produce the appearance of an identity, the 'foundational illusions of identity' (Butler 1990: 34), rather than a reflection of a pre-existing subject. It would follows then, that *all* identity representations are also performances.

Accounts of the epistemological development of the field of language and gender traditionally emphasize a distinction between gender as instantiated in interactional behavior and gender representation in written discourse (Sunderland and Litosseliti 2008: 4). This suggests a separation of 'real' or 'authentic' identities from imitations of these 'real life' gender performances, an idea which seems contrary to the CDA dictum that language simultaneously *reflects* reality ('the way things are') and *constructs* (*construes*) it to be a certain way' (Gee 1999: 82). In addition, the notion of text as performance also throws new light on Butler's assertion that gender is:

> a set of repeated acts within a highly rigid regulatory frame that congeal over time to produce the appearance of substance of a natural sort of being. (Butler 1990: 33)

Women's magazines repeatedly construct masculinity and femininity in limiting ways in line with the constraints of social norms, whilst simultaneously creating naturalized ideologies of gender though those very repetitions.

The idea of the text as a performance of gender is also helpful in explaining the presence of contradictory images of masculinity: contradictory images are present in women's magazines (and other texts) in part because '[p]erforming masculinity or femininity "appropriately" cannot mean giving exactly the same performance regardless of the circumstances' (Cameron 1997: 61). Just as the relationship between interlocutors and social context can have an effect on the type of gender identity performed in talk, texts' performances of gender are also dependent on their target audiences and the social purposes of text.

Performativity theory can, then, usefully be applied to the study of gender construction in text in three ways: (1) to account for the ways in which repeated ideas about gender come to *mean* masculinity or femininity, (2) to expose the ways in which sex, gender and sexuality are seen to inevitably coincide with one another, and (3) explore the subversive potential of a multiplicity of gendered identities, given that there is no inevitable link between 'sex' and 'gender'.

9.3 Combining Feminist Critical Stylistics with Corpus Linguistic Tools: Methodological Issues

Aside from questions relating to the representation of men and masculinity in women's magazines, this study also sought to investigate the applicability of the critical stylistics model to the study of large sets of data using corpus linguistic tools. This was no mean feat, particularly when incorporating a feminist post-structuralist approach to gender. This is partly because conventionally, corpus linguistic work on identity starts with pre-determined identity categories (such as 'man' or 'woman'). However, constraining the search to instances of lexical gender in this way would have set limits on my ability to uncover inter-esting connotative differences in how male entities are named, names that would reveal different ideologies of masculinity. I therefore decided *not* to begin my investigation using MAN/MEN as search terms. This meant that although I was able to uncover differences in naming strate-gies, I was unable to produce a comprehensive analysis of statistical col-locates, which would also have been illuminating for an analysis of the textual-conceptual function of describing.

The fact that a number of the textual-conceptual tools cannot be derived from specific linguistic features also made it difficult to use cor-pus linguistics to find relevant data. For example, as regards instances of appositional equivalence, I was only able to capture those that involved the conjunction *and*, which are likely much less frequent than those triggered by the juxtaposition of noun phrases. In addition, the open-ended nature of presupposition meant that although I was able to use Levinson's (1983) list of triggers as a guide for identifying instances of presupposition, I still could not do this automatically. The lexical form of different types of presupposition are varied, for example, the formal category 'factive verb' could contain a number of items, and to predict its members would involve having to predetermine a very narrow set of lexical items, which would inevitably result in missing a number of relevant presuppositions. However, the inbuilt automatic POS tagging program CLAWS in Wmatrix (Rayson 2008) facilitated my analysis of naming practices and transitivity, and having already filtered the data for the transitivity analysis made this more manual task significantly easier, as I had already been able to identify some relevant potential con-texts for presupposition and implicature.

One of the difficulties of combining different corpus linguistic tools with discrete functions of text (naming, opposition, transitivity and so on), is that it has the effect of compartmentalizing the analysis, such that it appears as though these different linguistic strategies work in iso-lation, when in reality of course they all work together to produce the ideological meanings discussed; the assumption that men are driven by sexual urges often also relies on naming choices in the noun phrase, for example. In the next section I present an analysis of an excerpt from a letters page, in order to demonstrate some of the ways in which the tools interrelate in the construction of ideational meaning.

9.3.1 Combining the Tools: 'Man Talk'

In the following section of a letters page from *Love It* magazine entitled 'Man Talk', the magazine writer poses a number of statements intended to reveal the 'mysteries of man':

(1a) HE SAYS: 'Why don't you have a bath, babe?'
(1b) HE MEANS: 'I've got a new PlayStation game and I need you out of the way at the moment.'

(2a) HE SAYS: 'I was listening, but I've got a lot on my mind.'
(2b) HE MEANS: 'I'm trying to watch SkySports.'

(3a) HE SAYS: 'I'm feeling ill – I think I might be dying.'
(3b) HE MEANS: 'I've just sneezed.'

(4a) HE SAYS: 'I've done the weekly shop.'
(4b) HE MEANS: 'I bought alcohol, a loaf of bread and a Pepperami.'

In terms of naming, the third person singular pronoun 'he' does not in fact refer to a particular identity, as the target referent is the (assumed) reader's partner, an example of 'synthetic personalization' (Fairclough 1989: 62), whereby a collective audience is referred to as an individual. The use of 'he' also constructs the reader as heterosexual. The parallel clause structure '*he* + present tense verb' creates oppositional meaning between the lexemes 'says' and 'means,' emphasizing a difference between semantic form and pragmatic function. The construction of SAYS/MEANS as an oppositional construct also implies that there *is* a difference between what men say and what they really think. This in turn implies that men's speech needs decoding, which contributes to a discourse of gender differences because it assumes that men's utterances are indecipherable to women. This also evokes the 'Mars and Venus' model of language and gender, whereby men and women are viewed as occupying wholly distinct 'worlds' (cf. Tannen 1990).

'SAYS' in the main clauses is a verbalization process, with the juxtaposing independent clauses providing the Verbiage (what is said). 'MEANS' could be categorized as a behavioral process, since it seems to fall somewhere between verbalization and cognition. The propositions expressed in the Verbiages draw on stereotypically gendered social practices, behaviors and attributes, where computer gaming and televised sports are constructed as stereotypical male pursuits (1 and 2), and men are perceived as heavy drinking, unhealthy hypochondriacs (3 and 4). As these are presented as categorical, unmodalized statements, they appear as universal truths, thus all men are assumed to behave in this way.

The locutions prefaced by 'HE SAYS' are intended as violations of the Co-Operative Principle. They are violations of the maxim of quality, in that they are presented by the magazine writers as lies; the 'HE MEANS' statements are expressions of the implied meanings of the 'HE SAYS' locutions. The 'HE SAYS' examples can also all be said to flout the maxim of quantity, in that they do not seem to provide sufficient information, which is subsequently supplied by the 'HE MEANS' statements. Example (3a) is an exaggeration, and therefore violates the maxim of quality. We could also interpret (4a) as a violation of the quality maxim on the same grounds: the implicature of (4b) is that this constitutes insufficient supplies, therefore the man in question's original statement in (4a) is also an exaggeration.

The use of 'HE' as a generic referent for men in these examples presuppose that all men exhibit the stipulated behaviors. However, this also has implications for how women are represented in the texts. For instance, the reader may infer from the declarative statement 'I've done the weekly shop' (4a) that it is women who usually carry out the task of food shopping, which implies that domesticity is the domain of women. The reader could also infer from (2a) that it is women who do most of the talking in relationships, drawing on folklinguistic stereotypes about women's loquacity (see, for example, Coates 1989; Cameron 1992).

9.4   Suggestions for Future Research

The Critical Stylistics tools I have used in this study were prior-
itized because of their relevance to the task at hand, but others would
undoubtedly help to illuminate how the texts construct ideologies of
masculinity. In particular, an analysis of 'Presenting Opinions', through
a consideration of modality and speech and thought processes, would
shed further light on how men's points of view, as well as those of the
text producers in relation to men, are constructed in the texts. For
example, my analysis of transitivity processes showed that the choice of
reporting verb can affect the writer's appraisal of the speaker.

Throughout my analysis, it also became clear that men are often presented in terms of what they are not; an analysis of the metafunction
of 'Negating' would also therefore be useful for examining what kinds
of qualities or behaviors are presented in the affirmative, and which
are constructed via negated forms. Additionally, the conceptual-textual
function of 'hypothesizing' would be useful for examining the kinds of
expectations of men that are set up by the texts, via, for example, the
use of *if*-clauses and epistemic modality.

Aside from the ideological meanings that cut across the different
tools outlined, I also found that metaphorical meanings intersected with
all four metafunctions. Future analyses could include metaphor as a useful additional category for the model. Cognitive metaphor theory posits
that representing X in terms of Y is an indication of how we actually
understand particular real-world concepts (Gibbs and Steen 1999). For
instance, choosing metaphors such as 'eye candy' and 'treat' to express
the physical attractiveness of men indicates that men are understood as
consumable objects. Conceptual metaphors are also often attempts to
construe complex aspects of the world in more 'familiar' terms (Gibbs
1994). These therefore reveal ideologies of how we conceptualize entities or events. If metaphorical meanings point to ideologies of how the
world is conceptualized, the construction of metaphor could be considered as another textual-conceptual function of text. Occurrences of
the conceptual metaphors for masculinity could also be further investigated in other kinds of (fictional and non-fictional) texts; this could

shed important light on how the complex notion of gender identity is reformulated into more familiar concepts for the reader.

Further studies of the textual representation of gender in women's magazines would also benefit from comparative analyses of constructions/representations of femininity and masculinity. They would also benefit from a triangulation of textual and ethnographic data, in order to understand the processes of how these texts are consumed and understood by their target audiences; specifically, how the ideologies identified in this book are negotiated by the reader. In addition, while my analysis has focused solely on the role of language in the construction of meaning, future treatment of magazines would benefit from a multi-modal approach, considering how text and image interact to perform gender identities, as has been done in other areas of critical linguistics (Machin et al. 2016; Caldas-Coulthard and Van Leeuwen 2002).

9.5   Concluding Remarks

This extended treatment of masculinity in women's magazines has demonstrated the importance of identifying and questioning representations of hegemonic masculinity in a genre which is assumed to be 'all about' femininity. Through an analysis of ideology construction in these texts, I have shown how written constructions of gender, like spoken discourse, can also be interpreted as performative mechanisms of gender identity. This offers a different perspective to that traditionally found in the field of language and gender, which has conventionally separated spoken performance from writing. In this book I question the assumption that these texts only tell women about how they should perform femininity; they also tell women how they can expect men to appear and behave, and thus what permissible performances of masculinity look like. The importance of feminist linguistic inquiry into texts such as these is not necessarily just to recognise how they propagate norms of femininity, but also their role in reiterating stereotypical images of men as (hetero) sexually motivated and threatening, resisting the possibility of subverting the gender order. In addition, although we might ordinarily think of 'lad culture' as residing in spaces like university campuses or in the pages of 'lads' mags' such as *FHM*, it's clear that tackling 'laddism' and other vehicles of sexism and misogyny also requires paying critical attention to female-targeted spaces such as the woman's lifestyle magazine.

As Gill (2007: 200) points out, unlike other feminist discourses, women's magazines promote individual, rather than a social transformation, despite the illusion of 'synthetic sisterhood' constructed via second person address and other tactics of 'synthetic personalization' (Fairclough 1989). Women's magazines are not critical of structural inequalities; they do not circulate around discourses of patriarchy, ideology and dominance. The only magazine to directly address gender inequality in politics or include items on women working in cultural industries in my corpus was *Diva*, a publication specifically marketed at lesbian readerships. This is worrying because it contributes to stereotypical views about lesbianism and 'militant' feminism, since there is an assumption that feminism isn't 'for everybody' (hooks 2000): the absence of such articles in magazines for heterosexual women assumes that straight women are not interested in these issues.

Women's magazines could contribute helpfully to feminist praxis if they acknowledged that men and women are more similar than different, rather than representing male and female subjects as innately different species, requiring dichotomous gender work. If it was consistently acknowledged that men do not all behave the same way in relationships and that a difference in sexual behavior between 'the sexes' is not natural and inevitable, then women's magazines would pose a challenge to the discourses of male (hyper)sexuality that serve to justify male sexual violence against women.

It is acknowledged by writers like Winship (1987) and McRobbie (1996) that women's magazines have great potential as carriers of feminist discourses, because of their celebration of women's lives to a mass audience. Glossy magazines such as *Marie Claire* and *Cosmopolitan* in particular have been praised for their increased focus on issues that extend beyond advertisements for the latest mascara or advice on how to get the new boy from the office to notice you (Gill 2007: 199). However, these magazines still promote heterosexual relationships as the end goal for any woman, and the kinds of men women are encouraged to pursue are those who conform to hegemonic masculine ideals; they don't work in low-paid jobs, they're not emotional and they don't wear eyeliner. For women's magazines to deconstruct and resist the gender stereotypes they promote would be an important way of contributing to a feminist understanding of gender and gender relations, and to progressive social change.

References

Benwell, B. (2004). Ironic Discourse: Evasive Masculinity in British Men's Lifestyle Magazines. *Men and Masculinities, 7*(1), 3–21.
Butler, J. (1990). *Gender Trouble: Feminism and the Subversion of Identity.* London: Routledge.
Caldas-Coulthard, C. R., & Van Leeuwen, T. (2002). Stunning, Shimmering, Iridescent: Toys as the Representation of Social Actors. In L. Litosseliti & J. Sunderland (Eds.), *Gender Identity and Discourse Analysis* (pp. 91–108). Amsterdam: John Benjamin.
Cameron, D. (1992). *Feminism and Linguistic Theory* (2nd ed.). Basingstoke: Macmillan.
Cameron, D. (1997). Performing Gender Identity: Young Men's Talk and the Construction of Heterosexual Masculinity. In S. Johnson & U. H. Meinhoff (Eds.), *Language and Masculinity* (pp. 47–64). Oxford: Blackwell.
Cameron, D. (Ed.). (2006). *On Language and Sexual Politics.* London: Routledge.
Coates, J. (1989). Gossip Revisited: Language in All-Female Groups. In J. Coates & D. Cameron (Eds.), *Women in Their Speech Communities* (pp. 94–121). London: Longman.
Fairclough, N. (1989). *Language and Power.* London: Longman.
Gee, J. P. (1999). *An Introduction to Discourse Analysis: Theory and Method.* London: Routledge.
Gibbs, R. W. (1994). *The Poetics of Mind: Figurative Thought, Language and Understanding.* Cambridge: Cambridge University Press.
Gibbs, R. W., & Steen, G. J. (1999). *Metaphor in Cognitive Linguistics.* Amsterdam: John Benjamins.
Gill, R. (2007). *Gender and the Media.* Cambridge: Polity Press.

Gray, J. (1992). *Men Are from Mars, Women Are from Venus*. New York: HarperCollins.

Hines, C. (1999). Rebaking the Pie: The WOMAN AS DESSERT Metaphor. In M. Bucholtz, A. C. Liang, & L. Sutton (Eds.), *Reinventing Identities: The Gendered Self in Discourse* (pp. 145–162). Oxford: Oxford University Press.

Holloway, W. (1984). Gender Difference and the Production of Subjectivity. In J. Henriques, W. Holloway, C. Urwin, C. Venn, & V. Walkerdine (Eds.), *Changing the Subject: Psychology, Social Regulation and Subjectivity* (pp. 227–339). London: Methuen.

hooks, b. (2000). *Feminism is for Everybody: Passionate Politics*. London: Pluto Press.

Levinson, S. C. (1983). *Pragmatics*. Cambridge: Cambridge University Press.

Machin, D., Caldas-Coulthard, C. R., & Milani, T. (2016). Doing Critical Multimodality in Research on Gender, Language and Discourse. *Gender and Language, 10*(3), 301–308.

McRobbie, A. (1996). '*More!*: New Sexualities in Girls' and Women's Magazines. In J. Curran, D. Morley, & V. Walkerdine (Eds.), *Cultural Studies and Communications* (pp. 172–194). London: Arnold.

Mills, S. (2008). *Language and Sexism*. Cambridge: Cambridge University Press.

Nash, W. (1990). *Language in Popular Fiction*. London: Routledge.

Rayson, P. (2008). From Key Words to Key Semantic Domains. *International Journal of Corpus Linguistics, 13*(4), 519–549.

Sunderland, J. (2004). *Gendered Discourses*. Basingstoke: Palgrave Macmillan.

Sunderland, J., & Litosseliti, L. (2008). Current Research Methodologies in Gender and Language Study: Key Issues. In K. Harrington, L. Litosseliti, H. Sauntson, & J. Sunderland (Eds.), *Gender and Language Research Methodologies* (pp. 1–18). Basingstoke: Palgrave Macmillan.

Tannen, D. (1990). *You Just Don't Understand*. London: Virago.

Winship, J. (1987). *Inside Women's Magazines*. London: Pandora.

References

Achugar, M. (2004). The Events and Actors of 11 September 2011 as Seen from Uruguay: Analysis of Daily Newspaper Editorials. *Discourse and Society, 15*(2–3), 291–320.

Attenborough, F. T. (2011). Complicating the Sexualisation Thesis: The Media, Gender and 'Sci-Candy'. *Discourse & Society, 22*(6), 659–676.

Attwood, F. (2005). "Tits and Ass and Porn and Fighting": Male Heterosexuality in Magazines for Men. *International Journal of Cultural Studies, 8*(1), 83–100.

Aubrey, J. S., Harrison, K., Kramer, L., & Yellin, J. (2003). Variety Versus Timing: Gender Differences in College Students' Sexual Expectations as Predicted by Exposure to Sexually Oriented Television. *Communication Research, 30*(4), 432–460.

Austin, J. L. (1962). *How to Do Things with Words: The William James Lectures Delivered at Harvard University in 1955*. Oxford: Clarendon Press.

Baker, P. (2003). No Effeminates Please: A Corpus-Based Analysis of Masculinity via Personal Adverts in Gay News/Times 1973–2000. In B. Benwell (Ed.), *Masculinity and Men's Lifestyle Magazines* (pp. 243–260). Oxford: Blackwell.

Baker, P. (2006). *Using Corpora in Discourse Analysis*. London: Continuum.

Baker, P. (2008a). *Sexed Texts: Language, Gender and Sexuality*. London: Equinox.

Baker, P. (2008b). "Eligible" Bachelors and "Frustrated" Spinsters: Corpus Linguistics, Gender and Language. In J. Sunderland, K. Harrington, & H. Saunston (Eds.), *Gender and Language Research Methodologies*. London: Palgrave Macmillan.

Baker, P. (2010). Will Ms Ever Be as Frequent as Mr?: A Corpus-Based Comparison of Gendered Terms Across Four Diachronic Corpora of British English. *Gender and Language, 4*(1), 125–149.

Baker, P. (2014). *Using Corpora to Analyze Gender*. London: Bloomsbury.

Baker, P., & Levon, E. (2015). Picking the Right Cherries?: A Comparison of Corpus-Based and Qualitative Analyses of News Articles About Masculinity. *Discourse & Communication, 9*(2), 221–236.

Baker, P., & Levon, E. (2016). 'That's What I Call a Man': Representations of Racialised and Classed Masculinities in the UK Print Media. *Gender and Language, 10*(1), 106–139.

Baker, P., Gabrielatos, C., & McEnery, T. (2013). Sketching Muslims: A Corpus Driven Analysis of Representations Around the Word 'Muslim' in the British Press 1998–2009. *Applied Linguistics, 34*(3), 255–278.

Baker, P., Gabrielatos, C., Khosravinik, M., Krzyzanowski, M., McEnery, T., & Wodak, R. (2008). A Useful Methodological Synergy? Combining Critical Discourse Analysis and Corpus Linguistics to Examine Discourses of Refugees and Asylum Seekers in the UK Press. *Discourse and Society, 19*(3), 273–306.

Baldry, A. (2000). *Multimodality and Multimediality in the Distance Learning Age*. Campobasso: Palladino.

Balirano, G., & Baker, P. (2018). *Queering Masculinities in Language and Culture*. Basingstoke: Palgrave Macmillan.

Ballaster, R., Beetham, M., Frazer, E., & Hebron, S. (1991). *Women's Worlds: Ideology, Femininity and Women's Magazines*. Basingstoke: Palgrave Macmillan.

Bates, L. (2014). *Everyday Sexism*. London: Simon & Schuster.

Benwell, B. (2001). Male Gossip and Language Play in the Letters Pages of Men's Lifestyle Magazines. *Journal of Popular Culture, 35*(1), 19–33.

Benwell, B. (2002). "Is There Anything 'New' About These Lads?" The Textual and Visual Construction of Masculinity in Men's Magazines. In L. Litosseliti & J. Sunderland (Eds.), *Gender Identity and Discourse Analysis* (pp. 149–174). Amsterdam: Benjamins.

Benwell, B. (Ed.). (2003a). *Masculinity in Men's Lifestyle Magazines*. Oxford: Blackwell.

Benwell, B. (2003b). Ambiguous Masculinities: Heroism and Anti-heroism in the Men's Lifestyle Magazine. In B. Benwell (Ed.), *Masculinity and Men's Lifestyle Magazines* (pp. 151–168). Oxford: Blackwell.

Benwell, B. (2004). Ironic Discourse: Evasive Masculinity in British Men's Lifestyle Magazines. *Men and Masculinities, 7*(1), 3–21.

Bing, J. M., & Bergvall, V. L. (1996). The Question of Questions: Beyond Binary Thinking. In V. L. Bergvall, J. M. Bing, & A. Freed (Eds.), *Rethinking Language and Gender Research: Theory and Practice*. London: Longman.

Braithwaite, B. (1995). *Women's Magazines: The First 300 Years*. London: Peter Owen.

Breazeale, K. (1994). In Spite of Women: *Esquire* Magazine and the Construction of the Male Consumer. *Signs, 20*(1), 1–22.

Brookes, G., Harvey, K., & Mullany, L. (2016). "Off to the Best Start"? A Multimodal Critique of Breast and Formula Feeding Health Promotional Discourse. *Gender and Language, 10*(3), 340–363.

Burton, D. (1982). Through Glass Darkly: Through Dark Glasses. On Stylistics and Political Commitment. In R. Carter (Ed.), *Language and Literature* (pp. 195–214). London: Allen & Unwin.

Butler, J. (1990). *Gender Trouble: Feminism and the Subversion of Identity*. London: Routledge.

Butler, J. (1993). *Bodies That Matter: On the Discursive Limits of "Sex"*. London: Routledge.

Butler, J. (1999). *Gender Trouble: Feminism and the Subversion of Identity* (2nd ed.). London: Routledge.

Caldas-Coulthard, C. R. (1996). "Women Who Pay for Sex. And Enjoy It": Transgression Versus Morality in Women's Magazines. In C. R. Caldash-Coulthard & M. Coulthard (Eds.), *Texts and Practices: Readings in Critical Discourse Analysis* (pp. 250–270). London: Routledge.

Caldas-Coulthard, C. R., & Moon, R. (2010). 'Curvy, Hunky, Kinky': Using Corpora as Tools for Critical Analysis. *Discourse and Society, 21*(2), 99–133.

Caldas-Coulthard, C. R., & Van Leeuwen, T. (2002). Stunning, Shimmering, Iridescent: Toys as the Representation of Social Actors. In L. Litosseliti & J. Sunderland (Eds.), *Gender Identity and Discourse Analysis* (pp. 91–108). Amsterdam: John Benjamins.

Cameron, D. (1992a). Naming of Parts: Gender, Culture and Terms for the Penis Among American College Students. *American Speech, 67*(4), 367–382.

Cameron, D. (1992b). *Feminism and Linguistic Theory* (2nd ed.). Basingstoke: Macmillan.

Cameron, D. (1997). Performing Gender Identity: Young Men's Talk and the Construction of Heterosexual Masculinity. In S. Johnson & U. H. Meinhoff (Eds.), *Language and Masculinity* (pp. 47–64). Oxford: Blackwell.

Cameron, D. (Ed.). (2006). *On Language and Sexual Politics*. London: Routledge.

Cameron, D. (2007). *The Myth of Mars and Venus: Do Men and Women Really Speak Different Languages?* Oxford: Oxford University Press.

Cameron, D. (2010, November 23). *Gendered Behaviour: What Can Science Tell Us?* Public Debate in Association with the University of Cambridge Centre for Gender Studies, King's Place. Available at http://www.guardian.co.uk/commentisfree/audio/2010/nov/24/gendered-behaviour-science-forum?popup=true. Accessed March 2018.

Cameron, D., & Kulick, D. (2003). *Language and Sexuality*. Cambridge: Cambridge University Press.

Campaign Against Living Miserably. (2014). Available at https://www.thecalmzone.net.

Canary, D. J., & Hause, K. S. (1993). Is There Any Reason to Research Sex Differences in Communication? *Communication Quarterly, 41*(2), 129–144.

Chapman, R., & Rutherford, J. (1988). *Male Order: Unwrapping Masculinity*. London: Lawrence and Wishart.

Clark, K. (1992). The Linguistics of Blame: Representations of Women in *The Sun's* Reporting of Crimes of Sexual Violence. In M. Toolan (Ed.), *Language, Text and Context: Essays in Stylistics* (pp. 208–224). London: Routledge.

Coates, J. (1989). Gossip Revisited: Language in All-Female Groups. In J. Coates & D. Cameron (Eds.), *Women in Their Speech Communities* (pp. 94–121). London: Longman.

Coates, J. (2001). Pushing at the Boundaries: The Expression of Alternative Masculinities. In J. Cotterill & A. Ife (Eds.), *Language Across Boundaries* (pp. 1–24). London: BAAL/Continuum.

Coates, J. (2003). *Men Talk*. Oxford: Blackwell.

Collins, R. L., Elliott, M. N., Berry, S. H., Kanouse, D. E., Kunkel, D., Hunter, S. B., et al. (2004). Watching Sex on Television Predicts Adolescent Initiation of Sexual Behavior. *Pediatrics, 114*(3), 280–289.

Connell, R. W. (1995). *Masculinities*. Berkeley: University of California Press.

Connell, R. W. (2005). Hegemonic Masculinity: Rethinking the Concept. *Gender & Society, 19*(6), 829–859.

Conradie, M. (2011). Masculine Sexuality: A Critical Discourse Analysis of *FHM*. *South African Linguistics and Applied Language Studies, 29*(2), 167–185.

Coy, M., & Horvath, M. A. H. (2011). Lads Mags, Young Men's Attitudes Towards Women and Acceptance of Myths About Sexual Aggression. *Feminism and Psychology, 21*(1), 144–150.

Crewe, B. (2003). *Representing Men: Cultural Production and Producers in the Men's Magazine Market*. London: Bloomsbury.

Crisp, P. (2002). Metaphorical Propositions: A Rationale. *Language and Literature, 11*(1), 7–16.

Cruse, A. (1986). *Lexical Semantics*. Cambridge: Cambridge University Press.

Cruse, A. (2004). *Meaning in Language: An Introduction to Semantics and Pragmatics*. Oxford: Oxford University Press.

Davies, M. (2013). *Oppositions and Ideology in News Discourse*. London: Bloomsbury.

de Beauvoir, S. ([1949] 1953). *The Second Sex* (H. M. Parshley, Trans. and Ed.). London: Jonathan Cape.

de Beauvoir, S. ([1949] 1988). *The Second Sex* (H. M. Parshley, Trans. and Ed.). London: Pan Books.

de Saussure, F. (1960). *Course in General Linguistics* (W. Baskin, Trans.). London: Peter Owen.

Delin, J. (2000). *The Language of Everyday Life: An Introduction*. London: Sage.

Del-Teso-Craviotto, M. (2005). Words That Matter: Lexical Choice and Gender Ideologies in Women's Magazines. *Journal of Pragmatics, 38*(11), 2003–2021.

Doty, A., & Gove, B. (1997). Queer Representation in the Mass Media. In A. Medhurst & S. R. Munt (Eds.), *Lesbian and Gay Studies: A Critical Introduction* (pp. 84–98). London: Continuum.

Duffy, E. (2013). *Women's Magazines in the Digital Age*. Urbana: University of Illinois.

Duke, L., & Kreshel, P. (1998). Negotiating Femininity: Girls in Early Adolescence Read Teen Magazines. *Journal of Communication Inquiry, 22*(1), 48–71.

Eckert, P., & McConnell-Ginet, S. (1992). Think Practically and Look Locally: Language and Gender as Community-Based Practice. *Annual Review of Anthropology, 21*(1), 461–490.

Eckert, P., & McConnell-Ginet, S. (2003). *Language and Gender*. Cambridge: Cambridge University Press.

Edelman, D. C. (2010). Branding in the Digital Age: You're Spending Your Money in All the Wrong Places. *Harvard Business Review, 88*, 63–69.

Edwards, T. (1997). *Men in the Mirror: Men's Fashion, Masculinity and Consumer Society*. London: Cassell.

Edwards, T. (2003). Sex, Booze and Fags: Masculinity, Style and Men's Magazines. In B. Benwell (Ed.), *Masculinity and Men's Lifestyle Magazines* (pp. 132–146). Oxford: Blackwell.

Eggins, S., & Iedema, R. (1997). Difference Without Diversity: Semantic Orientation and Ideology in Competing Women's Magazines. In R. Wodak (Ed.), *Gender and Discourse* (pp. 165–196). London: Sage.

Ehrlich, S. (2001). *Representing Rape: Language and Sexual Consent*. London: Routledge.

Fairclough, N. (1989). *Language and Power*. London: Longman.

Fairclough, N. (1992). *Critical Language Awareness*. London: Longman.

Fairclough, N. (1995). *Critical Discourse Analysis*. London: Longman.

Fairclough, N. (1996). A Reply to Henry Widdowson's "Discourse Analysis: A Critical Review". *Language and Literature, 5*(1), 49–56.

Fairclough, N. (2001). *Language and Power* (2nd ed.). London: Longman.

Farvid, P., & Braun, V. (2006). "Most of Us Guys Are Raring to Go Anytime, Anyplace, Anywhere": Male and Female Sexuality in *Cleo* and *Cosmo*. *Sex Roles, 55*, 295–310.

Favaro, L. (2017). Mediating Intimacy Online: Authenticity, Magazines and Chasing the Clicks. *Journal of Gender Studies*. Available at http://dx.doi.org/10.1080/09589236.2017.1280385. Accessed June 2017.

Fillmore, C. (1982). Ideal Reader and Real Readers. In D. Tannen (Ed.), *Analyzing Discourse: Text and Talk* (pp. 248–270). Washington, DC: Georgetown University Press.

Fine, C. (2011). *Delusions of Gender: The Real Science Behind Sex Differences*. London: Icon.

Firminger, K. B. (2006). Is He Boyfriend Material? Representations of Males in Teenage Girls' Magazines'. *Men and Masculinities, 8*(3), 298–308.

Fishman, P. M. (1980). Conversational Insecurity. In H. Giles, W. P. Robinson, & P. M. Smith (Eds.), *Language Social Psychological Perspectives* (pp. 127–132). New York: Pergamon Press.

Fishman, P. M. (1983). Interaction: The Work Women Do. In B. Thorne, C. Kramarae, & N. Henley (Eds.), *Language, Gender and Society*. Rowley, MA: Newbury House.

Foucault, M. (1972). *The Archaeology of Knowledge*. London: Tavistock.

Fowler, R. (1991). *Language in the News: Discourse and Ideology in the Press*. London: Routledge.

Frazer, E. (1987). Teenage Girls Reading *Jackie*. *Media, Culture and Society, 9*(4), 407–425.

Frederick, D., Fessler, D., & Haselton, M. (2005). Do Representations of Male Muscularity Differ in Men's and Women's Magazines? *Body Image, 2*(1), 81–86.

Friedan, B. (1963). *The Feminine Mystique*. New York: Dell.

Frosh, S., Phoenix, A., & Pattman, R. (2002). *Young Masculinities: Understanding Boys in Contemporary Society*. Basingstoke: Palgrave Macmillan.

Gabrielatos, C., & Baker, P. (2008). Fleeing, Sneaking, Flooding: A Corpus Analysis of Discursive Constructions of Refugees and Asylum Seekers in the UK Press, 1996–2005. *Journal of English Linguistics, 36*(1), 5–38.

García-Favaro, L. (2015). 'Porn Trouble': On the Sexual Regime and Travels of Postfeminist Biologism. *Australian Feminist Studies, 30*(86), 366–376.

García-Favaro, L., & Gill, R. (2016). "Emasculation Nation Has Arrived": Sexism Rearticulated in Online Responses to Lose the Lads' Mags Campaign. *Feminist Media Studies, 16*(3), 379–397.

Gee, J. P. (1999). *An Introduction to Discourse Analysis: Theory and Method*. London: Routledge.

Gibbs, R. W. (1994). *The Poetics of Mind: Figurative Thought, Language and Understanding*. Cambridge: Cambridge University Press.

Gibbs, R. W., & Steen, G. J. (1999). *Metaphor in Cognitive Linguistics*. Amsterdam: John Benjamins.

Gill, R. (2003). Power and the Production of Subjects: A Genealogy of the New Man and the New Lad. In B. Benwell (Ed.), *Masculinity and Men's Lifestyle Magazines* (pp. 34–56). Oxford: Blackwell.

Gill, R. (2007). *Gender and the Media*. Cambridge: Polity Press.

Gill, R. (2009). Mediated Intimacy and Postfeminism: A Discourse Analytic Examination of Sex and Relationships Advice in a Woman's Magazine. *Discourse and Communication, 3*(1), 345–369.

Gill, R. (2014). Powerful Women, Vulnerable Men and Postfeminist Masculinity in Men's Popular Fiction. *Gender and Language, 8*(2), 185–204.

Gill, R., & Elias, A. S. (2014). "Awaken Your Incredible": Love Your Body Discourses and Postfeminist Contradictions. *International Journal of Media and Cultural Politics, 10*(2), 179–188.

Glazer, N. (1980). Overworking the Working Woman: The Double Day in a Mass Magazine. *Woman's Studies International Quarterly, 3*(1), 79–93.

Gough-Yates, A. (2002). *Understanding Women's Magazines*. London: Routledge.

Gramsci, A. (1971). *Selections from Prison Notebooks* (Q. Hoare & G. Nowell-Smith, Trans.). London: Lawrence and Wishart.

Gramsci, A. (1985). *Selections from the Cultural Writings 1921–1926* (D. Forgacs & G. Nowell-Smith, Eds. & W. Boelhower, Trans.). London: Lawrence and Wishart.

Gray, J. (1992). *Men Are from Mars, Women Are from Venus.* New York: HarperCollins.

Greenfield, J., O'Connell, S., & Reid, C. (1999). Fashioning Masculinity: *Men Only*, Consumption and the Development of Marketing in the 1930s. *Twentieth Century British History, 10*(4), 457–476.

Grice, P. (1975). Logic and Conversation. In P. Cole & J. L. Morgan (Eds.), *Syntax and Semantics 3: Speech Acts* (pp. 41–58). New York: Academic.

Grice, P. (1989). *Studies in the Way of Words.* Cambridge, MA: Harvard University Press.

Gumperz, J. (Ed.). (1982). *Language and Identity.* Cambridge: Cambridge University Press.

Halliday, M. (1985). *An Introduction to Functional Grammar.* London: Arnold.

Halliday, M. A. K. (1994). *An Introduction to Functional Grammar* (2nd ed.). London: Arnold.

Halliday, M. A. K., & Matthiessen, C. (2004). *An Introduction to Functional Grammar* (3rd ed.). London: Arnold.

Hasinoff, A. (2009). It's Sociobiology, Hon! Genetic Gender Determinism in *Cosmopolitan* Magazine. *Feminist Media Studies, 9*(3), 267–283.

Hellinger, M., & Bussmann, H. (2001). Gender Across Languages: The Linguistic Representation of Women and Men. In M. Hellinger & H. Bussmann (Eds.), *Gender Across Languages: The Linguistic Representation of Women and Men* (Vol. 1, pp. 1–25). Amsterdam: John Benjamins.

Hellinger, M., & Bussmann, H. (2001–2003). *Gender Across Languages: The Linguistic Representation of Women and Men* (3 Vols.). Amsterdam: John Benjamins.

Henley, N., & Kramarae, C. (1991). Gender, Power and Miscommunication. In N. Coupland, H. Giles, & J. Wiemann (Eds.), *"Miscommunication" and Problem Talk* (pp. 18–43). Newbury Park, CA: Sage.

Hermes, J. (1995). *Reading Women's Magazines: An Analysis of Everyday Media Use.* Cambridge: Polity Press.

Hines, C. (1999). Rebaking the Pie: The WOMAN AS DESSERT Metaphor. In M. Bucholtz, A. C. Liang, & L. Sutton (Eds.), *Reinventing Identities: The Gendered Self in Discourse* (pp. 145–162). Oxford: Oxford University Press.

Holloway, W. (1984). Gender Difference and the Production of Subjectivity. In J. Henriques, W. Holloway, C. Urwin, C. Venn, & V. Walkerdine (Eds.), *Changing the Subject: Psychology, Social Regulation and Subjectivity* (pp. 227–339). London: Methuen.

Holmes, J. (1984). Hedging Your Bets and Sitting on the Fence: Some Evidence for Hedges as Support Structures. *Te Reo, 27*, 47–62.

Holmes, J. (2006). *Gendered Talk at Work*. Oxford: Blackwell.

Holmes, J. (2009). Men, Masculinities and Leadership: Different Discourse Styles at Work. In P. Pichler & E. M. Eppler (Eds.), *Gender and Spoken Interaction* (pp. 186–210). Basingstoke: Palgrave Macmillan.

hooks, b. (2000). *Feminism Is for Everybody: Passionate Politics*. London: Pluto Press.

Horne, S. J. (2011). *Judged by Their Covers: Robert Harrison's Girlie Magazines, 1941–1955* (Unpublished MA thesis). University of Missouri, Columbia.

Hyde, J. (2005). The Gender Similarities Hypothesis. *American Psychologist, 60*(6), 581–592.

Jackson, P., Stevenson, N., & Brooks, K. (2001). *Making Sense of Men's Magazines*. Cambridge: Polity Press.

Jamieson, D. (2007). Marketing Androgyny: The Evolution of the Backstreet Boys. *Popular Music, 26*(2), 245–258.

Jeffries, L. (2007). *Textual Construction of the Female Body: A Critical Discourse Approach*. Basingstoke: Palgrave Macmillan.

Jeffries, L. (2010a). *Opposition in Discourse*. London: Continuum.

Jeffries, L. (2010b). *Critical Stylistics*. Basingstoke: Palgrave Macmillan.

Jeffries, L. (2014). Critical Stylistics. In M. Burke (Ed.), *The Routledge Handbook of Stylistics* (pp. 408–420). London: Routledge.

Jenkins, M., & Kramarae, C. (1981). A Thief in the House: The Case of Women and Language. In D. Spender (Ed.), *Men's Studies Modified: The Impact of Feminism on the Academic Disciplines* (pp. 11–22). Oxford: Pergamon Press.

Jespersen, O. (1922). *Language, Its Origin and Development*. London: Allen & Unwin.

Johnson, F., & Finlay, F. (1997). Do Men Gossip? An Analysis of Football Talk on Television. In S. Johnson & U. Meinhoff (Eds.), *Language and Masculinity* (pp. 130–143). Oxford: Blackwell.

Johnson, S., & Meinhoff, U. (Eds.). (1997). *Language and Masculinity*. Oxford: Blackwell.

Jones, S. (2002). *Antonymy: A Corpus-Based Perspective*. London: Routledge.

Kehily, M. J. (1999). More Sugar? Teenage Magazines, Gender Displays and Sexual Learning. *European Journal of Cultural Studies, 2*(1), 65–89.

Kiesling, S. (2002). Playing the Straight Man: Displaying and Maintaining Male Heterosexuality in Discourse. In K. Campbell-Kibler, R. J. Podesva, S.

J. Roberts, & A. Wong (Eds.), *Language and Sexuality: Contesting Meaning in Theory and Practice* (pp. 249–266). Stanford, CA: CSLI Publications.

Kilgarriff, A., Rychlý, P., Smrž, P., & Tugwell, D. (2004). Itri-04-08 the Sketch Engine. *Information Technology.* Available at http://www.sketchengine.co.uk. Accessed September 2018.

Kitzinger, C., & Frith, H. (1999). Just Say No? The Use of Conversation Analysis on Developing a Feminist Perspective on Sexual Refusal. *Discourse & Society, 10*(3), 293–316.

Koller, V. (2004). Businesswomen and War Metaphors: "Possessive Jealous and Pugnacious"? *Journal of Sociolinguistics, 8*(1), 3–22.

Korte, B. (1997). *Body Language in Literature.* Toronto: University of Toronto Press.

Labov, W. (1990). The Intersection of Sex and Social Class in the Course of Linguistic Change. *Language, Variation and Change, 2*(2), 205–254.

Labov, W., & Waletzky, J. (1967). Narrative Analysis. In J. Helm (Ed.), *Essays on the Verbal and Visual Arts* (pp. 12–44). Seattle: University of Washington Press.

Lakoff, G., & Johnson, M. (1980). *Metaphors We Live By.* Chicago: University of Chicago Press.

Lakoff, R. T. (1975). *Language and Woman's Place.* New York: Harper & Row.

Lakoff, R. T. (2004). *Language and Woman's Place: Text and Commentaries* (M. Bucholtz, Ed., Rev. Exp. ed.). New York: Oxford University Press.

Lazar, M. (2005). *Feminist Critical Discourse Analysis.* Basingstoke: Palgrave Macmillan.

Lazar, M. (2009). Entitled to Consume: Postfeminist Femininity and a Culture of Post-Critique. *Discourse & Communication, 3*(4), 371–400.

Leech, G. (1969). *A Linguistic Guide to English Poetry.* London: Longman.

Leech, G., & Short, M. (2007). *Style in Fiction: A Linguistic Introduction to English Fictional Prose* (2nd ed.). Harlow: Pearson Education.

Leman, J. (1980). "The Advice of a Real Friend": Codes of Intimacy and Oppression in Women's Magazines 1937–1955. *Woman's Studies International Quarterly, 3*(1), 63–78.

Le Masurier, M. (2011). Reading the Flesh. *Feminist Media Studies, 11*(2), 215–229.

Levinson, S. C. (1983). *Pragmatics.* Cambridge: Cambridge University Press.

Levon, E., & Mendes, R. B. (2016). *Language, Sexuality and Power: Studies in Intersectional Sociolinguistics.* Oxford: Oxford University Press.

Litosseliti, L. (2006). *Gender and Language: Theory and Practice.* London: Hodder Arnold.

Litosseliti, L., Saunston, H., & Sunderland, J. (Eds.). (2008). *Gender and Language Research Methodologies* (pp. 211–226). Basingstoke: Palgrave Macmillan.

Livia, A., & Hall, K. (1997). 'It's a Girl!' Bringing Performativity Back to Linguistics. In A. Livia & K. Hall (Eds.), *Queerly Phrased: Language, Gender, and Sexuality* (pp. 3–18). Oxford: Oxford University Press.

López Maestre, M. D. (2013). Narrative and Ideologies of Violence Against Women: The Legend of the Black Lagoon. *Language and Literature, 22*(4), 299–313.

Lyons, J. (1977). *Semantics* (Vol. 1). Cambridge: Cambridge University Press.

Machin, D., & Thornborrow, J. (2003). Branding and Discourse: The Case of Cosmopolitan. *Discourse and Society, 14*(4), 453–471.

Machin, D., Caldas-Coulthard, C. R., & Milani, T. (2016). Doing Critical Multimodality in Research on Gender, Language and Discourse. *Gender and Language, 10*(3), 301–308.

Mahlberg, M. (2007). Corpus Stylistics: Bridging the Gap Between Linguistic and Literary Studies. In M. Hoey, M. Mahlberg, M. Stubbs, & W. Teubert (Eds.), *Text, Discourse and Corpora* (pp. 219–246). London: Continuum.

Mahlberg, M., & McIntyre, D. (2011). A Case for Corpus Stylistics: Ian Fleming's Casino Royale. *English Text Construction, 4*(2), 204–227.

Malkin, A., Wornian, K., & Chrisler, J. (1999). Women and Weight: Gendered Messages on Magazine Covers. *Sex Roles: A Journal of Research, 40*(7–8), 647–655.

Maltz, D., & Borker, R. (1982). A Cultural Approach to Male-Female Miscommunication. In J. Gumperz (Ed.), *Language and Social Identity* (pp. 196–216). Cambridge: Cambridge University Press.

Mautner, G. (2007). Mining Large Corpora for Social Information: The Case of Elderly. *Language in Society, 36*(1), 51–72.

Mautner, G. (2016). Checks and Balances: How Corpus Linguistics Can Contribute to CDA. In R. Wodak & M. Meyer (Eds.), *Methods of Critical Discourse Studies* (3rd ed., pp. 154–179). London: Sage.

McCracken, E. (1993). *Decoding Women's Magazines: From 'Mademoiselle' to 'Ms'.* London: Macmillan.

McEnery, T., & Wilson, A. (1996). *Corpus Linguistics.* Edinburgh: Edinburgh University Press.

McEnery, T., Xiao, R., & Tono, Y. (2006). *Corpus-Based Language Studies: An Advanced Resource Book.* London: Routledge.

McLoughlin, L. (2000). *The Language of Magazines.* London: Routledge.

McLoughlin, L. (2008). The Construction of Female Sexuality in the "Sex Special": Transgression or Containment in Magazines' Information on Sexuality for Girls? *Gender and Language, 2*(2), 171–195.

McRobbie, A. (1982). *Jackie*: An Ideology of Adolescent Femininity. In B. Waites, T. Bennett, & G. Martin (Eds.), *Popular Culture: Past and Present* (pp. 263–283). London: Croom Helm.

McRobbie, A. (1991). *Feminism and Youth Culture: From 'Jackie' to 'Just Seventeen'*. Basingstoke: Macmillan Education.

McRobbie, A. (1996). *More!*: New Sexualities in Girls' and Women's Magazines. In J. Curran, D. Morley, & V. Walkerdine (Eds.), *Cultural Studies and Communications* (pp. 172–194). London: Arnold.

Ménard, A., & Kleinplatz, P. (2008). "Twenty-One Moves Guaranteed to Make His Thighs Go Up in Flames": Depictions of 'Great Sex' in Popular Magazines. *Sexuality and Culture, 12*(1), 1–20.

Merriam-Webster Online. (2013). Available at http://www.merriam-webster. com. Accessed March 2013.

Mettinger, A. (1994). *Aspects of Semantic Opposition in English*. Oxford: Clarendon Press.

Milani, T. (Ed.). (2015). *Language and Masculinities: Performances, Intersections, Dislocations*. London: Routledge.

Mills, S. (1994). Close Encounters of a Feminist Kind: Transitivity Analysis of Pop Lyrics. In K. Wales (Ed.), *Feminist Linguistics in Literary Criticism* (pp. 137–156). Cambridge: D.S. Brewer.

Mills, S. (1995). *Feminist Stylistics*. London: Routledge.

Mills, S. (2003). Third Wave Feminism and the Analysis of Sexism. *Discourse Analysis On-line*. Available at https://extra.shu.ac.uk/daol/articles/ open/2003/001/mills2003001.html. Accessed January 2018.

Mills, S. (2008). *Language and Sexism*. Cambridge: Cambridge University Press.

Mills, S. (2012). *Gender Matters: Feminist Linguistic Analysis*. London: Equinox.

Mills, S., & Mullany, L. (2011). *Language, Gender and Feminism: Theory, Methodology and Practice*. London: Routledge.

Milroy, L. (1980). *Language and Social Networks*. Oxford: Basil Blackwell.

Molesworth, M., Nixon, E., & Scullon, R. (2010). *The Marketisation of Higher Education and the Student as Consumer*. London: Routledge.

Motschenbacher, H. (2009). Speaking the Gendered Body: The Performative Construction of Commercial Femininities and Masculinities Via Body-Part Vocabulary. *Language in Society, 38*(1), 1–22.

Murphy, L. (2003). *Semantic Relations and the Lexicon*. Cambridge: Cambridge University Press.

Nagel, J. (2003). *Race, Ethnicity and Sexuality: Intimate Intersections, Forbidden Frontiers*. Oxford: Oxford University Press.

Nash, W. (1990). *Language in Popular Fiction*. London: Routledge.

Naylor, B. (2001). Reporting Violence in the British Print Media: Gendered Stories. *The Howard Journal of Criminal Justice, 40*(2), 180–194.

Nicholson, L. (1994). Interpreting Gender. *Signs, 20*(1), 79–105.

Nixon, S. (1996). *Hard Looks: Masculinities, Spectatorships, and Contemporary Consumption*. London: UCL Press.

Nixon, S. (1997). Exhibiting Masculinity. In S. Hall (Ed.), *Representation: Cultural Representations and Signifying Practices* (pp. 291–330). London: Sage.

Nixon, S. (2001). Re-signifying Masculinity: From "New Man" to "New Lad". In D. Morley & K. Robins (Eds.), *British Cultural Studies* (pp. 373–385). Oxford: Oxford University Press.

Oakes, O. (2016). Magazine ABCs: Top 100 for First Half of 2016. *Campaign*. Available at http://www.campaignlive.co.uk/article/magazine-abcs-top-100-first-half-2016/1405423. Accessed June 2017.

O'Barr, W., & Atkins, B. (1980). "Women's Language" or "Powerless Language"? In S. McConnell-Ginet, R. Borker, & N. Furman (Eds.), *Women and Language in Literature and Society* (pp. 93–110). New York: Praeger.

Ochs, E. (1992). Indexing Gender. In A. Duranti & C. Goodwin (Eds.), *Rethinking Context: Language as an Interactive Phenomenon* (pp. 335–358). Cambridge: Cambridge University Press.

O'Hara, S. (2012). Monsters Playboys, Virgins and Whores: Rape Myths in the News Media's Coverage of Sexual Violence. *Language and Literature, 21*(3), 247–259.

Osgerby, B. (2001). *Playboys in Paradise: Masculinity, Youth and Leisure-Style in Modern America*. Oxford: Berg.

Oxford English Dictionary Online. (2017). Oxford University Press. Available at http://www.oed.com. Accessed June 2017.

Pearce, M. (2008). Investigating the Collocational Behaviour of MAN and WOMAN in the BNC Using Sketch Engine. *Corpora, 3*(1), 1–29.

Phipps, A., & Young, I. (2015). "Lad Culture" in Higher Education: Agency in the Sexualisation Debates. *Sexualities, 18*(4), 459–479.

Podhakecka, M., & Piotrowski, T. (2003). Russianisms in English (OED-BNC-LDOCE). In B. Lewandowska-Tomaszczyk (Ed.), *Practical*

Applications in Language and Computers (pp. 241–252). Frankfurt am Main: Peter Lang.

Rayson, P. (2008). From Key Words to Key Semantic Domains. *International Journal of Corpus Linguistics., 13*(4), 519–549.

Reisigl, M., & Wodak, R. (2001). *Discourse and Discrimination: Rhetorics of Racism and Anti-Semitism.* London: Routledge.

Ringrow, H. (2016). *The Language of Cosmetics Advertising.* Basingstoke: Palgrave Macmillan.

Sapir, E. (1929). A Study in Phonetic Symbolism. *Journal of Experimental Psychology, 12,* 225–229.

Sapir, E. (1944). On Grading: A Study in Semantics. *Philosophy of Science, 2,* 93–116.

Schegloff, E. A., & Sacks, H. (1973). Opening Up Closings. *Semiotica, 7*(1), 289–327.

Schulz, M. (1975). The Semantic Derogation of Women. In B. Thorne & N. Henley (Eds.), *Language and Sex: Difference and Dominance* (pp. 64–75). Rowley, MA: Newbury House.

Scott, M. (2008). *Wordsmith Tools Version 5.* Liverpool: Lexical Analysis Software.

Searle, J. R. (1969). *Speech Acts: An Essay in the Philosophy of Language.* Cambridge: Cambridge University Press.

Searle, J. R. (1979). *Expression and Meaning: Studies in the Theory of Speech Acts.* Cambridge: Cambridge University Press.

Searle, J. R. (1983). *Intentionality: An Essay in the Philosophy of Mind.* Cambridge: Cambridge University Press.

Searle, J. R. (1989). Consciousness, Unconsciousness and Intentionality. *Philosophical Topics, xxxvii*(10), 193–209.

Semino, E. (1997). *Language and World Creation in Poems and Other Texts.* London: Longman.

Semino, E., & Short, M. (2004). *Corpus Stylistics: Speech, Writing and Thought Presentation in a Corpus of English Writing.* London: Routledge.

Sigley, R., & Holmes, J. (2002). *Looking at Girls in Corpora of English, 30*(2), 138–157.

Simpson, M. (1994). *Male Impersonators: Men Performing Masculinity.* London: Cassell.

Simpson, P. (1993). *Language, Ideology and Point of View.* London: Routledge.

Simpson, P. (2004). *Stylistics: A Resource Book for Students.* London: Routledge.

Sinclair, J. (1991). *Corpus, Concordance, Collocation*. Oxford: Oxford University Press.

Smith, D. (1988). Femininity as Discourse. In L. G. Roman & L. K. Christian-Smith (Eds.), *Becoming Feminine: The Politics of Popular Culture* (pp. 37–59). New York: Falmer Press.

Soothill, K., & Walby, S. (1991). *Sex Crime in the News*. London: Routledge.

Stergiopoulos, G. (2008). *Treat Them Mean, Keep Them Keen*. London: Square Peg.

Stibbe, A. (2004). Health and the Social Construction of Masculinity in *Men's Health* Magazine. *Men and Masculinities, 7*(1), 31–51.

Stubbs, M. (2001). *Words and Phrases: Corpus Studies of Lexical Semantics*. London: Blackwell.

Sunderland, J. (2004). *Gendered Discourses*. Basingstoke: Palgrave Macmillan.

Sunderland, J. (2007). Contradictions in Gendered Discourses: Feminist Readings of Sexist Jokes? *Gender and Language, 1*(2), 207–228.

Sunderland, J., & Litosseliti, L. (2008). Current Research Methodologies in Gender and Language Study: Key Issues. In K. Harrington, L. Litosseliti, H. Sauntson, & J. Sunderland (Eds.), *Gender and Language Research Methodologies* (pp. 1–18). Basingstoke: Palgrave Macmillan.

Swann, J. (2002). Yes, but Is It Gender? In L. Litosseliti & J. Sunderland (Eds.), *Gender Identity and Discourse Analysis* (pp. 43–67). Amsterdam: John Benjamins.

Tabbert, U. (2016). *Language and Crime: Constructing Offenders and Victims in Newspaper Reports*. London: Palgrave Macmillan.

Talbot, M. (1992). The Construction of Gender in a Teenage Magazine. In N. Fairclough (Ed.), *Critical Language Awareness* (pp. 174–199). London: Longman.

Talbot, M. (1995). A Synthetic Sisterhood: False Friends in a Teenage Magazine. In K. Hall & M. Bucholtz (Eds.), *Gender Articulated: Language and the Socially Constructed Self* (pp. 143–165). London: Routledge.

Talbot, M. M. (1997). An Explosion Deep Inside Her: Women's Desire and Popular Romance Fiction. In K. Harvey & C. Shalom (Eds.), *Language and Desire: Encoding Sex, Romance and Intimacy* (pp. 106–122). London: Routledge.

Talbot, M. (1998). *Language and Gender: An Introduction*. Cambridge: Polity Press.

Talbot, M. (2010). *Language and Gender* (2nd ed.). Cambridge: Polity Press.

Talbot, M. (2014). Language, Gender and Popular Culture. In S. Ehrlich, M. Meyerhoff, & J. Holmes (Eds.), *The Handbook of Language, Gender and Sexuality* (pp. 604–624). Malden, MA and Oxford: Wiley-Blackwell.

Tannen, D. (1990). *You Just Don't Understand*. London: Virago.

Taylor, C. (2017). Women are Bitchy, but Men Are Sarcastic? Investigating Gender and Sarcasm. *Gender and Language, 11*(3), 415–445.

Taylor, L. D. (2008). Cads, Dads, and Magazines: Women's Sexual Preferences and Articles About Sex and Relationships. *Communication Monographs, 75*(3), 270–289.

Taylor, Y., & Sunderland, J. (2003). "I've Always Loved Women": The Representation of the Male Sex Worker in *Maxim*. In B. Benwell (Ed.), *Masculintiy and Men's Lifestyle Magazines* (pp. 169–187). Oxford: Blackwell.

Ticknell, E., Chambers, D., van Loon, J., & Hudson, N. (2003). Begging for It: "New Femininities", Social Agency and Moral Discourse in Contemporary Teenage and Men's Magazines. *Feminist Media Studies, 3*(1), 47–63.

Trudgill, P. (1972). Sex, Covert Prestige and Linguistic Change in the Urban British English of Norwich. *Language in Society, 1*(2), 179–195.

Trudgill, P. (1974). *The Social Differentiation of English in Norwich*. Cambridge: Cambridge University Press.

Tuchman, G., Daniels, A. K., & Benet, J. (1978). *Hearth and Home: Images of Women in Mass Media*. Oxford: Oxford University Press.

Uchida, A. (1992). When "Difference" Is "Dominance": A Critique of the 'Anti-Power-Based' Cultural Approach to Sex Differences. *Language in Society, 21*(4), 547–568.

The Urban Dictionary. (1999–2013). Available at http://www.urbandictionary. com. Accessed January 2018.

Van Dijk, T. (1991). *Racism and the Press*. London: Routledge.

Van Leeuwen, T. (1995). Representing Social Action. *Discourse & Society, 6*(1), 81–106.

Van Leeuwen, T. (1996). The Representation of Social Actors. In C. R. Caldas-Coulthard & M. Coulthard (Eds.), *Texts and Practices: Readings in Critical Discourse Analysis* (pp. 32–70). London: Routledge.

Wareing, S. (1990). Women in Fiction: Stylistics Modes of Reclamation. *Parlance, 2*(2), 72–85.

Wareing, S. (1994). And Then He Kissed Her.... In K. Wales (Ed.), *Feminist Linguistics in Literary Criticism* (pp. 117–136). Cambridge: D.S. Brewer.

Warner, M. (Ed.). (1993). *Fear of a Queer Planet*. Minneapolis: University of Minnesota Press.

Whelehan, I. (2000). *Overloaded: Popular Culture and the Future of Feminism*. London: Women's Press.

Widdowson, H. G. (1995). Discourse Analysis: A Critical Review. *Language and Literature, 4*(3), 157–172.

Winship, J. (1983). Femininity and Women's Magazines. Unit 6, *U221 The Changing Experience of Women*. Milton Keynes: Open University.

Winship, J. (1985). "A Girl Needs to Get Street-Wise": Magazines for the 1980s. *Feminist Review, 21,* 25–46.

Winship, J. (1987). *Inside Women's Magazines*. London: Pandora.

Wodak, R., & Meyer, M. (2009). Critical Discourse Analysis: History, Agenda, Theory and Methodology. In R. Wodak & M. Meyer (Eds.), *Methods of Critical Discourse Analysis* (2nd ed., pp. 1–33). London: Sage.

Woolls, D., & Coulthard, R. M. (1998). Tools for the Trade. *Forensic Linguistics, 5*(1), 33–57.

Xiao, Z., & McEnery, A. (2002, August 8–11). *A Corpus-Based Approach to Tense and Aspect in English-Chinese Translation*. Paper Presented at International Symposium on Contrastive and Translation Studies Between Chinese and English, Shanghai.

Ytre-Arne, B. (2011a). 'I Want to Hold It in My Hands': Readers' Experiences of the Phenomenological Differences Between Women's Magazines Online and in Print. *Media, Culture and Society, 33*(3), 467–477.

Ytre-Arne, B. (2011b). Women's Magazines and Their Readers: The Relationship Between Textual Features and Practices of Reading. *European Journal of Cultural Studies, 14*(2), 213–228.

Zimman, L. (2014). The Discursive Construction of Sex: Remaking and Reclaiming the Gendered Body in Talk About Genitals Among Trans Men. In L. Zimman, J. Raclaw, & J. Davis (Eds.), *Queer Excursions: Retheorizing Binaries in Language, Gender, and Sexuality* (pp. 13–34). Oxford: Oxford University Press.

Zimmerman, D., & West, C. (1975). Sex Roles, Interruptions and Silences in Conversation. In B. Thorne & N. Henley (Eds.), *Language and Sex: Difference and Dominance* (pp. 105–129). Rowley, MA: Newbury House.

Index

© The Editor(s) (if applicable) and The Author(s) 2019
L. Coffey-Glover, *Men in Women's Worlds*,
https://doi.org/10.1057/978-1-137-57555-5

Printed by Printforce, the Netherlands